Modern Business

A SERIES OF TEXTS PREPARED AS
PART OF THE MODERN BUSINESS
COURSE AND SERVICE OF THE
ALEXANDER HAMILTON
INSTITUTE

ALEXANDER HAMILTON INSTITUTE
NEW YORK

Modern Business

EDITOR-IN-CHIEF
JOSEPH FRENCH JOHNSON
Dean, New York University School of
Commerce, Accounts and Finance

MANAGING EDITOR
ROLAND P. FALKNER

ASSOCIATE EDITORS
LEO GREENDLINGER, CHARLES W. HURD

Volume	Titles	Authors
1.	BUSINESS AND THE MAN	Joseph French Johnson
2.	ECONOMICS OF BUSINESS	The Editors
3.	ORGANIZATION AND CONTROL	Charles W. Gerstenberg
4.	PLANT MANAGEMENT	Dexter S. Kimball
5.	MARKETING AND MERCHANDISING	The Editors
6.	ADVERTISING PRINCIPLES	Herbert F. de Bower
7.	SALESMANSHIP AND SALES MANAGEMENT	John G. Jones
8.	CREDIT AND THE CREDIT MAN	The Editors
9.	ACCOUNTING PRINCIPLES	The Editors
10.	COST FINDING	Dexter S. Kimball
11.	CORPORATION FINANCE	William H. Walker
12.	BUSINESS CORRESPONDENCE	Harrison McJohnston
13.	ADVERTISING CAMPAIGNS	Mac Martin
14.	RAILWAY TRAFFIC	Edwin J. Clapp
15.	FOREIGN TRADE AND SHIPPING	J. Anton de Haas
16.	BANKING	Major B. Foster
17.	DOMESTIC AND FOREIGN EXCHANGE	E. L. Stewart Patterson
18.	INSURANCE	The Editors
19.	OFFICE MANAGEMENT	The Editors
20.	THE EXCHANGES AND SPECULATION	Albert W. Atwood
21.	ACCOUNTING PRACTICE AND AUDITING	John T. Madden
22.	FINANCIAL AND BUSINESS STATEMENTS	Leo Greendlinger
23.	INVESTMENT	Edward D. Jones
24.	BUSINESS AND THE GOVERNMENT	Jeremiah W. Jenks

THE EXCHANGES AND SPECULATION

BY

ALBERT W. ATWOOD, A.B.
Associate in Journalism, Columbia University

MODERN BUSINESS

VOLUME 20

DR. NORMAN A. WIGGINS

ALEXANDER HAMILTON INSTITUTE

NEW YORK

COPYRIGHT, 1918, 1919, BY
ALEXANDER HAMILTON INSTITUTE

COPYRIGHT IN GREAT BRITAIN, 1918, 1919, BY
ALEXANDER HAMILTON INSTITUTE

The title and contents of this volume as well as the business growing out of it, are further protected by laws relating to trade marks and unfair trade. All rights reserved, including translation into Scandinavian.

Registered trade mark, Reg. U. S. Pat. Off., Marca Registrada, M. de F.

MADE IN U. S. A.

PREFACE

Whatever the merits or defects of this work may be, it embodies fairly continuous observation of the workings of the exchanges for more than twelve years by the author, who during seven years of that time was a financial writer for two New York newspapers, and for nearly the same length of time has lectured on the exchanges, to students at two universities in New York City. From the keen questions and discussions of scores of these students, many of whom have been and are connected with banking and brokerage concerns, much of the material in this book has been threshed out, and it has been my effort to discuss the very questions that such teaching experience indicates are of vital interest to young men in the business world.

In a small degree I have drawn on the former Modern Business Text on "Investment and Speculation." This Text is the joint product of Professor Thomas Conway Jr. and myself. At this time it would be very difficult to trace the authorship of the different sections of this book, but I am relieved from the necessity of so doing by the courteous consent of Professor Conway, for which I am grateful, to use any portions of the Text which I might desire to incorporate in the present volume. Mr. Louis Gottlieb, Fellow in Economics, Sociology and Politics in Columbia University, has been of assistance in gathering material for the book, and has been especially painstaking in handling difficult subjects. I am most indebted to my wife, whose encouragement and practical help have at all times been essential.

ALBERT W. ATWOOD.

Princeton, N. J.

TABLE OF CONTENTS

CHAPTER I

THE MARKET

SECTION		PAGE
1.	Why Exchanges Exist	1
2.	Why Exchanges Are Limited to Securities and Agricultural Products	2
3.	The Three Great Exchanges	4
4.	New York Stock Exchange	5
5.	Beginnings of the New York Stock Exchange . .	5
6.	Functions of the Stock Exchanges . . .	6
7.	Providing Ready Transfers of Securities . . .	6
8.	Real and Quoted Price Brought into Harmony .	8
9.	Trend of Business Indicated	9
10.	Other Functions of the Stock Exchange . . .	10
11.	Evils of the Stock Exchanges	10
12.	Why New York Is Supreme	12

CHAPTER II

THE NEW YORK STOCK EXCHANGE

1.	Membership	14
2.	The Building	16
3.	The Floor	17
4.	Method of Purchase and Sale of Securities . .	18
5.	Floor Members	20
6.	Classes of Brokers	22
7.	Commission Brokers	22

SECTION		PAGE
8.	"Two-Dollar" Brokers	23
9.	"Odd-Lot" Brokers	23
10.	Room Traders	25
11.	Specialists	26
12.	Number of Trading Members	26
13.	Government of the Exchange	27

CHAPTER III

LISTING SECURITIES ON THE STOCK EXCHANGE

1.	What Listing Means	29
2.	Classes of Securities Listed	31
3.	Machinery of Listing	32
4.	No Supervision After Listing	33
5.	Safeguards Maintained	33
6.	Advantages of Listing	34
7.	Value of Listing for Bank Loans	37

CHAPTER IV

MARGINS

1.	Two Classes of Security Buyers	50
2.	Why Margins Are Used	53
3.	Danger of Margins	54
4.	Amount of Margin	55
5.	Interest Rates	55
6.	Partial Payment Method	56
7.	When a Broker May Close a Transaction	57
8.	Legal Relation of Broker and Customer	60

CHAPTER V

RELATION OF BANKS TO THE SECURITY MARKET

1.	Amount of Loans to Brokers	62
2.	Source of Brokerage Loans	63

CONTENTS

SECTION		PAGE
3.	Kinds of Loans to Brokers	64
4.	Call Loans	65
5.	How Brokers' Loans Are Made	66
6.	Collateral for the Loan	67
7.	Banks and Speculation	69
8.	Securing the Loan, "Over-Certification"	70
9.	One-Day Unsecured Loans	73
10.	Interest Rates	75
11.	Renewal Rates	76
12.	Weaknesses and Services of the Call Loan System	77
13.	Effect of Money Rates on Stocks	78

CHAPTER VI

THE WAYS OF WALL STREET

1.	Four Methods of Trading	80
2.	Commissions	82
3.	"Bulls" and "Bears"	83
4.	Process of Selling Short	85
5.	A Short Sale Briefly Stated	88
6.	Loaning Rates	89
7.	Broker and Customer	90
8.	Market Effects of Short Selling	91
9.	Dangers and Advantages of Short Selling	92
10.	Loaning Rate as a Market Index	93
11.	Legal Prohibitions	93
12.	Functions of Short Selling	94
13.	Arguments Against Short Selling	96

CHAPTER VII

THE WAYS OF WALL STREET (*Continued*)

1.	Puts, Calls and Straddles	101
2.	Puts	102

SECTION	PAGE
3. Calls	103
4. Straddles and Spreads	104
5. Price of Privileges	105
6. Stop-Orders—or Stop-Loss Orders	107
7. Averaging	107
8. Pyramiding	108
9. Arbitrage	108
10. London and New York Prices	109
11. Delivery of Stock	111
12. Stock Clearing House	112
13. Speculation and the Clearing House	113
14. Transfers	114
15. When Brokers Fail	115

CHAPTER VIII

USE OF INFORMATION ON THE EXCHANGES

1. Value of News	118
2. The Ticker	119
3. Stock Abbreviations	120
4. Use of the Ticker	121
5. Quotation Companies	122
6. News Tickers	124
7. Bulletin Service	124
8. Newspapers	126
9. Reading the Financial Page	127

CHAPTER IX

THE CURB MARKET

1. Physical Characteristics	130
2. The Great Open Market	131

CONTENTS

SECTION		PAGE
3.	Organization and Membership	132
4.	Present Importance	133
5.	Relation of the Stock Exchange to the Curb	134
6.	Functions of the Curb	135

CHAPTER X

OTHER AMERICAN STOCK EXCHANGES

1.	Consolidated Stock Exchange of New York	140
2.	History and Description	141
3.	Stock Exchanges Outside New York	142
4.	Services of the Smaller Exchanges	143
5.	Boston Stock Exchange	144
6.	Chicago Stock Exchange	146
7.	Philadelphia Stock Exchange	147
8.	Pittsburgh Stock Exchange	147

CHAPTER XI

THE LONDON STOCK EXCHANGE

1.	Importance of the London Stock Exchange	149
2.	Effect of the War	149
3.	International Scope of the London Exchange	151
4.	Lombard Street	152
5.	Organization and Machinery	153
6.	Brokers and Jobbers	156
7.	How Jobbers Operate	157
8.	Publicity	159
9.	Settlements	160
10.	Commissions	162
11.	Listing Securities	163

CHAPTER XII

THE CONTINENTAL BOURSES

SECTION		PAGE
1.	How They Differ from American Exchanges	165
2.	Berlin Bourse	166
3.	Paris Bourse	168
4.	Membership and Government	169
5.	Prerogatives of Stock Brokers	170
6.	Kinds of Dealings	172
7.	Margins and Commissions	173
8.	Clearings and Deliveries	174
9.	The "Coulisse"	174

CHAPTER XIII

THE PRODUCE EXCHANGES

1.	Importance of the Exchanges and of Their Speculative Activity	177
2.	Types of Produce Exchanges	178
3.	"Spots" and "Futures"	180
4.	Future Trading Illustrated	181
5.	"Contract" Trade, Another Name for Future Trading	181
6.	Terms of Sale	184
7.	Legal Status of Futures	185
8.	Warehouse Receipts	186
9.	Inspection and Grading	187
10.	State Bureaus of Inspection	190
11.	Chicago and Liverpool Grades of Wheat	191
12.	Federal Grain Inspection Law of 1916	192
13.	General Methods of Inspection and Grading	193

CHAPTER XIV

THE PRODUCE EXCHANGES (*Continued*)

SECTION		PAGE
1.	Hedging	195
2.	Relation of Hedging to Future Trading	196
3.	How Millers Hedge	197
4.	Shifting the Risk	199
5.	Future Trading Steadies Prices	199
6.	Service of Future Trading Illustrated by the Grain Business	200
7.	Adjusting Prices	201
8.	What the Farmers Think of the Exchanges	201
9.	Activities of the Exchanges	202
10.	Farmers' Participation in the Business of Exchanges	204
11.	Influences That Govern the Price of Grain	206
12.	Foreign Influences: The Liverpool Market	208
13.	Sources of Market Information	209
14.	Newspaper Accounts of Market Fluctuations	210

CHAPTER XV

THE CHICAGO BOARD OF TRADE

1.	Why Chicago Has the Largest Market	213
2.	Methods of Trading, Spot and Cash	215
3.	Methods of Payment	217
4.	Ringing Out	220
5.	Clearing-House	221
6.	Commissions	222
7.	Government and Management	223
8.	Other American Grain Exchanges	224

CHAPTER XVI

THE NEW YORK COTTON EXCHANGE

1.	Importance of Cotton	227

SECTION		PAGE
2.	Primary Markets	228
3.	Government and Membership	229
4.	Unit of Trading	229
5.	Methods of Settlement	230
6.	Cotton Futures	231
7.	The Grades	232
8.	Cotton Futures Act	233
9.	Use of Futures	236
10.	Factors That Determine Cotton Prices	237
11.	Reading the Cotton Market	238

CHAPTER XVII

ABUSES OF SPECULATION — THE BUCKET SHOP

1.	Speculative Refinements Lead to Abuses	242
2.	What Is a Bucket Shop?	243
3.	Extent of Bucketing	246
4.	Margins or Stakes	247
5.	When Bucketers Flourish	247
6.	Bucket Shops and Quotations	249
7.	Evils of Bucket Shops	250

CHAPTER XVIII

MANIPULATION

1.	Difficulty of the Subject	253
2.	What Is Manipulation?	255
3.	Kinds of Manipulation	256
4.	Extreme or Excessive Speculation	257
5.	Rumors	257
6.	Pools	258
7.	Directors' and Officers' Manipulations	258
8.	Wash Sales	259

CONTENTS

SECTION		PAGE
9.	Matched Orders	260
10.	Defense of Matched Orders	261
11.	Evils of Manipulation	262
12.	Prohibition of Manipulation	262
13.	Some Celebrated Plungers; James R. Keene	264
14.	A. O. Brown & Co.	265
15.	Matched Orders, American Ice	265
16.	The Hocking Pool	266
17.	California Petroleum Case	268

CHAPTER XIX

SPECULATIVE FEATS AND EXCESSES — CORNERS

1.	Corners Defined	271
2.	How Corners Are Worked	272
3.	Corners in Stock	273
4.	Northern Pacific Panic	274
5.	Harlem Corner	275
6.	Gold Corner of 1869	278
7.	United Copper Corner	279
8.	Corners in Products	280
9.	Speculative Corners	281
10.	Corners in Wheat	282
11.	Leiter Corner	282

CHAPTER XX

BENEFITS AND EVILS OF SPECULATION

1.	Investment, Speculation and Gambling	284
2.	Speculation Defined	285
3.	Safety and Risk	287
4.	Income and Profit	288
5.	Method of Purchase	289

xx—2

SECTION		PAGE
6.	Ownership of Capital	290
7.	Duration of Investment	290
8.	Bonds or Stocks	291
9.	Gambling Defined	292
10.	Method of the Speculator	293
11.	Evils of Speculation	294
12.	Excessive Speculation	295
13.	Effect of Speculation on Stocks	296
14.	Effects of Speculation in General	297
15.	Survey of Restrictions on Speculation	298
16.	Experience of Germany	300
17.	Why the German Law Failed	302
18.	Conclusion	304

CHAPTER XXI

INFLUENCES THAT GOVERN STOCK PRICES

1.	How Far Is Speculation Scientific?	306
2.	Influences Affecting Speculation	307
3.	Extrinsic Influences	308
4.	Technical Conditions	309
5.	Importance of Extrinsic Influences	311
6.	Intrinsic Influences	312
7.	Business and Money Market Conditions	313
8.	Business Barometers	314
9.	Management and Character of the Company	318
10.	Limitations	319
11.	Potential Factors	319
12.	Classification of Price Movements	321
13.	Mistakes of Speculators	325
14.	Qualities Necessary for Success	326

THE EXCHANGES AND SPECULATION

CHAPTER I

THE MARKET

1. *Why exchanges exist.*—Any two persons may strike a bargain. One buys and the other sells. There is a meeting of the minds, a contract is effected, a sale or transaction made. Two savages meet in the jungle and instead of killing one another they exchange cocoanuts and sharp stones. In such an incident we have an early stage of barter and a step toward civilization as well. Later on men use money in their dealings. More than two men come to the same place to trade. As commerce grows, the place becomes a centre of trade, a market. Ultimately fairs are held there, annually or perhaps oftener.

Finally, the market passes under the control of a regular organization or association of brokers. They pass rules and regulations and form an "exchange," one of the most important institutions in modern business and the most highly organized and delicately adjusted market in the world.

There are two kinds of exchanges, one deals in stocks and the other in commodities. The first is an organization which conducts speculation and investment in stocks and bonds. It is made up of professional traders, who buy and sell on their own account, and of brokers, who buy and sell for others. The commodity exchange is an organization of the same kind, tho instead of dealing in securities, which are the paper representatives of corporations, it provides a place for dealing in grain, cotton or other agricultural produce. It is with these two great groups of institutions that this book deals.

2. *Why exchanges are limited to securities and agricultural products.*—Now at first thought it might seem a curious fact that organized markets, or exchanges, should exist only for securities and agricultural products. Why are there exchanges for stocks, wheat and cotton but none for safety razors, typewriters or cigarettes? The reasons are simple and obvious. As regards agricultural products, it would be a great economic loss if the manufacturer, for the purpose of collecting his material, were obliged to travel over a territory large enough to supply the required amount of raw wheat, corn and cotton. Such products are shipped from country to country in vast quantities. Exporters and importers cannot go from place to place to buy and sell a few bushels at a time. Further, the commodities can be handled in bulk without injury. They can be stored away for long periods of time without deterioration. They are easily graded into certain standard qualities. The raw material is gathered from many scattered sources for mass pro-

duction. Dealers meet at a common, central point and compete for the concentrated raw material.

But the producer of manufactured articles, of typewriters, automobiles and the like has a different problem. No one purchaser wants many articles, and each buys only after personal inspection and a series of bargainings. The products are unlike, and the buyer of a Packard would be dissatisfied with a Ford. The problem is just the reverse of that in the agricultural field. With the manufactured article it is more economical to break up the market into many small distributing points. In the case of cigarettes the finished product is distributed among tens of thousands of retail stores.

The conditions, as regard securities, are not unlike those in the agricultural markets. It is not necessary to see each stock or bond certificate. Each share of common stock of the United States Steel Corporation is like hundreds of thousands of others. Like bushels of wheat or bales of cotton, such securities can be dealt in by the mass. Given only the name, price and quantity, men can "trade."

"The market" is a term which has come to mean something more than a place. It is used to describe the collective mind that finds expression in the fluctuating prices at which property is bought and sold. One of the leading financial dictionaries defines the word "market" as follows: "in general the meaning is the predominating feeling as to values." We speak of the market as a person.

"Thus we say," writes Theodore H. Price in the *Outlook*, "that the market is 'strong' or 'weak' or 'panicky,' 'unreasonable' or 'suspicious,' 'enthusiastic' or 'tired,' 'hungry' or 'asleep,' and attribute to it almost every emotion felt by the individual."

In this sense the word "market" has come to be synonymous with "exchange." When we say "the stock market," we mean the stock market on the stock exchange, and nine times out of ten, we mean the stock market on the largest stock exchange. There are many dealings in stocks, bonds, wheat, cotton and other produce off the exchanges. One authority has estimated that of the entire commerce in stocks, grain and cotton that is generated by the nation, probably less than five per cent is conducted on the exchanges, "and yet all the business of the country is attuned to the tone of these exchanges and reflects the confidence or doubt of the collective public mind to which they give expression. . . . It seems reasonable to assume that the American public directly affected by the changes in value registered on our exchanges include about 11,000,000 people."

3. *The three great exchanges.*—The first part of this book deals with stock exchanges, the second part with commodity exchanges. In this country there are three great organized markets, the New York Stock Exchange, the Chicago Board of Trade and the New York Cotton Exchange. It is with these that we are chiefly concerned, altho comparisons must be made with similar institutions abroad. There are smaller

stock exchanges in almost every city of metropolitan aspirations, grain exchanges in numerous middle western and Canadian cities and an important cotton exchange in New Orleans. But other markets are all more or less responsive to the influences that affect the three larger exchanges.

4. *New York Stock Exchange.*—By far the largest single market for stocks and bonds in the country is the New York Stock Exchange. Here, as on all exchanges there is a large element of speculation, and as speculation is more extensive in stocks than in bonds, sales of stock far exceed those of bonds. Over a period of years the average annual turnover in stocks on the New York Exchange exceeds sixteen billion dollars, while that in bonds is about one billion. Many classes of bonds are indeed more extensively bought and sold off than on the Exchange. Yet half a billion dollars of new bonds are "listed" yearly and in no single place off the Exchange does such a huge market for bonds exist.

5. *Beginnings of the New York Stock Exchange.*—In 1792, twenty-four men who called themselves "Brokers for the Purchase and Sale of Public Stocks" met under an old tree on Lower Wall Street and formed the organization which was destined to play by far the most important rôle in the financial history of the United States. The business of the organization remained small until the year 1817 when the public debt had increased to $109,000,000. Later the discovery of gold in California gave impetus to specula-

tion and the increase in national wealth enlarged the volume of trading done on the Exchange. When the period of the Civil War was reached it became an essential factor, the expansion of our national debt and the suspension of specie payments all helping to whet the speculative appetite. After the war, railroad construction went on at an increasing pace and the industrial development of the country received more and more attention. The creation of corporations and combinations made the Exchange an extremely busy place and the centre for trading in the United States.

6. *Functions of the stock exchanges.*—Stock exchanges have come into existence because of the enormous increase in stocks and bonds; because of the growing ratio they bear to the world's total wealth; because of the wide distribution of their ownership among millions of persons; and on account of their increasing use as security for bank loans. The chief functions which stock exchanges perform may now be considered.

7. *Providing ready transfers of securities.*—Of first importance is the ready means afforded the exchange of transferring stocks and bonds from hand to hand, an element which is vitally essential to the creation of corporations. The stock exchange renders this service because it provides at all times a wide, permanent and easily available market for the sale of securities, and establishes the current prices for such securities, based on the best available information. The exchange provides a central market where quick sales

may be made. Without organized stock exchanges it might take days to sell stocks, where now transactions are made in seconds and minutes. Professor S. S. Huebner describes this function in an excellent passage:

Without an organized market for corporate securities, the average individual holder would stand in a most defenseless position. He could not learn their price from day to day, because transactions, if private, would not be recorded, might be designed to mislead and, certainly would not be representative of the general judgment. He would be exposed to a hundred times the fraud of today. He would be at the mercy of every rumor. He would be unable to place a correct estimate of the importance of current events upon the price of his securities. He could be easily misled by unscrupulous counselors into selling his securities far below their fair value.

Today, however, every newspaper of any importance in the country gives daily the quotations of leading securities for the day before, and the holder cannot be deceived as to the price. These quotations represent the average combined judgment of many minds, which is given concrete expression in actual transactions on the floor of the Exchange. Thru the widespread publicity of stock exchange quotations the world over, the holders of securities are given gratis the combined opinion of the most competent financiers as to the value of those securities at present and their prospective value in the future.

The predominance in the business of dealing in securities held by such stock exchanges as those of New York, London and Paris in their respective countries make these markets the most important news centers of the world in respect to everything which has a price making quality. By the aid of myriads of news agency activities of international scope, the exchanges are able to approximate to what is accepted as actual value. Prices made on the great exchanges in this country are published in newspapers with a circulation of at least ten million copies; these same prices are printed within a few minutes of their making by thousands of "tickers" in scores of cities; they are sent over hundreds of private wires leased by brokers to all parts of the United States and Canada; they are cabled to all the leading cities of Europe. Thus we are led to the second function performed by the stock exchange.

8. *Real and quoted price brought into harmony.*— The exchange tends to bring real and quoted prices into the nearest possible agreement. The fact that open public markets exist where prices are immediately recorded thruout the civilized world, brings to these exchanges as buyers and sellers countless thousands of speculators and investors who are constant students of conditions and present and prospective influences. Naturally they seek to "discount," anticipate or take advantage of these conditions. From hour to hour the average of the best expert opinion as to what values to place upon properties is thus registered. The stock market is the best collective body of opinion in this country. More than anything it represents the collective mind on practical business subjects. If you want to know what the real value of a stock is, "list" it on the stock exchange, leave it there a few years, and you will find out.

9. *Trend of business indicated*.—The stock exchange indicates the directions in which capital may be most profitably employed. It prevents the misdirection of investments into unnecessary ventures. It brings into sharp relief the errors of capitalists and the misapplications of money. Nowhere does the changing value of property become so quickly known to all who read. The exchange thus acts as a barometric indicator of future conditions. It anticipates or discounts the ebb and flow of prosperity. Those who trade or operate upon the exchange have in mind the future rather than the present, and their every action in buying and selling tends to discount coming events. Prices reflect, not so much present as future dividends, not so much actual as potential earning power.

Speculation from the very nature of the case deals with the future. Among the first speculators were middlemen or jobbers who undertook to pay the growers of wheat the current price and take the risk of selling at a higher price later on. As one authority says:

The stocks and bonds of our corporations aggregate so large a proportion of the world's wealth, and represent such a variety of industries, that a marked rise or decline in the general level of prices is the surest indication, in fact an almost unfailing index, of coming prosperity or depression. And the all-important fact is, that such changes of prices on the exchange always precede, that is to say, discount the event, and do not follow, or occur concurrently. Without an exception every business depression in this country had been discounted in our security markets from six months to two years before the depression became a reality.

If the happenings of the exchanges affected only the speculators themselves, they would deserve little consideration. Whether these markets act as barometers because of the superiority of the speculative vision in anticipating future conditions, or because of the hypnotic, psychological influence of the stock market upon industry in general, it is hard to say. Probably the former is nearer the truth, because the collective opinion of minds trained to correlate economic phenomena is exceptionally acute and well informed.

10. *Other functions of the stock exchange.*—Other functions are performed by the stock markets, such as the assistance that it renders in promoting very large corporations and the part that it plays in transferring credit to one country from another without the movement of gold. If there were not a great mass of sound securities which are quoted in international markets, an adverse trade balance against a country could be settled only by the shipment of goods or gold. This fact has been brought out in a most striking manner since the war, but a detailed consideration of the subject belongs to the text on "Domestic and Foreign Exchange."

11. *Evils of the stock exchanges.*—There are those who maintain that the exchanges should not be allowed to exercise such power and influence as they do. But there seems to be no way to prevent it.

For nearly half a year after the war started, the stock and cotton exchanges were closed, but the stoppage of practically all business in securities and cotton was accompanied by a depression in nearly all business. The opening of the exchanges was a signal for general rejoicing and the resumption of industrial activity. The grain exchanges had remained open and the largest wheat crop ever produced was marketed with extraordinary rapidity.

There are, of course, those who dishonestly abuse the facilities of the exchanges, but their number is not great. There are far more, unhappily, who ignorantly and foolishly abuse these facilities. These are people who approach the market in a gambling spirit, who know nothing of its purposes and are incapable of understanding the mighty influences which dominate it. They seek to become wealthy over night, without work, by merely playing with the fluctuations in the quotations made on the exchanges.

It is not to be wondered at that in the free buying and selling of such a vast amount of flexible and easily transferable property as corporate shares, many questionable practices should arise. Yet the exchanges have thrown about the whole business of stock dealing so many safeguards and protections, they have so regulated the brokerage business and forced so much higher standards of business honor among brokers than would otherwise prevail, that it is probable all the evils are more than offset by the benefits. And this without considering the fact that the economic functions of the exchanges must be performed somehow, no matter what the evils may be.

12. *Why New York is supreme.*—The New York Stock Exchange is supreme in this country, as are the London and Paris exchanges in Europe, altho those of Berlin, Frankfort, Brussels, Antwerp, Amsterdam, Vienna and Petrograd are fairly important in their own countries. The New York Stock Exchange overshadows all others in this country because New York is the financial center of the nation.

As the other cities are becoming important financial centers the prestige of the New York Stock Exchange not only remains but increases relatively faster than the city itself. While other cities become great centers for a particular locality, New York remains the national financial center, the national center for corporation headquarters and banking on a large scale. What perhaps is even more important is that New York obviously has the closest and most extensive commercial and financial relations with other countries. This fact alone would raise its stock exchange far above all others.

REVIEW

What do you consider the value of organized markets for securities and produce?

What functions does the stock exchange exercise?

What are considered the most important exchanges in the United States?

What methods would you suggest to prevent abuse of the stock exchange facilities?

Much adverse criticism is directed against the exchanges. Assuming that these were to be permanently done away with, how do you think the economic functions of the exchanges might be exercised?

How do you account for the development of the New York Stock Exchange?

CHAPTER II

THE NEW YORK STOCK EXCHANGE

1. *Membership.*—The New York Stock Exchange is a very exclusive organization—in reality, a club. Membership is limited to 1,100, and has been full for many years. The cost of a membership varies with the supply and the demand. The supply consists of the "seats" of members who retire, who desire to sell, or who die; there is no other way of obtaining entrance but by obtaining their seats, since all seats have already been purchased. The demand, of course, consists of the number of persons desiring to become brokers on the Exchange. The price of memberships, or seats, as they are commonly called, has ranged in recent years from about $35,000 to $95,000, the usual price is from $55,000 to $75,000.

The word seat is a misnomer. In early days the brokers had seats in a room arranged like the ordinary legislative chamber, but at the present time the business of the Exchange is handled upon a great floor, where the brokers transact their business standing.

The applicant for admission to the Stock Exchange must be a citizen of the United States, and at least twenty-one years of age. In order to have his application considered by the Secretary of the Exchange he must indicate two sponsors who will vouch for his honesty, integrity and financial responsibility. Having fulfilled this requirement, he must then begin negotiations with the Secretary concerning a seat on the Exchange. After the payment of the initiation fee of $2,000, he and his sponsors are summoned before the Committee on Admissions for examination. His personal history, condition of health and business experience are examined in elaborate detail and, if everything proves satisfactory, he is elected to membership and required to sign the constitution. The authorities are especially inquisitorial regarding the source of the funds which the candidate employs to buy the seat. This is because the Exchange fears that he may use money to which some "string," or condition, is attached, and that the supposed owner, if he should get into trouble, might not have the capital with which to meet his obligations.

In brief, the reason for such painstaking exclusiveness is that the Stock Exchange desires a high degree of financial responsibility in those who join. Members cannot make distinctions in their operations. They must accept the first bargain offered—provided, only, the price is acceptable. Unlike most lines of business, the buyer or seller cannot draw any personal lines whatever, even when he thinks the other person's credit is not good. Nor is there any method by which this rule can be evaded. Since they are required to do business with the first fellow-member who presents himself, the members, as a rule, are naturally very careful whom they admit.

Dr. Weld in his "Marketing of Farm Products" gives an excellent summary of the advantages of insisting upon high membership values on the produce exchanges. His remarks apply equally well to stock exchanges. He says:

> The principal reasons for maintaining high membership values, are, to make it necessary for an individual to have some means before assuming the financial obligations incumbent on members, and to increase the disciplinary power of the exchange over its members. . . . It is necessary for the exchange to hold some club over its members to enforce its rulings. If a membership is valued lightly a member may be willing to run the risk of expulsion in order to be able to stoop to some illegitimate practice. If his membership has a high financial value, he will be held more easily to the rules. Expulsion from one of the large exchanges carries with it not only financial loss but business disgrace. The more severe the restrictions on admission, the greater the disgrace from expulsion.

2. *The building.*—Outsiders were formerly admitted to a gallery where they might view the Stock Exchange in action, but this is no longer permitted. Those who have business at the Secretary's office, and newspaper men are the only persons who enter the building, except members, officers and employes. Newspaper men are never allowed to go on the main floor of the Exchange; they may enter only the Secretary's office or the library on the fifth floor, both far away from the place in which business is transacted.

© *Brown Bros., N.Y.* FLOOR OF THE NEW YORK STOCK EXCHANGE

THE NEW YORK STOCK EXCHANGE 17

The present building of the New York Stock Exchange is a large and ornate structure, running thru from Broad to New Street. Only the first floor is used for trading; it is, however, an immense inclosure, with ample space for the transaction of business. The other five floors and the basement are used for the elaborate mechanical apparatus, including the complex cable, telegraphic and telephonic connections; for meeting rooms, committee rooms, officers' and employes' accommodations (members never have offices in the building unless they are also officers of the Exchange or of the building company), a luncheon club, smoking and lounging rooms, libraries, and similar comforts and conveniences.

3. *The floor.*—The main floor of the Exchange is surmounted by a high dome which admits a generous supply of light and air. An air-cooling plant was installed recently which minimizes the effects of excessive humidity and keeps the floor of the Exchange well-ventilated in spite of the crowds. Around the walls is a seemingly limitless number of telephone booths each of which is leased to some member of the Exchange. The members and their clerks use these telephones many times a day to communicate with their offices for the purpose of receiving orders and reporting the success of negotiations.

On the "floor" of the Exchange there are scattered posts, at each one of which there are the names of the stocks that are bought and sold at that point. The number of stocks thus enumerated ranges from twenty to forty. There is, therefore, some particular place in the room for the purchase and sale of each listed security which, when once designated, is seldom changed.

For example, Atchison, the first stock on the alphabetical list, is at post 5; New York Air Brake at 14; and American Brake Shoe at 8. The broker soon learns where the securities are dealt in, and automatically turns in the right direction whenever he has occasion to trade. One post at the northeast corner, No. 4, gets considerable attention, because here the "loan crowd" is situated; stocks and money may be borrowed and lent. These operations are explained in later chapters. Still another portion of the floor on a raised platform, under a gallery, is given up to bonds; and on one side of the room, close to the cable instruments, are the "arbitrage" brokers, who buy from, and sell to, London brokers.

Brokers tend to gather in crowds. Around or near each post are several of these crowds, which naturally vary in size as the popularity of the various securities changes. Thus, one hears such expressions as the "Steel Crowd," the "Reading Crowd," and so on.

4. *Method of purchase and sale of securities.*—To the average visitor who formerly made the rounds of the Stock Exchange, the whole affair was a puzzle. He did not understand what took place on the floor, and he left the place with wonderment. Altho pandemonium seems to exist, the machinery of business runs so smoothly that to the layman it is incredible

that transactions involving hundreds of millions of dollars are carried thru without a hitch every day.

When a member secures an order to buy, he goes to the proper post where the security is dealt in, and calls out how much he desires to buy and the price he is willing to pay. The price named will of course be at the last "quotations" or below it. The brokers who have that stock for sale gather around the post, each shouting out the price at which he will sell the quantity desired. At first the buyer and the sellers may be far from a common ground of agreement, but gradually they approach each other until some broker offers the stock at the price which is agreeable to the buyer.

The first bid and offer to buy or sell, takes precedence when it can be heard, and if there is a dispute as to which particular bid or offer was first, a committee decides. Prices are made by eighths of one dollar, never less. The fractions are $\frac{1}{8}, \frac{1}{4}, \frac{3}{8}, \frac{1}{2}, \frac{5}{8}, \frac{3}{4}, \frac{7}{8}$; no other fractions are used. An eighth is the equivalent of $12\frac{1}{2}$ cents. Stocks are also spoken of as rising or falling one or two or any number of "points." A point is one dollar, unless the stock happens to be selling at less than a dollar, in which case a point would be one cent.

Formerly the basis of quoting stocks was percentages instead of dollars, as now. It was all very well if the par value happened to be $100, but it was very confusing if the par value was $50. According to both the old and the new system a $100 par stock selling at 75¾ and at $75.75 is the same thing, but a $50 par stock which sold at 160 under the old system really was selling at $80 a share.

In the process of bidding and asking above described, the seller finally offers a price that is agreeable to the buyer. The latter shouts "Take it," and each makes a simple memorandum upon a little pad which he carries in his hand, as to the number of shares "bought" or "sold," as the case may be, the price, the name of the security and the name of the broker with whom the deal is closed.

It must be understood that no stocks or bonds ever appear on the floor. They are not transferred or delivered there. The only business which takes place on the Stock Exchange is that of making contracts to buy and sell securities and money at some later date; the actual delivery and payment always takes place elsewhere. These contracts are commonly known as "sales." They are also called "transactions," or "dealings." The total sales of any one stock or of all stocks, in any given period of time, is known as the "volume."

Newspapers, tickers and all other reporting agencies in adding up the total, properly take one side of the account only, altho for every buyer there is a seller, and for every seller, a buyer. If A sells 100 shares of Union Pacific to B, they are not counted as 200 shares, because A has sold B 100 shares and B has bought 100; they are recorded simply as 100.

5. *Floor members.*—The brokers who actually buy

and sell on the Exchange are known as "floor brokers." A Stock Exchange firm may have a score of broker partners, only one of whom is a member of the Stock Exchange. The partners who are not members would no more be admitted to the floor than an outsider. This fact cannot be too strongly emphasized. The firm of J. P. Morgan & Company belongs to the Stock Exchange, but only one of the dozen partners, thru membership in the Exchange, would be admitted there. On the other hand, some firms have six or seven Exchange or floor members.

Except in dull markets, floor brokers do not walk back and forth from the Exchange to their offices to get their orders; they communicate by means of the private telephones already referred to. Their attention is called to their telephones by means of a simple device: each member has a number high on the wall of the floor room usually covered by a disk, and when any one in his office wants to give him an order, a telephone operator at the Exchange presses a button which drops the disk and reveals the number. The floor broker who is constantly on the watch is thus notified. He does not even need to leave the floor to go to his telephone, perhaps fifty feet away, for there are hundreds of messenger boys who dart to and fro between brokers on the floor and the clerks who operate the telephones. Thus floor brokers can get into touch with their partners, customers and offices almost instantaneously, and without leaving the floor at any time.

The brokers usually gather about 9.30 a. m. The Exchange opens for business at 10 a. m., at the ringing of a bell, and closes at 3 p. m., except on Saturday, when it closes at noon. There is usually a rush of orders to execute at the "opening," which means the first few minutes after ten o'clock, and the "tone" of the market at the opening is considered important.

6. *Classes of brokers.*—After a man becomes a member of the Exchange, there is no hard-and-fast rule whatsoever as to the particular kind of business he shall engage in. There are many different kinds of transactions, however, to be carried on, and each broker generally confines his activities to one or two classes. Some of the nine important classes of brokers may be considered.

7. *Commission brokers.*—The most common type of broker, the member who, by himself, or in partnership with other brokers, devotes the greater part or the whole of his time to the execution of orders for buying or selling for customers, is called a commission broker. He maintains a large office and a considerable force of employes by means of the commissions and the other items received from his transactions. Very often the commission brokers have so many accounts and so many customers that it is impossible for them to execute all their orders. This is especially the case when the market is active. The floor member, or members, of a firm may find that there is an overwhelming rush of orders especially at the "open-

ing." At such time they employ "two-dollar" brokers to help them.

8. *"Two-dollar" brokers.*—The member who executes orders for other members formerly for $2, now $2.50, for every hundred shares, is known as a "two-dollar" broker. At first glance it would seem strange that any broker should take the trouble to execute orders for other members at this rate, when he could get $15 for doing the same amount of work for outside clients. There are, however, a considerable number of brokers who do not care for a business that involves a large number of negotiations and accounts with customers and the maintenance of a more or less expensive establishment, but who would rather execute the floor business of other members who have a large clientele. It is obvious that because of the low rate of commission that these men charge for performing this function, they must transact a large volume of business in order to secure a fair amount of profit. Reliance on efficiency and celerity in the execution of orders is their means of securing business and the proficiency they display, especially during periods of activity, is often astonishing. There are several hundred "two-dollar" brokers.

9. *"Odd-lot" brokers.*—Those members who are purchasers and vendors of fractional lots of securities, are called "odd-lot" brokers. They are about fifty in number. These men charge no commission, because they are allowed to make profits by trading against their commitments when these occur, that is, the

brokers do not have to turn the stock over to their customers at precisely the same price that the former paid for it. It must be understood that these odd-lot brokers have no dealings whatever with any outsiders. Their business consists in buying from, or selling to, commission brokers from one to ninety-nine shares of stock, and then putting these small lots together into 100-share certificates, or splitting up 100-share certificates, as the case may be.

On the Stock Exchange the "unit" of trading is one hundred shares of stock and $10,000 in bonds. Unless otherwise specified, that amount is always understood when a broker buys or sells. By specifying, he can buy any number of shares less than one hundred, but it has not generally been found practical to conduct business on the floor on the basis of ten-share or one-share units. Indeed, the whole huge fabric of stock-trading would probably break down if all the brokers had usually to deal in small lots among themselves. But there are millions of investors and speculators thruout the country who own less than one hundred shares. This is made possible by the odd-lot brokers. The outsider does not come into contact with these brokers, who are wholesalers on a large scale, but goes to his regular broker, who buys for his client the three or seven shares, as the case may be, from the ever ready odd-lot man.

The odd-lot brokers usually secure the cooperation of a large number of floor members, because of the enormous detail of their work. Their expenses are heavy, since upon them falls the burden of having 100-share certificates split up into small lots. An odd-lot therefore costs the outsider one-eighth more than a 100-share lot, and it can be sold, generally, only for one-eighth less. Odd-lot brokers transact fully one-fifth of the total business that is done on the floor.

10. *Room traders.*—Those operators who do business independently, go by the name of room traders. They do not carry on transactions for others, but speculate or "trade" on their own account. Room traders do not try to make large profits on any one transaction, for they rely upon their volume of trade to yield an adequate income. Since they are on the floor of the Exchange at all times, and do not have to rely upon mechanical devices to bring them information concerning the movement of prices—which, in rush hours, cannot be secured until several minutes after a transaction is concluded upon the floor of the Exchange—they are able to take advantage of every slight fluctuation, and can therefore sell upon the slightest upward movement and buy again when prices begin to sag. Their usual procedure is to specialize in a few stocks, so as to guard against being caught in any general movement of prices. In order to use as little cash as possible in settlement, they try each day to make their sales and purchases as nearly equal as they can under the circumstances. There are possibly one hundred room traders, and they, together with the arbitrageurs [1] transact nearly one-third of the entire business of the Exchange.

[1] See p. 108.

11. *Specialists*.—Those members who make a specialty of a few selected securities are called specialists. Like the room traders, they have no dealings with the public at large. In some cases, one security is the object of their attention or study, altho usually they confine their operations to three or four. In most cases, because of their expert knowledge, the business of these brokers comes from the fulfilment of orders given by other brokers.

In the case of inactive stocks—that is, those infrequently dealt in—the commission brokers would almost always seek out a specialist rather than another commission broker. Specialists are always supposed to know the last price of their particular securities, and it is largely from them that the quotations are obtained. The fact that a broker is specializing in any given stock is always well known to other brokers.

12. *Number of trading members*.—The 1,100 members represent between 500 and 600 firms aggregating about 2,000 partners. Rarely more than 500 or 600 brokers are on the floor at any one time. There are several members of the Exchange who have rarely been there. Among the 1,100 members are a great many who never buy or sell for outsiders, and in fact who never themselves buy or sell on the floor. They have become members merely because they realized that membership enables them to buy securities much more cheaply and sell them with more profit than they otherwise could. This is true even when they employ a two-dollar broker. Such men as John D. Rockefeller, J. P. Morgan, George J. Gould, August Belmont and other leading financiers, belong to the Exchange partly in order to lend to it their sanction.

13. *Government of the Exchange.*—The government of the Exchange rests in an all-powerful governing committee, composed of the President, the Treasurer and forty members. There are also paid officials, and a secretary and an assistant secretary, who are not members. The assistant secretary is the chief authority on technical details and both have many important duties. The governing committee is the final authority on nearly all matters; there are, in fact, few instances where such a committee is vested with such practically unlimited jurisdiction. This body resembles the board of directors of a corporation. It has power to appoint all committees and regulate their jurisdiction; it may also try all members for alleged offences and punish them if they are found guilty. It controls the finances of the Exchange, and since the Exchange is not incorporated, the committee may mete out punishment to offenders without being hindered by court action. It is thus free of all legal embarrassments and technicalities, and can enforce its rulings rigidly. By way of discipline, according to the offense, the committee removes a member's telephone, suspends him or expels him.

There are some fifteen committees in all, chosen from among the members of the governing committee. This organization of the government of the Exchange at first glance seems complicated; in realty it is very simple, considering the magnitude of the business involved, and the complexity of the questions that constantly arise. The Exchange is a wholly self-governing body, a fact that is remarkable when one considers the vastness of the operations conducted there.

There is no necessity of describing the work of all the committees. The Committee on Admissions not only passes on all applications for transfer of seats, but has charge also of the reinstatement of suspended members. While the Governing Committee is exceedingly strict about dropping an insolvent member, they often offer opportunity for reinstatement. There are also committees that are concerned respectively with law, business conduct (the ethics of transactions), arbitration (disputes), the clearing house, stock list (admission of securities), and many other subjects. The work of the Committee on Stock List concerns matters which require detailed consideration and which will be treated in the next chapter.

REVIEW

How does a firm gain admission to the New York Stock Exchange?
How is the business of the Exchange actually conducted?
What classes of brokers do business on the Exchange?
Why is membership in the Stock Exchange valuable?
How is the Exchange governed?

CHAPTER III

LISTING SECURITIES ON THE STOCK EXCHANGE

1. *What listing means.*—Before we discuss the further operations and trading methods on the stock exchanges, it is desirable to explain in some detail the admission or "listing" of the securities on the "Board," which is the Wall Street nickname for the Stock Exchange. This subject is far more important than it appears at first, and its numerous ramifications can be suggested only in this place. The Stock Exchange is as exclusive in regard to admitting stocks as it is in regard to admitting members.

While the Stock Exchange is a very efficient organization created for the purpose of trading in securities, it is to be noted that these securities are of selected classes. The floor has been compared to a vast auction room, but its wares differ radically from those of the usual auction room in that they are gathered together systematically.

The Exchange does not permit the broker-member to buy or sell any securities other than those which have received approbation from the exchange as well as the privilege of being listed. Many believe that every stock which has any real value is dealt in on the Exchange but this is far from correct. There are many securities which are more valuable from the investors' point of view and desirable from the standpoint of the public, than those which are listed. Another common error is the belief that securities traded in on the Exchange having been selected impartially because of their merit, those which are not listed must have been denied the privilege because of some inherent defect. This idea is inaccurate. Listed securities range from one extreme to the other in point of desirability. Some are of the highest grade while others are practically worthless.

It cannot be too strongly emphasized that listing a security does not prove its worth. It may be neither safe nor desirable. The Stock Exchange assumes no responsibility and affords absolutely no guarantee. But in the great majority of cases, companies whose stocks are listed must be important and sufficiently established to furnish the most exhaustive information. No stock or bond has gone on the Stock Exchange in recent years unless all the information reasonably and humanly possible to furnish, as far as the Exchange authorities could then determine, had been given. A few cases where accountants' reports were found later to be either misleading or totally inaccurate prove nothing except that perfection is impossible and that no one can foretell absolutely the future movement of securities, or estimate exactly the value of good-will and other intangible items.

This much may be said of listed securities: the investor has all the available facts upon which to form an opinion; how far these facts extend will be shown later on in this chapter. It is true that numerous companies whose stocks and bonds are listed have been ruined by high finance or mismanagement; but even in these cases the companies have had enormous amounts of actual property, and have not been patently fraudulent schemes, mere paper projects, such as are offered to the investor outside the stock exchange, literally by the scores of thousands.

2. *Classes of securities listed.*—It is neither possible nor necessary to name the various securities listed on the Stock Exchange. Reference to a daily newspaper will quickly afford practically a complete list. Most of the great, interstate corporations are listed. Particularly are the stocks of very large companies with a widely diffused ownership listed upon the Board. No stock held by a few owners will be admitted. Nor does the Stock Exchange care to take in even the largest corporations during their period of inception and incubation. It prefers to leave these to the curb market. It wants the stock to be at least a year old.

Until recently very few foreign securities were admitted to the New York Exchange, because American capital was not available for them and American investors took no interest in them. But the European war has brought about a great change. Increased attention has been given to the few foreign securities that were listed and several new ones have gone on the Board. In this respect the New York Stock Exchange differed radically in the past from the European exchanges, especially the London Exchange where thousands of foreign securities were actively traded in.

3. *Machinery of listing.*—The Stock Exchange maintains a Committee on Stock Listing, consisting of five members, to which are referred all applications for listing securities. A high-salaried clerk, in reality an important expert with a staff of assistants and offices of his own, is employed by the Committee to go over the reports in minute detail.

Even after the Committee on Stock Listing has granted its permission to list the stock its action must be reviewed by the Governing Committee. The Stock Listing Committee presents to the Governing Committee the full statement of the capital, number of shares, resources, etc., of the corporation making the application. This evidence is reviewed by the Governing Committee and if it gives its consent the stock may then be placed upon the list of the Exchange. It will be seen, therefore, that to gain admission any security must pass the scrutiny of two committees, one of which is the supreme body in the government of the exchange.

It is further maintained by the Stock Exchange that the function of determining the merit of new security issues is one that does not properly belong to the Stock Exchange, but to the government itself. If laws could be enacted which as in England, Germany and France place the burden of this responsibility upon the shoulders of competent departments of the government, the Committee on Stock Listing of the New

York Stock Exchange could go out of business. It would say to applicant companies, "Here is the government's blank provided for your purpose; fill it out." The public would know at once that no security could be admitted to the Exchange list that had not complied with these requirements. In the absence of such a law, the Committee on Stock Listing goes farther today than it ever went before to protect the public.

4. *No supervision after listing.*—The requirements for listing securities are strictly enforced by the committee. After the corporation secures admission to the list, however, this supervision virtually ceases. There is little checking up of its affairs and no further statements are made compulsory until further issues are listed. It is this fact that justifies the previous assertion that the mere fact of being listed on the Exchange does not guarantee the merit of the security in question.

The corporation may drift into an unsatisfactory condition without any official objection being raised by the Exchange and its securities may drop from a high value to a practically worthless condition.

5. *Safeguards maintained.*—It would be inaccurate to say, however, that the Exchange does nothing at all by way of supervision. On the contrary, it recommends that the listed corporations publish and distribute to the stockholders an annual report with full details concerning the income and expenditures of the corporation and a balance sheet showing the true financial condition at the end of the fiscal year. Ob-

servance of this rule is not compulsory, but the recommendation has almost the force of law and nearly all the corporations comply with it.

Nor will the Exchange allow any listed company to declare secret dividends by which only "insiders" profit. Due notice must be given of all dividends, new stock issues and other essential details. Anything in the nature of actual fraud in the issue of stock, forged stock, illegal issue of stock, improperly engraved certificates, overissue of stock and other actually fraudulent measures are forbidden by the exchange in a long list of rules and regulations which are rigidly enforced. It compels all companies to maintain in the city of New York two separate offices, one where stock can be transferred and the other where this process is checked up. This rule prevents any possible delay or fraud in having securities transferred to a new owner's name.

In other words while practically guaranteeing the *physical genuineness* of its securities, the Stock Exchange consistently refuses to guarantee their *worth*. If the Exchange were to attempt such a colossal task it would undertake one of the biggest problems and burdens in the whole of modern industrial life. It is absurd to expect such a thing.

6. *Advantages of listing.*—The marketability of any security is obviously increased by listing. Yet it must not be supposed that no unlisted securities have a broad, active market. Many unlisted securities en-

joy an excellent market. Indeed there are listed bonds whose chief market is not on the Stock Exchange at all, but "over the counter," which means by telephone from broker to broker. But such a market is not dependable. The outside buyer is wholly at the mercy of the dealer. He has few published quotations to go by. There is nothing open about the dealings even if the outsider knows to what dealer to go, which is rarely the case.

The Exchange is a great market to which any one can bring his securities, confident that he will here find a buyer who will purchase at some price. The advantage of this position is well known and highly appreciated. A man, for example, who owns a piece of real estate and who desires to sell it must first of all make a long and laborious search to find a person who is willing to buy real property. There may be many people who would like to buy real estate but few perhaps are interested in property in his locality. When it comes to find customers who would be interested in his particular property he finds that the number is still further reduced. Finally it is necessary for him to come to an agreement concerning the price. There is no market where he can go and be certain of finding a customer.

In the case of securities, the situation is altogether different. The peculiar advantages or disadvantages which are inherent in every piece of real estate give to it individual characteristics. Every share of stock, on the other hand, is like every other share of stock of the same company. Its value is exactly the same. Any one, therefore, who is familiar with the value of the stock of a given corporation and who desires to purchase it cares absolutely nothing about receiving any particular share. The situation in the case of the stock is the same as if every piece of real estate in the same locality were of equal desirability and value. The market for securities, therefore, is much broader than for any other classes of property. No individual search is necessary except for the general purpose of ascertaining the value of any given security. It is possible, therefore, to maintain a market such as the Stock Exchange for the purchase and sale of property where men decide in the fraction of a second to accept or reject the offer as it is made on the floor. This gives the Stock Exchange its great value and commands for it the enormous volume of business annually transacted.

Now the owner of the security which is not listed on the Exchange finds himself in a position similar to that of the real estate owner. He knows not where to go to find his market. Many people may be interested in his stock, but for him to ascertain their whereabouts is difficult, requires much time, expense and above all, causes delay and uncertainty. He feels keenly the need of a market where he can take his stock and where he knows that the prospective buyer of suck stock would be making inquiries for it. This is furnished by the Stock Exchange. For this reason it comes about that the securities of most corporations of any considerable size are listed upon one or more exchanges.

7. *Value of listing for bank loans.*—Listing on the New York Stock Exchange gives a security a wide market and a definite current value, making it easier to sell and *always easier to borrow upon.* In fact, securities are not generally available as collateral for Stock Exchange loans unless they are listed. Banks accept the quotations on this Exchange as the basis for computing how much they will lend upon given securities; the practice is to value the securities at 10 points below the quotations and lend 80 per cent of such valuation. In advertisement and circulars describing securities offered for sale it is always stated as an inducement to purchasers that they are listed on the New York Stock Exchange when such is the case.

The usual method of describing the listing requirements on the Stock Exchange is to give them in detail. But a long list of rules is frequently confusing and meaningless. It seems wiser in the present instance to reprint an actual report which was recently furnished to the Stock Exchange in compliance with these rules. These publications are furnished to all members and to newspapers. As in the case of many other companies whose securities have been listed, very little of the complete and detailed information that follows was available to investors before the stock was listed. A typical listing on the New York Stock Exchange is here given:

COMMITTEE ON STOCK LIST,
NEW YORK STOCK EXCHANGE.

THE OWENS BOTTLE-MACHINE COMPANY.

(Incorporated under the laws of Ohio.

SEVEN PER CENT CUMULATIVE PREFERRED STOCK.
COMMON STOCK.

Toledo, Ohio, June 12, 1916.

The Owens Bottle-Machine Company hereby applies to have listed upon the New York Stock Exchange temporary certificates for

$6,957,400 Seven Per Cent Cumulative Preferred Stock (69,574 shares par value $100 each), being the total amount issued and outstanding of an authorized issue of $20,000,000.

$9,000,000 Common Stock of an authorized issue of $30,000,000, consisting of 360,000 shares of the par value of $25 each, on official notice of issuance in exchange for present outstanding Temporary Certificates of the par value of $25 per share or in exchange for outstanding certificates for Common Stock of the Company of the par value of $100 per share;

with authority to substitute permanent engraved interchangeable certificates for Preferred and Common Stocks on official notice of issuance in exchange for outstanding interchangeable temporary certificates therefor.

All of said stock, the listing of which is now applied for, is fully paid and non-assessable, and no personal liability attaches to its ownership.

The Owens Bottle-Machine Company was incorporated under the laws of the State of Ohio on December 13, 1907, succeeding a corporation of the same name which had been incorporated September 3, 1903, under the laws of New Jersey. Its charter is perpetual. The charter provided for an authorized capitalization of $2,500,000 Common Stock and $500,000 Preferred Stock. On December 13,

1912, the authorized Common Stock of the Company was increased to $15,000,000. On February 14, 1916, the authorized Common Stock of the Company was reduced from $15,000,000 to $7,500,000, and the nominal value of each share from $100 to $25. On March 23, 1916, the authorized Common Stock of the Company was increased to $30,000,000 and the authorized Preferred Stock was increased to $20,000,000, exclusive of the $500,000 Preferred Stock authorized by the original charter of the Company, which is to be redeemed and cancelled by the Company on September 30, 1916, in cash, at 115.

$300,000 of said Common Stock was issued on account of the original subscriptions made at the time of the organization of the Company in 1907; $2,200,000 thereof was issued as part payment of the assets of Owens Bottle-Machine Company, of New Jersey, the predecessor of the present Company; $5,000,000 thereof was issued ($1,250,000 in each of the years 1912 to 1915 respectively) as dividends to the Common stockholders, and $1,500,000 thereof, for which listing is now applied, was issued and sold for cash to existing Common stockholders, at the rate of Two Hundred and Twenty-five per cent of par. The $6,957,400 of Preferred Stock was issued in exchange for stock of The American Bottle Company of Ohio, at the rate of one share of The Owens Bottle-Machine Company for one share of The American Bottle Company of Ohio.

In accordance with the terms of its Certificate of Incorporation, the Company is engaged in the manufacture and sale of bottles. The Owens Bottle-Machine Company is the owner of the United States right to use and license other manufacturers to use the Owens bottle-machine, which is the only wholly automatic bottle-making machine in the world, the patents covering which are held by the Toledo Glass Company, an Ohio corporation. The United States patent rights on the bottle-machine and allied appliances which are thus controlled by this Company number fifty-six and expire on various dates from 1920 to 1933. Most of these represent important improvements on the original invention.

Patent applications covering other inventions and improvements for the benefit of this company are now pending.

For a statement of the rights, privileges, preferences and voting powers of the Preferred and Common Stocks of the Company and the restrictions and qualifications thereof, reference is hereby made to Article Fourth of the Certificate of Incorporation as set forth in the certificate of increase of the Capital Stock filed March 24, 1916, in the office of the Secretary of State of Ohio. As provided in and subject to said Article Fourth:

I. The holders of the preferred stock shall be entitled to receive, out of the surplus profits of the Company, dividends when and as declared, at the rate of seven per cent per annum and no more, payable quarterly on the first day of each January, April, July and October, in preference to all other stockholders and such dividends shall be cumulative. Dividends on any share of such stock shall begin to accrue from the quarterly dividend date next preceding the date of the original issue thereof, unless such share shall be issued on a dividend date, and in such case, from such date. The holders of said preferred stock shall not, as such, be entitled to receive any other or further dividends of any kind whatsoever.

II. Upon not less than ninety (90) days' previous notice given both by mail to the record holders of the preferred stock to be redeemed and by publication, the Company may, by such method as shall be provided from time to time by resolution of the Board of Directors or by the By-Laws, redeem, on the first day of January, April, July or October in any year, the whole or any part of the preferred stock at one hundred and fifteen per cent of the par value thereof, plus accrued unpaid dividends.

III. The preferred stock shall be preferred as to both earnings and assets. In the event of any voluntary liquidation or dissolution or winding up of the Company, each registered holder of any share of the preferred stock shall be paid a sum equal to its redemption price, or, if such liquidation or dissolution or winding up be involuntary, a sum equal to its par value, in each case with all accrued unpaid dividends, before anything shall be paid to the holders of the common stock; and the holders of the common stock shall be entitled to the entire assets remaining after such payment to the holders of the preferred stock.

IV. So long as any of the preferred stock shall be outstanding, the Company, out of any remaining surplus profits, shall, annually on or before the first day of November, in the year 1916, and in each year thereafter, set aside, for the redemption or purchase of the preferred stock, a sum equal to three per cent of the maximum amount of preferred stock at any time issued and this obligation shall be cumulative.

V. Without the affirmative vote or written consent of the holders of at least three-fourths in amount of its outstanding preferred stock the Company shall not create nor by vote of or upon any shares owned by it, authorize any other corporation, a majority of the voting stock of which is then owned by it, to create any mortgage or other lien to secure an issue of bonds or otherwise, or issue or authorize any such other corporation to issue any additional bonds under any present mortgage or any evidence of indebtedness maturing later than one year after the issuance thereof.

VI. No more than $7,000,000 par value of the preferred stock shall at any time be issued, unless at the time of such issue the Company's net earnings for the last preceding fiscal year, or its average annual net earnings for the last preceding three fiscal years (whichever shall be the greater), applicable to the payment of dividends, shall be not less than two and a half times the aggregate amount required for the payment of all dividends for the entire year next ensuing upon both the preferred stock then outstanding and the preferred stock then to be issued.

VII. In no event shall any preferred stock be at any time issued to an extent which will make the total amount of the outstanding preferred stock, at its par value, exceed seventy-five per cent of the net assets of the Company, including assets to be acquired from the issuance of additional preferred stock.

VIII. The holders of the common stock shall exclusively possess voting powers for the election of directors and for all other purposes, and the holders of the preferred stock shall have no voting powers, except as herein stated; provided, that in case the Company shall have failed in respect of four quarterly periods to declare and pay the full regular quarterly dividend on the preferred stock, then, and in every such case, so long as there shall be any accrued unpaid dividends upon the preferred stock, the holders of the common stock shall have no voting powers and the holders of the preferred stock shall exclusively possess voting powers for the election of directors and for all other purposes.

IX. The holders of the preferred stock shall not be entitled to subscribe for or to acquire from the Company any stock, either preferred or common, which the Company may, from time to time, issue or offer for subscription or sale.

X. Out of the surplus profits of the Company remaining after full cumulative dividends on the preferred stock shall have been paid for all cash quarterly dividend periods and full dividends for the current quarterly dividend period shall have been declared and paid, or provided for, and the requirements under Clause V. of said Article Fourth (briefly stated in Clause IV. hereof) have been compiled with in respect of any and all amounts then or theretofore required to be set aside or applied, then, and not otherwise, dividends may be declared upon the common stock, provided, however, that no dividends shall be declared upon the common stock unless, at the time of said declaration, the surplus profits of the Company remaining, after payment of such dividend, shall be at least equal to seven per cent of all the preferred stock then outstanding.

In addition to the regular dividends of seven per cent per annum on the Preferred Stock, the Company has paid cash dividends on its Common Stock as follows: Fiscal year 1909, six per cent; fiscal year 1910, eight per cent; fiscal year 1911, ten per cent; fiscal year 1912 to date, twelve per cent.

The Company has also paid four stock dividends of $1,250,000 each on the Common Stock in the calendar years 1912–1915, inclusive.

As stated above, the Company owns the United States rights to use and licence other manufacturers to use the Owens bottle machines. Prior to 1908, the business of the Company had been almost exclusively restricted to the licensing of such machines upon a royalty basis. In 1908, the Company entered upon the manufacture of bottles, and the growth of the business is outlined in the following statement of the output of the Company for the past six years:

	Bottles	Net Profits
Fiscal year ending September 30, 1911	52,890,192	$713,919.99
" " " " 30, 1912	79,329,600	1,238,738.35
" " " " 30, 1913	109,529,280	1,812,154.68
" " " " 30, 1914	131,529,600	2,222,972.59
" " " " 30, 1915	133,421,328	1,644,518.58

The Owens Bottle-Machine Company owns securities in the following companies:

Name of Company	Incorporated under laws of	Date		Duration of Charter
American Bottle Co.	Ohio	August,	1905	Perpetual
The Chas. Boldt Co.	Ohio	April,	1900	Perpetual
Hazel-Atlas Glass Co.	West Va.	October,	1901	50 Years
Thatcher Manufac'g Co.	New York	February	1905	99 Years
Whitney Glass Works	New Jerse	August,	1887	Aug. 31, 1937
Welch Grape Juice Co.	New York		1903	99 Years
Mid-West Box Co.	Indiana	July,	1914	50 Years
Fairmont Glass Works	Indiana	August,	1900	50 Years
The Buckeye Clay Pot Co.	Ohio	August,	1909	Perpetual
The Toledo Owens Glass Sand Co.	Ohio	May,	1913	Perpetual

LISTING SECURITIES

The capitalization of such companies is:

Name of Company	Preferred Stock Authorized	Outstanding	Owned by Owens Bottle-Machine Co.
American Bottle Co.	$4,000,000	$3,719,500	$3,719,200
The Chas. Boldt Co.	250,000	250,000	7,500
Hazel-Atlas Glass Co.			
Thatcher Manufacturing Co.	500,000	317,000	5,000
Whitney Glass Works	500,000	*3,600	
Welch Grape Juice Co.	1,000,000	646,500	500,000
The Toledo Owens Glass Sand Co.			
The Buckeye Clay Pot Co.			
Mid-West Box Co.			
Fairmont Glass Works			

Name of Company	Common Stock Authorized	Outstanding	Owned by Owens Bottle-Machine Co.
American Bottle Co.	$4,000,000	$4,000,000	$3,999,200
	Special Stock		
American Bottle Co.	$2,000,000	$700,000	700,000
	Common Stock		
The Chas. Boldt Co.	750,000	700,000	700,000
Hazel-Atlas Glass Co.	6,000,000	4,131,200	1,886,200
Thatcher Manufacturing Co.	1,000,000	874,900	5,000
Whitney Glass Works	500,000	496,400	387,800
Welch Grape Juice Co.	500,000	470,000	20,000
The Toledo Owens Glass Sand Co.	200,000	168,500	155,000
The Buckeye Clay Pot Co.	100,000	94,200	20,000
Mid-West Box Co.	100,000	61,600	41,000
Fairmont Glass Works	250,000	250,000	

* The capital stock of Whitney Glass Works was originally $500,000. Later it was increased to $1,000,000, all outstanding, of which $500,000 was preferred stock and $500,000 was common stock. Thereafter all of the common stock was retired by consent, with provision for the conversion of the preferred stock into common stock. All of it has been so converted except $3,600, which is in process of being converted.

The Owens Bottle-Machine Company owns no stock in Fairmont Glass Works, but does own $95,000 of bonds of an outstanding issue of $142,500.

STATEMENT OF PHYSICAL PROPERTIES OF THE OWENS BOTTLE-MACHINE COMPANY.

Location of plant	Acres of land Occupied	Sq. ft. of Factory Floor space	Approximate Annual Capacity Bottles	Character of buildings
Toledo, O.	2.2	75,000	14,400,000	Brick
Toledo, O.	5.5	49,000	7,200,000	Concrete ware-sheds of wood
Clarksburg, W. Va.	15.7	163,800	86,400,000	Steel and brick
Fairmont, W. Va.	19.5	345,000	115,200,000	Steel frame and siding

The number of employees at the several plants of The Owens Bottle-Machine Company is approximately 700.

STATEMENT OF PHYSICAL PROPERTIES OF CONTROLLED COMPANIES.

Location of plant	Acres of Land Occupied	Sq. ft. of Factory Floor Space	Approximate Annual Capacity Bottles	Character of Buildings
American Bottle Co., Streator, Ill.:				
Upper Plant	41.7	462,935 }	129,600,000	Brick, concrete and corrugated iron
Lower Plant	13.6	262,623 }		
Newark, Ohio	44	519,183	158,400,000	Brick, concrete and corrugated iron
Whitney, Glassboro, New Jersey	11.2	116,000	57,600,000	Brick, corrugated iron and wood
The Toledo Owens Glass Sand So., Silica, O.	80	31,600	200,000 tons glass sand	Concrete

The American Bottle Company owns hand plants at Newark, Ohio; Massillon, Ohio; Wooster, Ohio; Streator, Ill., and Belleville, Ill. The Belleville and Wooster plants have been partly dismantled and are carried on the Company's books simply at the value of the land. The Massillon plant has not been operated for several years, and is carried on the books simply at the value of the land. There are five hand-blown furnaces at Newark, some of which have been operated within the past two years, but the values of the buildings and equipment were all charged to depreciation reserve before closing books August 31, 1915, and the land values only are carried in the appraisal of the Newark machine plant property. There is one hand-blown factory at Streator, Ill., which is, however, so closely identified with the Streator lower machine plant that it is considered a part of the machine plant. The acreages of the several hand plants are as follows: Massillion, Ohio, 15 acres; Wooster, Ohio, 12 acres; Belleville, Ill., 12.58 acres.

The number of employees of The American Bottle Company at the several plants is approximately 1,200.

The number of employees of the Whitney Glass Works is approximately 275.

The plant of the Toledo Owens Glass Sand Company is not being operated at present.

The American Bottle Company has no funded or mortgage debt.

LISTING SECURITIES

The Whitney Glass Works has a mortgage debt of $95,000.

THE OWENS BOTTLE-MACHINE COMPANY.

INCOME AND EXPENSES FOR THE FISCAL YEAR ENDED SEPTEMBER 30, 1915.

Manufacturing income:		
Net sales $2,025,971.96		
Cost of sales 1,344,319.24		
	$681,652.72	
Royalties received	1,054,382.62	
Manufacturing profit and royalty		$1,736,035.34
Other income:		
Dividends:		
Buckeye Clay Pot Co.... $1,000.00		
Hazel-Atlas Glass Co..... 327,402.00		
Thatcher Mfg. Co. 350.00		
Welch Grape Juice Co.... 875.00		
Chas. Boldt & Co., Com... 16,660.00		
Chas. Boldt & Co., Pref... 450.00		
	$346,737.00	
Interest on bonds owned	6,000.00	
Interest on loans, etc.	40,146.10	
Miscellaneous	5,962.46	
Total other income		398,845.56
Total income		$2,134,880.90
Expenses:		
General, administrative and selling		224,747.60
Net operating profit		$1,910,133.30
Other deductions:		
Experimental, bad accounts, licensed machines —depreciation, etc.	$33,982.02	
Special depreciation provisions	231,632.70	$265,614.72
Net profit		$1,644,518.58

SUMMARY OF INCOME FOR THE FOUR MONTHS ENDED APRIL 30, 1916.

Gross profit	$93,802.86	
Deduct cash discount and drayage.	3,654.30	
	$90,148.56	
Deduct interest	1,451.60	
		$88,696.96
Deduct bad debts		122.92
		$88,574.04
Deduct selling, management and office expenses		17,464.99
		$71,109.05
Miscellaneous profits		
Purchased share	$1,785.43	
Rental	1,014.68	
		2,800.11
		$73,909.16
Deduct maintenance		9,443.39
		$64,465.77
Deduct depreciation		17,013.27
		$47,452.50

BALANCE SHEET AS AT APRIL 30, 1916
ASSETS.

Permanent (Book Value):			
Real estate and buildings	$303,610.36		
Machinery and equipment	247,027.18		
		$550,637.54	
Less: Reserve for Repairs—Unused		30,250.00	$520,387.54
Current:			
Cash on hand and on deposit		$36,186.92	
Customers' Accounts	$94,311.78		
Less: Allowance for doubtful, etc.	1,200.00		
		93,111.78	
Inventory—Merchandising and supplies at cost		153,249.70	282,548.40
Investments			9,544.03
Deferred:			
Prepaid insurance			4,599.88
			$817,079.85

LIABILITIES.

Capital Stock—Common, authorized and issued		$500,000.00	$500,000.00
Currents:			
The Owens Bottle-Machine Co.—			
For royalty		$14,111.89	
Accounts payable		24,672.36	
Accrued taxes and interest		4,862.46	43,646.71
Bonded debt:			
First Mortgage 5 per cent coupon Bonds due July 1, 1931—Authorized		$250,000.00	
Less: Retired		155,000.00	95,000.00
Profit and Loss—Surplus			178,433.14
			$817,079.85

NOTE.—It is estimated that there are included in Permanent Accounts as carried on the books an amount not to exceed $150,000, representing good-will.
Copyright by Brown Bros., N. Y.

The Owens Bottle-Machine Company agrees with the New York Stock Exchange as follows:

Not to dispose of its stock interest in any constituent, subsidiary, owned or controlled Company, or allow any of said constituent, subsidiary, owned or controlled companies to dispose of stock interests in other companies unless for retirement and cancellation, except under existing authority or on direct authorization of stockholders of the Company holding the said companies.

To publish and submit to the stockholders, at least fifteen days in advance of the annual meeting of the corporation, a statement of its physical and financial condition, an income

LISTING SECURITIES

account covering the previous fiscal year, and a balance sheet showing assets and liabilities at the end of the year; also annually an income account and balance sheet of all constituent, subsidiary, owned or controlled companies.

To publish quarterly an income account and balance sheet.

To maintain in accordance with the rules of the Exchange, a transfer office or agency in the Borough of Manhattan, City of New York, where all listed securities shall be directly transferable, and the principal of all listed securities with interest or dividends thereon shall be payable; also a registry office in the Borough of Manhattan, City of New York, other than its transfer office or agency in said city, where all listed securities shall be registered.

Not to make any change in listed securities of a transfer agency or of a registrar of its stock, or of a trustee of its bonds or other securities, without the approval of the Committee on Stock List, and not to select as a trustee an officer or director of the Company.

To notify the Stock Exchange in the event of the issuance of any rights or subscriptions to or allotment of its securities and afford the holders of listed securities a proper period within which to record their interests after authorization, and that all rights, subscriptions or allotments shall be transferable, payable and deliverable in the Borough of Manhattan, City of New York.

To publish promptly to holders of bonds and stocks any action in respect to interest on bonds, dividends on shares, or allotment of rights for subscription to securities, notices thereof to be sent to the Stock Exchange, and to give to the Stock Exchange at least ten days' notice in advance of the closing of the transfer books, or extensions, or the taking of a record of holders for any purpose.

To redeem Preferred Stock in accordance with the requirements of the Stock Exchange.

The Directors (elected annually) are: Edward D. Libbey, William S. Walbridge, Clarence Brown, Michael J. Owens, Frederick L. Geddes, William H. Boshart, John D. Biggers,

Tunus H. Miller, all of Toledo, Ohio, and Elisha Walker, of 25 Broad Street, New York.

The Officers are: Edward D. Libbey, President; Clarence Brown, William S. Walbridge and William H. Boshart, Vice-Presidents; William S. Walbridge, Secretary; John D. Biggers, Treasurer; Michael J. Owens, Factories Manager; Frederick L. Geddes, John D. Biggers and Tunis H. Miller, Assistant Secretaries.

The fiscal year ends on September 30.

The annual meeting of the stockholders is held at the Company's principal office, 1401–1434 Nicholas Building, Toledo, in Lucas County, Ohio, on the second Tuesday in November in each year.

Certificates of stock are interchangeable between New York and Toledo.

The Transfer Agents for the Preferred Stock and Common Stock are The New York Trust Company, New York, and The Ohio Savings Bank & Trust Company, Toledo, and the Registrars are the Liberty National Bank, New York, and Northern National Bank, Toledo.

THE OWENS BOTTLE-MACHINE COMPANY,
By WM. S. WALBRIDGE, *Secretary*.[1]

This Committee recommends that the above-described Temporary Certificates for $6,957,400 Seven per Cent Cumulative Preferred Stock and $1,500,000 Common Stock be admitted to the list, on official notice of issuance and payment in full, with authority to add $7,500,000 Common Stock upon official notice of issuance in exchange for outstanding Common Stock of the par value of $100, also with authority to substitute permanent engraved interchangeable certificates for Preferred and Common Stock respectively, upon official notice of issuance, in exchange for temporary certificates therefor; making the total amount authorized to

[1] Additional financial statements relating chiefly to the subsidiary companies which are attached to the application in the manner of a postscript are omitted here.

be listed $6,957,400 Preferred Stock and $9,000,000 Common Stock.

GEORGE W. ELY, *Secretary.*

WM. W. HEATON, *Chairman.*

Adopted by the Governing Committee
July 25, 1916
GEORGE W. ELY, *Secretary.*

REVIEW

What is a "listed" security?

What responsibility does the exchange assume for its listed securities?

What advantage has a listed security over a non-listed security?

What information regarding a security does the exchange require before listing?

Is it, in your opinion, desirable to list foreign securities on the New York Stock Exchange?

CHAPTER IV

MARGINS

1. *Two classes of security buyers.*—Very little of the complicated machinery of Wall Street which is so difficult for the layman to understand, would exist at all if every patron of the Stock Exchange paid for securities entirely with his own money. The numerous technical terms which puzzle the uninitiated arise largely from the fact that the outsider, as well as the "insider," has fallen into the habit of both buying and selling securities with the use of borrowed money, and that a huge machine must be created and kept running to provide the means.

It is usual and in some ways convenient to divide buyers of stocks into two groups. To the first group belong those who pay outright in cash or its equivalent the total amount involved in the purchase of the securities, just as a man who buys a $20 suit of clothes hands to the salesman a twenty-dollar bill or a few days later sends him a check. In the second group are found those persons, by far the more numerous, who buy securities largely on borrowed money. They furnish a part only of the means necessary to buy the stock and rely on the broker to secure the balance. In common parlance the customer trades on a "margin." Ex-

MARGINS

pressed in another way the broker "carries" the customer for all except a small part of the cost.

It is assumed in both cases that the broker actually buys these securities, paying for them in full with his own resources, or with money which he has borrowed, usually from a bank. Such is the general practice. Now it may be said that a person who pays for stock in full is a conservative investor and that the person who buys on a margin is a speculator. As a generalization this is well enough, for even a moment's reflection will show the novice that an outright purchase is safer and more conservative than the other. But it must not be supposed that there is any hard and fast line between margin dealing and outright purchase.

It is easy enough to draw a line between the man who regularly "trades" on a 10 per cent margin at a broker's office, and the outright investor who never borrows a cent. But there are innumerable gradations between these two transactions. There is the man well known to his broker who desires to buy a stock today but who has not sufficient means to pay for it, altho tomorrow he will have a note of many thousands of dollars coming due and he will then complete the purchase. A man of large wealth, also well known to his broker may wish to buy a stock at once, but may not have even a check book with him. Another man buys on a margin and the next day decides to complete the purchase in full. Again, the man who buys, for example, 100 shares of stock on a 10 per cent margin, and after a few days instructs his broker, as he has a perfect right to do, to reduce the account to 10 shares, in which case he is no longer a margin trader at all but the outright owner of 10 shares, provided of course, there has been no decline in price and he has paid all the expenses.

Then again there is the customer who buys 100 shares of stock at $100 a share on—say a 50 point margin—and the stock goes to $200 a share after his purchase has been made. As all the profits of a transaction go to the customer, it is apparent that such a man could sell out, buy again and become the owner of 75 shares. And finally, there is the man who buys outright and the next month goes to his bank and borrows 80 per cent of the value of the stock. He is no longer an outright owner but a margin operator. These illustrations show the danger of generalization about margin trading and indicate also the dangers attendant upon the passage of any legislation on the subject. A law might be passed forbidding margins of less than 20 per cent, but in an active market a man might have a 25 per cent margin one moment and regard himself as both within the law and safe. The next moment his margin might be 19 per cent and he would be a criminal even before he could write out a check. In other words it is dangerous to legislate or generalize on the question of how much credit a broker may extend to a customer.

There is nothing inherently wrong about a margin operation. It is a question of one's resources and ability to meet inevitable debts. It is no more wrong in itself to contract a margin operation in stocks than to purchase real estate on a mortgage or to contract any other debt. It is solely a personal question, to be decided on its individual merits. But unfortunately thousands of persons do operate on margins who have not sufficient resources, and consequently much loss and suffering results.

2. *Why margins are used.*—Most speculators naturally, even tho in countless cases unwisely, desire to operate with as little money of their own as possible. They realize that their profits, in proportion to the capital invested, would be greater were a smaller amount invested than if they bought their stocks outright. A man, for instance, who would buy 100 shares of some stock at 150 would have $15,000 invested. If the stock rose to 160 he would make $1,000, or a profit of about one-fifteenth of his capital. If, however, he bought stock on a margin he could probably be able to buy 100 shares with an advance on his part of $1,500, the balance being furnished thru the agency of the broker. The profit upon the transaction would remain approximately the same, but instead of making one-fifteenth of his capital his profits would now equal two-thirds of the amount of his original investment. Speculators usually prefer, even when they have large financial resources, to buy stock on margin.

It is also true that by trading on a margin a speculator can naturally diversify his purchases much more widely. He can operate not only on a wider scale, but also with a larger reserve. He can equalize or mitigate his losses by operating in other directions.

3. *Danger of margins.*—The unfortunate side of margin, or as it is sometimes called "account" dealing, is that if the stock declines the loss is proportionately large, just as the profit is proportionately large if the stock goes up. There is danger that if margined stock falls far enough the speculator will lose everything he has invested unless he puts up more margin, for unless he does so the broker sells the stock for what it will bring and retains the proceeds, thus "wiping out" the speculator. The broker is obliged to do this in order to protect himself with the bank from which he has borrowed.

Just how much additional margin a speculator is obliged to put up; how big a decline is necessary before he should be asked to put up "additional"; how long a period of time the broker should give the customer to comply with the call for more margin; how much notice the broker should give before selling the customer out—all these are questions the answers to which in thousands upon thousands of cases vary with circumstances. The courts have been called upon repeatedly to decide them. These points will be treated in greater detail in following paragraphs.

In general brokers do not call for "additional" unless a stock has declined a full point or more. The broker must always give "reasonable" notice. In giving notice everything depends upon the credit and resources of the speculator. Unless the speculator is convinced that he has bought a worthless stock or one which will never again rise in price, he shows only the most rudimentary common sense in keeping his margin ample at all times to protect himself against any decline that may take place.

4. *Amount of margin.*—The most usual margin on the Stock Exchange, averaged over a period of years, is ten points, or $10 a share. In abnormal times much larger margins are required. Some brokers require more margin than others. Well-known, wealthy and highly responsible persons will be allowed smaller margins than others. Highly speculative stocks are not bought on margin at all by responsible brokers. Very high-priced stocks are not safe to buy on margins. Low priced, but steady stocks, do not require large margins. In buying on margin, therefore, everything depends not only on the quality of the stock and its marketability, but also on the extent of its fluctuations.

5. *Interest rates.*—The rate which a broker charges for carrying stocks for a customer, that is, for the money which he supplies him, also varies. If a customer has a big and active account the rate may be reduced, just as a large railroad is able to buy lubricating oil at a lower price than a small mechanic. Brokers try to make a profit on their "interest account," which is the technical expression for the money they loan customers. They usually charge a trifle more interest for money loaned than they themselves pay to the bank for it, and they are not permitted by the Stock Exchange to charge less. Customers are often

charged six per cent. As an offset the customer is invariably credited with all dividends and interest on the stock, no matter how small his margin.

6. *Partial payment method.*—A variation of the margin system is found in the partial payment method of buying stocks. Legally and technically it is the same, but it varies in certain details. Besides the original margin, which is usually at least $20 a share, the customer agrees to pay about $5 a month until the stock is fully paid for. If the method is followed properly, only high grade, non-fluctuating stocks are purchased. As a result this plan is very safe because the large initial payment is added to regularly on the first of each month, thus constantly bulwarking the stock from being wiped out by a decline in the market.

By the partial payment method a person with $100 is able to buy five shares of a standard stock and pay for it by saving only $20 a month. He will become the owner of stock costing $100 a share in a year and eight months. The investor can always increase his payments, and if he discontinues them his status does not differ from that of the regular margin buyer.

In any margin operation the broker invariably reserves the right to call for "additional" at any time, and the customer always has the right to demand delivery of the stock whenever he is prepared to pay for it. In the vast majority of marginal operations customers never see the stock because they never pay for it. Margins, it should be noted, may consist of securities as well as cash. "Paper profits," the name for an advance in price which has not been cashed in, may also serve as margin.

7. *When a broker may close a transaction.*—In speculative dealings of the above character, it is always assumed, unless otherwise stipulated, that the broker has a right to close any transaction with his customer at will, provided he gives reasonable notice of the time and place of sale. The procedure is merely to hand the customer the securities dealt in with the request that the balance due on the securities be paid. No reason for this action is required.

Whether the amount of time and notice of sale is reasonable or not depends upon the circumstances relating to each case. Consideration must be given to the location of the parties, physical possibility of the client to meet the demand (he may be out of town and cannot be reached), the condition of the market itself, and the nature of the stock. In some cases the courts have held one hour to be sufficient notice while in others a week was considered a fair time limit.

The fact that a patron has paid down a margin entitles him to partial ownership of the securities, and so long as the margin is sufficient for the purpose the broker is not allowed to sell them without receiving direct permission from the customer. When a broker wishes to sell out a customer, he does not have to wait until the price falls so low as to make him incur a loss but he may sell out before that point is reached. The reason for this interpretation of the law is that inasmuch as the device of requiring margins was created to protect the broker, no protection is afforded him by forcing him to suspend judgment and action until a loss is incurred.

If a broker decides that a larger margin is necessary, he must notify his customer in exact terms of the amount required to carry his account still further. Reasonable time must be given to the customer to make good the additional margin. The period varies from one hour to two days. Before the broker ultimately sells, notice of the time and place of sale must be given to the customer, provided the security is held as pledge. When this is found to be impossible, after making every effort to find his customer, a broker is then free from the obligation actually to serve notice concerning the time of sale and also from the obligation to give the customer reasonable time within which to advance the sum requested as additional margin.

Very often brokers who conduct extensive transactions with the public print at the foot of their notices of purchases and sales the following sentences or others to a similar effect:

It is agreed between broker and customer that (1) all transactions are subject to the rules and customs of the . . . exchange and its clearing house; (2) all securities from time to time carried on the customer's account may be loaned by the broker or may be pledged by him either separately or together with other securities, either for the sum due thereon, or for a greater sum, all without further notice to the customer and (3) in all marginal business the broker may close transactions by the sale or purchase of securities at his discretion when the margin is near exhaustion, without further notice to the customer.

MARGINS

The safest way for a broker to carry on transactions with a customer is to secure in writing from his customer, every time business dealings are carried on with him, the permission to use the securities he buys, whenever an exigency arises, to best protect the former's interest.

The whole question of margins is succinctly described in a legal decision, that of Markham vs. Jaurdon (41 N. Y. 235):

> The customer employs the broker . . . to buy certain stocks for his account, and to pay for them, and to hold them subject to his order as to the time of sale. The customer advances 10 per cent of their market value and agrees to keep good such proportionate advance according to the fluctuations of the market. . . . The broker undertakes and agrees (1) at once to buy for the customer the stocks indicated; (2) to advance all the money required for the purpose, beyond the 10 per cent advanced by the customer; (3) to carry or hold such stocks for the benefit of the customer so long as the margin of 10 per cent is kept good or until notice is given by either party that the transaction must be closed. An appreciation in the value of the stocks is the gain of the customer and not of the broker. (4) At all times to have in his name or under his control, ready for delivery, the shares purchased or an equal amount of other shares of the same stock. (5) To deliver such shares to the customer when required by him upon the receipt of the advances and commissions accruing to the broker; or (6) to sell such shares upon the order of the customer, upon payment of the like sums to him, and account to the customer for the proceeds of such sale. Under this contract the customer undertakes (1) to pay a margin of 10 per cent on the current market value of the shares, (2) to keep good such margin according to the fluctuations of the market and (3) to take the shares so purchased on his order whenever re-

quired by the broker, and to pay the difference between the percentage advanced by him and the amount paid therefor by the broker.

8. *Legal relation of broker and customer.*—From this outline of the duties and relationship of customer and broker it will be observed that there are three steps in the trade which involve different legal rights; (1) there is the relationship of principal and agent. The broker is ordered by his client to make purchases of certain securities which he should proceed to do with diligence and care. For his trouble in performing the duties of agent he receives a stipulated rate of commission. His task once performed he assumes immediately a different legal rôle.

(2) His functions are then transferred from the territory of agency into the field of credit. His principal is now the debtor and he becomes the creditor. Inasmuch as his customer merely pays down ten per cent or thereabouts and leaves the remaining sum to be raised in some way or other by the broker, the latter becomes the creditor of the former.

(3) The final transformation takes place when the securities the broker has purchased are delivered to him. While the customer is the legal owner of the securities they remain in the possession of the broker because he has a lien on them for all the money he has advanced directly or indirectly and for his unpaid commission charges. Here we have the relation of pledger and pledgee. The total sale price less interest on the sum advanced, the principal itself and com-

mission fees are turned over to the client in case of sale. When purchases are involved, the account of the customer is debited with the interest on the 90 per cent or so borrowed, and credited with interest on the margin.

As a result of so many complicated relationships, disputes frequently arise between brokers and customers. As already stated a large body of legal decisions has been built up around these many points. But on the other hand the actual transaction of business proceeds far more smoothly than might be supposed. Disputes are relatively few considering the immense volume of business. The average stock operator never suspects the intricate legal, financial and accounting relations that exist between him and his broker, for the simple reason that the machinery takes care of them without a hitch. On the Stock Exchange such disputes as do arise are far more often settled by the Committees of the Exchange than by recourse to law.

REVIEW

What is meant by buying on "margin"?

Under what circumstances would you find it desirable to trade in securities on margin?

What risk does a speculator assume in buying on margin?

What interest should a broker charge on any marginal transaction?

How does the "partial payment" plan differ from ordinary marginal purchasing?

How does an advance or a decline in the value of the security affect a marginal transaction?

CHAPTER V

RELATION OF BANKS TO THE SECURITY MARKET

1. *Amount of loans to brokers.*—The fact that a large part of all dealings in stocks is carried on with borrowed money, or on margin, raises the interesting question: where does this money come from? In brief, the brokers, who in the aggregate, supply vast sums to their customers, usually obtain it from the banks. There are no data to indicate how extensive a business this is, but it is so large that it forms one of the most important financial activities in the country.

The amount of loans made to brokers on "call," which is only one of three kinds of ways in which brokers negotiate, has been estimated all the way from one hundred to seven hundred million dollars outstanding at any one time in the New York market. In a single day as much as $50,000,000 has been loaned on call on the Stock Exchange floor, while the extent of loans directly made by banks to brokers off the floor is unknown.

Another way of finding the size of this business is to note the extent of speculative stock transactions, the majority of which are carried on margin. Taking an extreme case, we find that in a single year, 1906, more than forty-three million shares of Reading stock

BANKS AND THE SECURITY MARKET 63

were "sold" on the stock exchange and hardly more than three million shares were transferred on the books of the company. While many investors who pay for their stocks in full do not have them transferred on the companies' books, most investors do take this precaution, and it is safe to infer that the bulk of the sales which did not result in transfers were margin operations and therefore required borrowed money. As Reading stock sold at an average price of perhaps $70 a share in 1906, the enormous total of money involved, even after making every conceivable allowance, is apparent. And Reading was, and is, only one of scores of active stocks.

It is safe to assume that customers do not supply on the average more than 10 to 15 per cent of the money required to carry thru a margin operation, leaving the remainder to be supplied by brokers. In some cases the broker is rich enough to supply the entire sum out of his own resources. In the majority of instances, however, a bank is the usual resort, the broker using the stock which he has purchased for his customer as collateral security for the loan.

2. *Source of brokerage loans.*—It must not be supposed that money loaned for this purpose comes from any one source. Much of it is supplied by wealthy corporations with surplus funds available for temporary investment. The United States Steel Corporation, for example, has had at one time more than $100,000,000 in ready cash. The General Electric Company, the Singer Manufacturing Company and

many other large corporations likewise have big sums available in cash; rich individuals, such as John D. Rockefeller, as well as many wealthy estates, also have much ready cash. Russell Sage frequently loaned as much as $20,000,000 at one time to brokers, and Hetty Green was supposed to engage in the same business.

But nearly all the money finds its way thru the channels of the big New York banks. Not only do these banks lend their own surplus funds and those of wealthy individuals and estates, but for many years they have loaned the funds of thousands of banks located in other parts of the country, altho this practice has been somewhat altered by the Federal Reserve Act. In testimony before a Congressional committee [1] in 1913 it was brought out that the chief lenders at that time were J. P. Morgan and Company, First National Bank of New York City, National City Bank of New York, Lee Higginson and Company of Boston and New York, Kidder Peabody and Company of Boston and New York and Kuhn, Loeb and Company. Several of the trust companies in New York City have grown enormously since 1913, and are large lenders to brokers.

3. *Kinds of loans to brokers.*—Loans to brokers are of three kinds, time, call and one-day unsecured. The first named are for a definite period of time, stated at the moment of borrowing. With a time loan the

[1] Report of the committee appointed pursuant to House Resolutions 429 and 504 to investigate the concentration and control of money and credit, Feb. 28, 1913. Pujo Report, Page 56.

BANKS AND THE SECURITY MARKET 65

broker is certain that nothing will be required by the bank until the end of the stipulated period. Normally time loans cost more than call loans, but the rate fluctuates less. They are usually issued for thirty, sixty or ninety days.

The call loan, as its name implies, is much more temporary. Consequently the broker must use much good judgment in his borrowing. If he takes on a number of time loans at say 5 per cent when call money is at 2 per cent he may seem to use poor judgment, but if call money suddenly rushes up to 10 per cent his foresight is obviously rewarded. If money rates promise to advance in the future a broker does well to rely on time loans, whereas if money gives indication of remaining stationary it is evident that he does well to take on call loans. The rate on time money remains the same thruout the life of the loan, whereas the rate of most call loans is "renewed" from day to day. Many brokers regard 65 per cent in time loans and 35 per cent on call as a wise division of their borrowing.

4. *Call loans.*—Call or demand loans are theoretically callable at any time. In the New York market, however, certain customs have developed governing the conditions under which the banks may call loans. The call is usually made in the morning and the money must be repaid, not during the same day but the following day by 2.15 p.m., when the broker receives back the collateral he gave in support of his loan.

It has also become an unwritten rule that if a loan

made today is to be called on the following day it must be called at or before 1 p.m. If not called by that time the understanding is that the loan will run until at least the second day following. Theoretically, as already stated, call loans are made subject to payment on demand. In practice, they are at least one day loans, but may run on for many weeks or months. There are instances on record where banks have allowed call loans on gilt edge securities to run for years. Indeed, in one case a call loan ran for forty years.

5. *How brokers' loans are made.*—The business of making loans by the bank is carried on in two ways. The first is by direct connections with the stock brokers, and the second by the use of middle men or money brokers who act as intermediaries between the lenders and the borrowers. Most of the loans are made by so-called money brokers, who are to be found at a regular place in the board room where loans are made. The rate for call money varies from day to day. Sometimes it is very low, while again it soars to almost prohibitive heights. The charge which is made, however, is definitely established on the Stock Exchange and is quoted upon the ticker tape just as are the security quotations.

The bank officer as soon as he ascertains at the beginning of the day how much money he has at his disposal for loaning, will call in one of the money brokers whom he regularly employs, and ask him to find a market for it. In most cases the broker serves the banker gratuitously because it gives him a standing with the banks and makes it easier for him to get time loans, thereby making him of greater use to his customers and consequently increasing his profits. The money broker then takes his place on the floor of the Exchange and offers his cash for sale. All that he really does is to find some one who desires to borrow money and then to agree with the customer upon the rates which shall be charged, in the same way as we saw was done with the sale of securities.

When the transaction is closed the money broker hands to the stock broker a slip containing the name of the bank for whose account the loans are made. The money broker's connection with the transaction now ceases and all further negotiations are made with the bank.

6. *Collateral for the loan.*—The call loan is negotiated upon the security of collateral which is furnished. In the transactions between the stock broker and the money broker nothing is said about the character of the collateral which is to be furnished. This is a matter, however, which is of the utmost importance to the bank. When the broker comes to make his loan he offers collateral as security. The banker will carefully scrutinize this collateral. All the securities deposited must be satisfactory and must be "good delivery" according to the rules of the Stock Exchange—that is to say, they must be in good form, and there must be nothing which would cloud or raise a question concerning this title or the ability of the holder to transfer them to subsequent buyers.

As collateral, the banks look with disfavor upon stocks and bonds which seldom change hands because it is difficult to find a buyer quickly for such securities when they are offered for sale. Active securities are preferred to those which are inactive because in a panicky market, when stocks are rapidly declining, all banks are forced to drop huge quantities of collateral upon the market in order to protect themselves. Their contracts with the brokers are such that at any time they can either demand immediate repayment for the loan or an increase in the amount of collateral which is furnished for its security; but, in case neither request is honored, the bank will immediately sell the securities thru some broker upon the Exchange, in order to dispose of them before a fall in price will carry their value below the amount which the bank has loaned upon them. It is of the utmost importance, therefore, that the bank make sure to find a ready market for the collateral which it holds, not only in good financial weather, but also when the stress and storm of a panic is at hand. The rule deciding the value of a security in the minds of the banker, therefore, is not what it will sell for under good conditions, but what it will bring under adverse conditions. Bankers also usually discriminate against the stock of manufacturing companies at least to the extent that they will not make a loan on collateral which consists of industrial stocks alone. If they make a loan upon this kind of collateral they will frequently charge a much higher rate of interest, or they will ask a much larger margin than the customary 10 or 20 per cent. In many cases, however, the brokers give collateral which consists of both railroad securities and industrial securities. In the case of United States Government bonds, which are considered so secure and their market so uninterrupted, bankers as a rule require little or no margin.

7. *Banks and speculation.*—In an ordinary market there are millions of securities purchased and held on speculation. While these securities are regarded as belonging to the speculator who has bought them, they are in reality in possession of the banks which hold them as collateral for loans they have made upon them. The money lenders and bankers, therefore, have the largest amount of money invested in speculative securities, and the greater proportion of this money, it must be remembered, is the surplus funds of the country banks and a portion of their reserve loaned to the New York banks.

So-called country banks, which include not only those in rural districts but also those in towns and cities having but a small population, have during a large part of the year, surplus funds for which they cannot find a profitable investment. The surpluses of the farmer, the merchant and the manufacturing company have given the country banks deposits in excess of the demand for money. This is particularly true in the agricultural districts of the middle west and south where the banks have difficulty in finding a sufficient quantity of three and four months promissory notes to keep their funds employed. On the other hand the banks in large reserve and central reserve cities, particularly those in New York, are almost always in the market for purchasing the surplus funds of country banks, either upon time or call—that is, for a certain period of thirty, sixty or ninety days,—or for borrowing with the understanding that the money will be returned immediately upon demand. The interest paid for these surplus funds is usually low, averaging about 2 per cent. The country bank, however, is willing to invest its surplus money in this manner, if no other use can be found for its funds, for the low rate is attractive. It happens, therefore, that not only the percentage of the reserve of the bank which under the law can be sent to reserve agents but also the unloaned funds of the bank are sent to the large cities. A very large percentage of this surplus money goes to New York. It is estimated that under normal conditions over 200 million dollars coming from this source alone are in the hands of the New York banks.

We recollect that a very large proportion of the loans of the New York banks are made to stock brokers. This class of business men forms the most important customers of the bank, in fact, some of the largest banks of the country have few customers except the brokers. It is the brokers who create the enormous demand for money which enables the New York banks under ordinary times to absorb the surplus funds which are offered to them from all other sections of the country.

8. *Securing the loan, "over-certification."*—Sup-

pose a broker has purchased $100,000 of stock for a customer. He contemplates securing an $80,000 loan from the bank on this stock. In order to negotiate the loan he must have the stock in his possession so as to be able to offer it as collateral at the time the application is made. On the other hand, however, before he can get possession of the stock from the seller he will be called upon to make payment in full. In the meantime it is probable that the broker will have a balance in bank which is much too small to enable him to draw a check for the amount of the purchase price of the stock. Here is a gap which must be bridged in some way. The broker must get the money and it is only the banks which can supply it. Without some arrangement the whole business of speculation would cease. Until a few years ago this gap was bridged by the practice of over-certification. Under this arrangement when the broker is called upon to pay for the $100,000 of stock he draws a check upon his bank to the order of the firm from whom he has purchased the stock for $100,000. This check is sent to the bank where the broker keeps his account for certification. This is a practice which is quite common in all banking communities.

Certification consists of a formal indorsement of the check of the bank guaranteeing that it will be paid when presented. It is intended to be a certification by the bank that the broker has sufficient funds on deposit to meet the check when it is presented. This guarantee is affixed by the cashier or paying teller of the bank, who endorses the check across its face certifying that the signature is correct and also that the bank is willing to pay the check upon presentation and identification, or when it comes thru the clearing house. This process is explained in greater detail in the Text on Banking. The broker's balance is perhaps only $25,000, nevertheless the bank has certified a check for $100,000. This is called over-certification and is simply one form of the great system of credit existing in the banking and brokerage business.

The practice of over-certification amounts to a temporary loan. In order to secure this privilege from the bank the broker has entered into an agreement which provides that, in return for a certain minimum balance which the broker shall keep at all times, the bank will over-certify his checks up to a certain specified amount. It is also understood that as soon as the stock is secured from the seller, it is to be taken to the bank and offered as collateral for a call loan. The temporary loan which the broker had made by the over-certification of his check is therefore transferred into a regular call loan. But this practice of over-certification is now largely extinct. It existed for many years in direct violation of the National Bank Act, which provides

That it shall be unlawful for any officer, clerk or agent of any National Bank to certify any check drawn upon the Association unless the person or company drawing the check has on deposit with the Association at the time an amount of money equal to the amount specified in said check.

In spite of the provision of the law and the punishment which is provided for its disobedience, over-certification went on for years. The magnitude of the practice can be judged from the fact that in a single year it is estimated that more than fourteen billion dollars of checks were over-certified in this manner.

9. *One-day unsecured loans.*—At the present time the bankers and brokers escape the law by a practice which in reality is little different from the former one. The broker who desires a certified check for an amount in excess of that which he has on deposit will go to the bank and present his own note for discount, drawn to himself and indorsed only by him. This note is made payable the same day on which it is presented and it is understood that it will be taken up before the close of banking hours by the broker, who will deposit the collateral which he had purchased and make call loans for the amount of his indebtedness. The bank discounts this note and places the proceeds to the credit of the broker. This gives him a balance on the books of the bank equal to, or in excess of, the amount for which he has asked certification. The officers of the bank are therefore relieved of the necessity of over-certifying his checks, for the broker's balance is now equal to the amount for which he desires certification.

In spite of the apparent laxity of this arrangement very few losses have resulted. The banks are extremely conservative about extending the privilege and before doing so make rigid investigations. They must have intimate knowledge of the broker's character, his judgment and his business methods, and if he fails to meet the standard in any particular the privilege is refused. In the second place the bank stipulates that the broker must keep a minimum deposit—for example, $50,000—in order to have the privilege of making one day loans to the extent of one million dollars. They count upon having the use of the $50,000 of the broker at all times, thus making the customer provide at least a portion of the 25 per cent reserve which must be held against his deposit. The banks pay no interest to the brokers on their balances, and charge no interest for one day unsecured, or clearance, loans, as they are sometimes called. They are also known as day-to-day loans.

Finally, it is understood that the broker must make his deposits at the bank as frequently as he receives checks in payment for the securities which he sells. Frequently he makes deposits six or seven times a day. As a result the broker, while he has received a large unsecured loan, is on the other hand, receiving at frequent intervals, deposits representing payments from firms which have bought securities from his house.

The practice of over-certification still exists to some extent in the case of state banks and trust companies. In this class of institutions the prohibition against it is not so strict and the state banks therefore continue the practice. Two large brokerage failures a few years ago have made the banks more careful than ever. In these cases the United States Supreme Court held that the banks were not preferred creditors. Several of the national banks no longer make one day unsecured loans.

10. *Interest rates.*—Money lent on call loans yields a rate that fluctuates normally around 2 or 3 per cent. Here the law of demand and supply clearly operates to determine the amount of business to be done. Occasionally when money is scarce, the rate rises considerably higher than the figures quoted and causes embarrassment in financial circles. When the interest charges are high, business will decrease.

Three terms are employed in connection with the trend of rates. If the rates are normal, that is to say range from 1 to 3 per cent, call money is "easy"; it becomes "firm" when it rises to 6, 7, 8 or 9 per cent. If call money proceeds higher, the word "stringent" is applied.

Call loans sometimes jump to 100 per cent or higher. For a few minutes during the height of the panic of 1907, call loans were not to be had at any price. The President of the Stock Exchange rushed across the street to J. P. Morgan's office and said that if money was not forth-coming immediately the Exchange would be obliged to close, or brokers would fail in a wholesale manner. Thru J. P. Morgan's influence a banking syndicate was formed at once and within a few moments the brokers were able to obtain $25,000,000.

When rates rush up to 100 per cent or more it is only the few weaker brokers who pay the highest figures. The more far sighted ones have sometimes previously borrowed enough time money at lower rates to enable them to do business. Some banks will not loan to brokers above 6 per cent, regardless of what the prevailing rates may be. If the banks have no money to lend they withdraw from the market, but they never charge more than their fixed maximum.

The reader might be led to believe that a high rate of interest benefits the banks, yet the contrary is often true. The banks' available resources for borrowing purposes consist in considerable part of large deposits of individuals or corporations. It is obvious that when the interest rate rises, perhaps to 20 or 25 per cent, the latter can derive greater profits by withdrawing their funds from banks paying 3½ to 4 per cent and lending them directly to willing speculators and brokers. Consequently it is to the interest of the banks to keep the rate down to a point where it will not encourage the withdrawal of individual or corporate resources.

11. *Renewal rates.*—Call loan interest rates are usually subject to change, according to market fluctuations. If, for example, the bank agrees at 11 a. m. to lend a certain sum of money on stock given as collateral at, say 2½ per cent, and if the market rate rises to 3 per cent, the bank immediately proceeds to notify the borrower that a 3 per cent rate will be charged. The statement would read thus: "If agreeable, we mark your loan of $10,000 dated February 16, 1916, as renewed at 3 per cent from this date." If this is satisfactory to the person concerned he merely stamps the perforated slip attached to this statement and

sends it back to the bank as an indication of acquiescence.

12. *Weaknesses and services of the call loan system.*—The practice of lending money on call to brokers has been much criticized. That funds from all parts of the country should be absorbed by stock speculation seems wrong to many persons. No doubt much of the sentiment which led to the passage of the Federal Reserve Act received its impetus from this criticism. Curiously enough the operation of the Federal Reserve Act, far from curtailing the amount of money available for brokers' loans, has thus far had the opposite tendency. This is due to the fact that with the much smaller reserves required under the Act, the banks have larger funds available for the purpose, at least temporarily.

It is the purpose also of the Federal Reserve Act to build up a market in bills, or discounts, similar to that which existed in London before the war, in order to furnish temporary investments for banks other than call loans. It is doubtful, however, if any short term investments are safer for banks than call loans. The reason money flows to Wall Street from all parts of the country is simply because the stock market furnishes plenty of loans at all times which are quickly convertible into cash. A country bank prefers to send its spare cash to New York to loan to a broker rather than let a farmer or merchant or contractor have it, for the reason that these business men cannot repay the loan in ten days if necessary, whereas the broker, as a matter of course, repays it when demanded.

Call loans furnish the banks with a safe means of using surplus funds, the great advantage being that if regular customers need or desire money the call loans can always be cashed in at once. Unlike nearly all other bank investments, call loans can be cashed in without loss, trouble, ill feeling or expense. They are completely liquid, which is a great essential in the banking business.

13. *Effect of money rates on stocks*.—Possibly the relationship between stock speculation and the banks is too close. Certainly the stock market depends very largely upon the banks for existence and in turn the banks possibly depend too much upon the market. This relationship is a most important force in causing changes in stock prices. When money is easy, prices naturally rise and when rates become firm they tend to fall. Brokers and speculators naturally take an intense interest in the condition of the banks and the rates for money.

Aside from the quoted rates, the surest indication of money market conditions is contained in the weekly statement of the Bank Clearing House in New York. In normal times the statement of the Bank of England is also of importance.[1] The relationship between money rates and speculation is discussed also in a later chapter of this book.

While many forces operate to influence money

---

[1] See also the Modern Business Texts on "Banking," p. 143, and on "Investment," p. 269.

rates, the one which most commonly engages the attention of stock operators has to do with the seasonal influences, especially the flow of currency in the autumn to "move" the crops.[1]

REVIEW

Who supplies the money for security transactions?

What different kind of loans are available for brokers?

If you were a stock broker, how would you distribute the money you borrowed from the banks among the different kind of loans?

What would you offer as collateral for the loans?

What is your opinion of the present practice which involves the money of persons who never saw Wall Street in speculative transactions?

What was the danger in over-certification?

What do you understand by "easy" money?

[1] See the Modern Business Text on "Banking," pp. 227, 251.

CHAPTER VI

THE WAYS OF WALL STREET

1. *Four methods of trading.*—As far as the Stock Exchange is concerned, there are four ways in which "bids and offers"—that is, buying and selling—may be conducted. These methods are (1) cash, (2) regular way, (3) at three days, (4) buyers' and sellers' option.

In "cash" transactions on the Exchange the securities must be delivered by the seller to the buyer and paid for upon the same day that they are sold. Payment is usually made by certified check, not by cash in the strict sense of the word. The London Stock Exchange has a similar method of business, known as "for money."

"Regular" or "regular way" transactions are made with the understanding that the delivery and the payment are to take place before 2.15 p. m. on the day following the date of the sale, unless the sale is made on Friday or Saturday, when delivery and payment take place on Monday.

In transactions "at three days," delivery is made upon the third day after the contract is made.

"Buyers' and sellers' option" must be for a period of not less than four days and not more than sixty days.

By far the greatest amount of business, probably more than 95 per cent of the whole, is done by the second method—"regular," or "regular way." If the seller fails to deliver the security at 2.15 p. m. on the day after the sale, according to the contract, the proper committee of the Exchange is immediately notified and thereupon proceeds to purchase the securities in question "under the rule," i.e. on the open floor of the Exchange, and if a greater price is demanded for them than that of the original sale, the difference must be covered by the person who failed to keep the terms of the contract. If the latter fails to meet these terms, he is liable to be suspended or expelled from the Exchange.

The fourth method of trading—"buyers' and sellers' option"—involves contracts by the terms of which the buyer has the right to a certain number of shares, at a specified price, at any time within the period of the option. This system corresponds roughly to that of "futures," which is so extensively used in the case of produce speculation. Futures are fully described in Chapter XIII.

The rule of the Exchange in regard to agreements involving more than three days, is that they must be in writing and must be exchanged before the close of the day after the sale, and that interest charges are permissible in this case. If the party owning the option should desire to have the securities, due notice must be given before 2.15 p. m. of any day, and the request must be complied with on the following day.

Until the beginning of the great European war, this fourth method, "buyers' and sellers' option," was practically obsolete. But owing to the delay in shipments, and other war-time disturbances, a large amount of business in seller's options in bonds has been carried on of late. For the first time in many decades these transactions have been important, and are indicated in the reports by such figures as "S2O" or "S3O," meaning seller's option to deliver within twenty or thirty days, as the case may be. Unless otherwise specified at the time, all transactions are understood to be "regular way."

2. *Commissions.*—It is a universally accepted rule, to which all members must strictly adhere, that commissions shall be charged on all sales or purchases in securities that are made for others. Rebates, either by direct action or by indirect means are forbidden, and any violation of this rule brings serious punishment. For the first offense, the penalty is suspension for a period ranging from one year as a minimum to five years as a maximum, according to the facts of the case, and any member who is guilty of a second offense is expelled. A member who fails to charge a customer with the commission authorized by the Exchange, is considered as having granted a rebate and is punishable accordingly. When a member is suspended for this or a similar offense, he is not permitted, during the period of suspension, to avail himself of the reasonable rate of commission charged to members.

There is a rule of the Exchange, that all business,

whether in buying or selling, transacted for parties who are not members of the Exchange, and for firms in which the Exchange member is only a special partner, is chargeable at the rate of not less than $\frac{1}{8}$ of one per cent; $7.50 is charged for 100 shares of stock selling under $10; $15 for stocks selling at $10 and under $125; $20 for stocks selling at $125 and higher. While the commissions named in this rule are the minimum, and members are permitted to charge as much more as they desire, competition makes the charges uniform. An exception is that for less than ten shares brokers shall make a uniform charge of $1.50 for their services, whether the transaction involves one share or nine.

The second rate is for the member of the Exchange who purchases securities for other members. If the name of the principal for whom the broker acts is not disclosed, the rate is $3.75 for each 100 shares. Otherwise, the rate allowed by the exchange is $2.50 for the purchase or sale of every 100 shares. On all organized exchanges, no matter what the exchange may deal in, whether it be stocks, cotton, coffee, produce or any other commodity, very low commission rates are afforded to those members who have occasion to employ other members to transact their business for them, but who wish to attend to the delivery themselves, that is to say, to allow their names to be "given up."

3. *"Bulls" and "bears."*—Speculators or brokers' customers are often classified as "bulls and "bears,"

according to their attitude toward the future movement of the prices of securities. The bulls are those who buy because they expect prices to go higher, and the bears are those who sell in anticipation of falling prices. The market is therefore called "bullish" or "bearish," as one or the other class predominates in trading at any one time.

Buyers are called "long" of stocks or "long" of the market. Those who have stocks of their own to sell are simply sellers. Those who have stocks to sell, which they do not own, are "short" sellers, or are "short" of stocks or "short" of the market.

Now the buyers of stock who are contemplating a rise in its value may purchase their shares in one of two ways. The first way is to buy the securities outright, paying the full purchase price for them. Those who do this are either investors or conservative speculators. They take their securities, lock them up in a vault and go on attending to their everyday affairs until such time as their expectations have been realized, when they take the securities to the broker's office, have them sold and pocket the profit they have waited for. If their judgment has been erroneous and the value of the securities declines instead of advances, they can either hold the securities until the price rebounds, which very frequently happens, or they can have them sold and suffer the loss. These persons, as a rule, are little concerned with the banking or brokerage interests. Their stocks having been paid for outright, they require no money to carry them in a falling market. This class of buyer, however, is in the minority. The great majority of those who purchase in anticipation of a rise in the prices of stocks, do so upon a margin by which they advance a small part of the value of the stock, the greater portion of the funds being secured by the broker. The method by which such transactions are carried on has already been explained.

4. *Process of selling short.*—Those on the other side of the market—the persons who are counting upon a fall in the value of stock—can operate only in one way. Evidently no one could make a profit by buying stock outright, paying for it and then locking it up in anticipation of a fall in its value. It is possible, however, for a man to make money if he can foresee a fall in the value of a security and govern his transactions accordingly.

It is believed in Wall Street that the public is made up for the most part of bulls, or those who play for a rise in the value of stocks, while the professional traders are more frequently the bears, or those who anticipate a fall in the value of securities. This belief is founded upon the fact that the public, as a rule, does not speculate upon a falling market. Indeed not many understand how the transaction is carried thru. The operation of speculating on a falling market is known as selling "short," sometimes called "selling securities, seller short." This practice is carried on very extensively.

In order that the short sale method may be made

clear, let us take an illustration. Suppose a man believes that he has inside information that a decision will be rendered by the Supreme Court of the United States which will be very disastrous to the interests of a certain railroad company. He reasons that as soon as the decision is announced it will immediately cause a sudden fall in the value of the stock of this corporation. The market is quick to learn of every favorable or unfavorable condition that may affect the securities which are handled upon the Exchange. Now if the man desires to take advantage of the opportunity which he believes is presented, he will sell short—let us say—300 shares of this company's stock in order to make a profit from the fall in price which he feels certain will come. The broker, having been directed to make this sale, and having received the funds needed for the transaction, now proceeds in the regular way provided for under the rules of the Exchange. He sells 300 shares of the railway company's stock for the customer, knowing that at that time the customer in all likelihood does not own or intend to purchase the 300 shares of stock which the broker must deliver. Under his contract, the broker must turn over the stock to the buyer before 2.15 p. m. on the day following the sale. Before this time arrives the broker borrows the stock.

There are a number of persons in Wall Street, and some connected with every exchange who make a business of loaning stock to brokers who desire to put thru short sales. In the New York Exchange there is a post on the floor, around which those who wish to loan stock or to borrow it can gather and effect their transactions. It may upon first thought seem strange that any one should desire to loan stock, yet such a transaction is not without its advantages. The borrower of the stock must deposit with the lender a sum of money equal to the market value of the stock at that time. In other words, he must deposit the equivalent of its purchase price in the open market. This deposit gives to the lender the full value of the stock, and at the same time entitles him to demand at any time, upon short notice, that the stock be returned. If he had decided to borrow money upon the stock as collateral, instead of loaning it, and had taken it to a bank, he could not have secured its full value, but perhaps would have been given only 80 per cent of the full amount. He, therefore, can raise 20 per cent more money upon his security by loaning it than he can by using it as collateral for loans. It is largely because of this fact that there are usually many lenders of securities in the market.

The broker now has in his possession stock which he has borrowed. He takes this and makes delivery in accordance with the rules of the Exchange. The transaction between the selling and the buying broker seems regular in every way, and there is nothing on the face of it to indicate that the sale was at all extraordinary. The fact is, however, that the broker's customer has sold and delivered stock which he did not own, but which he hopes to be able to buy later at a lower price. If the expectations of the customer come true and the court decision, rendered in accordance with his forecast, causes the value of the stock to decline, he will be in a position to profit by the perspicacity that led him to take the risk, for he can go into the open market and purchase 300 shares of the railway stock at a lower price than that at which he sold it. As soon as he secures delivery of the securities, which he now buys, his broker takes them to the firm from which the stock was originally borrowed, returns them and receives a check for the amount of money originally deposited, together with interest upon the sum at the prevailing rate for the time during which it was in the hands of the lenders of the securities.

But the customer, on the other hand, may have inaccurately forecasted the nature of the court's decision and the stock may advance, upon the strength of the favorable ruling. In this case he would endeavor to cover his "short" sale. He would do this by buying stock in the open market as speedily as possible. He would, of course, have to pay more for it than the amount for which he sold it. The broker would turn the securities over and get back his original deposit, and the customer would lose the difference between the amount that he was forced to pay for the stock, plus costs and charges and the amount for which he sold it.

5. *A short sale briefly stated.*—The course of a short sale can be made graphic by an illustration:

1. A sells stock, which he does not own, to B.

2. A borrows stock from C and delivers to B, who never learns that it was borrowed stock, and does not care, since he actually has possession of the stock.
3. A goes into the open market and buys an equal amount of the same stock from any broker, D, and hands it over to C, thus covering and completing the transaction.

6. *Loaning rates.*—It must be remembered that when C lends stock to A, he receives as security its full market value at the time, in a certified check, which must be kept "market to market," that is, if the stock goes up several points, C receives a check for the difference from A, if it goes down, he sends a check for the difference to A. To put it in other words, payments are made either way, as prices fluctuate, in order that the lender of the stock may always have the cash equivalent of the present market value of his stock. But C pays A interest on this cash at a trifle more than the prevailing call-loan rate. He is willing to make this arrangement for reasons already mentioned.

If, however, the stock that C lends is very scarce and hard for "shorts" like A to borrow, C may pay a very low rate of interest indeed—far less than the call-loan rate. He may even pay nothing at all, in which case the stock is said to loan "flat." This happens only when that particular stock is very hard to borrow. Finally, the stock may become so scarce that C, instead of paying interest, may actually receive interest.

Then the stock is said to loan at a "premium." In that case, C, the fortunate possessor of stock, not only gets the full cash market value for the temporary use of his stock, but a commission for its use besides. These interest rates and premiums are expressed in percentages such as $\frac{1}{32}$ per cent (per day).

7. *Broker and customer.*—When a customer issues an order to his broker to sell short securities on margin, the understanding is that the broker shall obtain them and deliver them to the buyer. The interesting question is, Where does the broker secure stocks to be delivered? There are four possible sources: (1) other brokers; (2) outsiders; (3) such securities as the broker carries for other customers, if these customers permit him to use them, and (4) whatever securities the broker himself may have.

The customer must pay all interest charges during the period of sale, as well as all premiums that the broker may have to pay in the process of borrowing securities on the market. The lender of the stocks—not the short-seller who is borrowing the stocks—gets all the dividends that they pay. The broker cannot terminate his loan of securities to the customer whenever he desires, and if, after he borrows from another member of the Exchange, his loan is called in, he must replace it in some way or other.

In regard to interest on the proceeds of the short sale, no definite, clear-cut custom has been adopted. As a rule, no interest is allowed; but where large transactions are involved, special arrangements are made for the distribution of interest charges between the two parties. In the case of the margin that the customer advances, however, no question arises, since it is taken for granted that interest will be paid him on this sum.

8. *Market effects of short selling.*—In any normal market there is always a considerable "short" interest; in other words, there are a considerable number of persons who are selling stock short in anticipation of a decline. There is likely to be a considerable "long" interest at the same time; that is, it is likely that there will be a number of persons who have bought stock in anticipation of being able to sell it at a higher price. The conflict between these two interests, together with the influence exerted by those who buy outright, is the force which largely fixes the price of securities. A very active long interest,—the purchase of stock in large amounts will force prices up. On the other hand, large short sales result in heavy offers, and buyers can sometimes be found only when the price concessions have been secured. When, however, the market is dominated by either one or the other interest, a reaction in the prices of stocks will usually follow immediately.

The hammering of the prices of securities, caused by constant short selling, drives prices so low that the bulls see a chance to make an advance. Their efforts are frequently aided by the outside buyer, who figures that the existing price of the security offers him a desirable investment. The buying done by these two parties in the transaction immediately absorbs all the stock that the shorts offer. As soon as this movement begins—in fact, sometimes before the price of the security has been advanced—the short interest "scrambles to cover," buying in stock to close up their transactions.

9. *Dangers and advantages of short selling.*— Short selling is dangerous for the seller unless there is plenty of stock available for borrowing purposes. This is because lenders of stock can call in their loans at any time. Thus the short seller may be faced with ruin unless there is another lender ready. As a matter of fact, loans of stock are constantly being called in, renewed or placed with other lenders.

Short selling is safe only when the stocks that are sold have a large "floating supply"—in other words, only when a large proportion of the outstanding stock is available for speculation, instead of being locked up in the vaults of investors. The only kind of stock which it is really safe to sell short is that which is constantly in the hands of brokers and actually entered, in their names, on the company's books. For many years United States Steel, common, was such a stock, because most of it was held by brokers, in their own names, for customers who had bought it on margin. The largest lenders of stock are brokers, and the stocks that are most available for lending are those which brokers hold on margin for speculators.

Preferred stocks, choice investment stocks and those that are very high-priced are not suitable for selling short. When shorts cannot borrow stocks at all, a corner exists. Corners are described in detail in Chapter XIX.

10. *Loaning rate as a market index.*—Attempts are often made to judge the condition of the market by the extent of the existing short interest as reflected in the demand for loans, which in turn is shown by the rate charged. But conditions in the "loan crowd" are misleading for a number of reasons, the most important of which—a curious one—is the following. Many sellers of stocks, in order to conceal their operations, actually borrow in the loan crowd, and then when the time comes to cover their short contract, deliver their own stocks out of their strong boxes. This is true of corporation directors and others who do not wish to have it known that they are selling out.

11. *Legal prohibitions.*—Few operations have been more criticised than short selling. Laws have been passed prohibiting it, but these are not at present in operation, and the practice is now entirely legal. In New York State, the legislature passed a law, in 1812, declaring void any contracts for the sale of securities which the seller did not actually own or have in his possession at the time when the contract was made. Forty-six years later however, this section was repealed and the following substitution was made:

> An agreement for the purchase, sale, transfer or delivery of a certificate or other evidence of debt, issued by the United States or any state, or municipal or other corporation, or any share or interest in the stock of any bank, corporation or joint stock association, incorporated or organized under the laws of the United States, or of any state, is not void or

voidable, because the vendor, at the time of making such contract, is not the owner or possessor of the certificate or certificates, or of other evidence of debt, share or interest.

The fact that a short sale is effected thru a broker on margin does not operate to make the transaction illegal and the contract void. This fact has been upheld by the courts again and again.

Judge Barnard, of the Circuit Court of the District of Columbia, commented upon this point as follows:

A short sale is not a gambling operation. The law defines a gambling operation to be where the parties make a contract of purchase and sale, without intent on the part of either, to deliver or receive the article which is the subject of the contract. . . . This is a mere bet—a gamble. But where actual delivery is made of the goods contracted to be sold and received, the transaction becomes a commercial one.

12. *Functions of short selling.*—As regards the actual effect of short selling, the weight of argument seems to be in its favor. The point is important from a practical standpoint, and has been hotly debated for more than one hundred years. The committee appointed by Governor Hughes of New York to investigate conditions in Wall Street, reported on this subject as follows:

Short sellers endeavor to select times when prices seem high in order to sell, and times when prices seem low, in order to buy, their action in both cases serving to lessen advances and diminish declines of price. In other words short selling tends to produce steadiness in prices, which is an advantage to the community. No other means of restraining unwarranted marking up and down of prices has been suggested to us.

In justification of short selling, Professor S. S. Huebner writes in the *Annals of the American Academy of Political and Social Science:*

Short sellers do not determine prices. By selling they simply express judgment as to what prices will be in the future. If their judgment is wrong, they will suffer the penalty of being obliged to go into the market and buy the securities at higher prices. Nine-tenths of the people are by nature "bulls," and the higher prices go, the more optimistic and elated they become. If it were not for a group of "short sellers" who resist an excessive inflation, it would be much easier than it is now to raise prices thru the roof; and then when the inflation became apparent to all, the descent would be abrupt and likely unchecked until the basement was reached. The operations of the "bear," however, make excessive inflation extremely expensive and similarly tend to prevent a violent smash because the "bear," to realize his profits, must become a buyer.

The writer has been told by several members of the New York Exchange that they have seen days of panic when practically the only buyers who were taking the vast volume of securities dumped upon the Exchange, were those who had sold short, and who now turned buyers as the only way of closing their transactions. They were curious to know what would have happened in those panic days when everybody wishes to sell and few cared to invest, if the buying power had depended solely upon the real investment of the outside public. . . . Short selling is thus a beneficial factor in steadying prices and obviating extreme fluctuations. Largely thru its action the discounting of serious depressions does not take the form of a sudden shock or convulsion, but, instead, is spread out over a period of time, giving the actual holder of securities ample time to observe the situation and limit his loss before ruin results. In fact, there could be no organized market for securities worthy of the name if there did not exist two sides, the "bull" and the "bear." The constant contest between their judgments is sure to give a much saner and truer level of prices than could otherwise exist.

13. *Arguments against short selling.*—Examining the case in more detail, and restating some of the arguments noted by Professor Huebner, we find that three valid arguments against short selling present themselves:

(a) It tends to depress prices.

(b) There is a temptation to keep on selling after prices have fallen. Short selling may be used to disorganize an already dangerous and panicky market.

(c) Professional speculators, the only ones who sell short, do not necessarily confine their efforts to stocks which should sell lower, but attack two or three active securities, thus tending to upset the whole market.

But balanced against the adverse arguments just given there are the following arguments in favor of short selling.

(a) No human being can undertake to say whether short selling tends more to advance or lower prices in the long run. Every short seller *must* buy. The man who buys, sells later. The man who sells short must buy later. It is only a question of sequence, and there is no moral element involved in that. The ordinary buyer is a free agent; he can change his mind, withdraw at any time, stay out of the market. But the short is compelled to buy or go bankrupt. It is an absolute commonplace of Wall Street that the stocks in the strongest position

are those with a large short interest, because every
one knows there is bound to be support which cannot
be withdrawn. The short seller never backs out, altho
future-delivery contractors in other lines of trade
often do.

(b) Shorts buy when support is most needed—
when prices are low. They sell when prices are highest, or at least they try to. Thus extremes are curtailed. When stocks are topheavy the shorts try to
sell. In other words, they supply stock when the demand is most urgent, just as they make the strongest
demand for stock when there is an over-supply.
Short selling takes the sharpness out of nearly every
movement. It distributes losses over a period of time
on the downward side. It shifts the risk from investors to professional speculators. It provides a stepping-off place all the way down. It spreads the loss
over a wider surface. It prevents a sudden slump
from a high price to relatively no price at all. These
statements I think are amply proved by the gradual
decline in New Haven stock, in which there has been
plenty of short selling, as compared with the sickening slumps in the shares of Boston and Maine leased
lines, in which there was little if any short selling.
Dr. Henry C. Emery, a leading authority on speculation, declares that short selling performed the same
function in the '90's in the case of Atchison. On the
other hand, where there is an active demand for stocks
for any reason, the advances are far more rapid if
there are no bold spirits to sell short.

(c) Far more harm is done by putting stocks too high than by driving them too low. More money is lost on the bull than on the bear side. Panics come from over-doing and not from underdoing. There are laws to punish those who circulate rumors to depress bank stocks, but there are no laws to punish the man who circulates a false rumor to put stocks up. Most persons prefer the bull rather than the bear side, and there are plenty of manipulators to take advantage of human nature. Thus there are a hundred false rumors that a stock is going up, to one that it is going down.

Every time a stock goes down the bears are blamed, like the ogres in the fairy tales. This is silly, and every sensible man knows it. The shorts, or bears, are needed, just as a minority party is needed. There could be no active, organized market without short selling, so violent would be the movements without the check that it affords.

(d) Much of the objection to short selling comes from the fallacy that high prices are always beneficial. It may be just as advantageous to buy cheap as to sell dear; therefore, it may be just as desirable for the community to have a force that depresses prices as it is to have one that raises them, altho the real function of short selling is to eliminate extremes—at one period it depresses prices, and later it advances them.

(e) Any sweeping prohibition of short selling would cripple the investment share markets; a large part of the technical short selling at present is not for the purpose of taking advantage of lower prices at all. A man in Chicago telegraphs his brokers in New York to sell one hundred shares of stock, which he has with him. He sends the stock by express, but until the certificates arrive the brokers are short. When receivership for the St. Louis and San Francisco Railroad was first rumored, a flood of selling orders were received in New York from London, Antwerp, Berlin and Paris. To execute the orders, brokers here had to borrow stock to deliver, and remain short for a week, until the steamers arrived.

(f) Short selling is a necessary adjunct of the odd-lot business, the least speculative on the Exchange. Odd-lot brokers buy and sell on the Stock Exchange in 100-share lots, the regular unit of trading, and then break up these lots into one, ten, seventeen, or any other number of shares, for investors who desire to buy. Small investors do most of their buying when the market is falling, and if the odd-lot broker first buys and then sells to the investor, with the market falling all the time, he loses all the time. But by selling first and buying afterwards (short selling), he avoids loss.

The practice of short selling often affords a means of hedging. As the miller must sell futures when he buys spots (or speculates), so persons who have occasion to use the stock market are often obliged to sell short. This may be true of dealers or bankers who introduce a new issue of securities. What the uninformed consider speculation is often a safeguard, or hedge, against risks which have to be taken. Naturally this is not an amusement for amateurs to engage in. Short selling is serious business and is for professionals. Stocks may be cornered or almost cornered, and the short may be squeezed. But he is no more foolish than the man who buys something that he cannot pay for.

REVIEW

Explain how buying and selling on the stock exchange is conducted. Which method is most frequently used and what is the procedure followed?

In your opinion has the European war affected trading methods? If so, in what way?

What is meant by being "long" or "short" on stock?

Trace the operations in a short sale.

Who pays the interest charges and premiums on a short sale? Who gets the dividends? Who receives the interest on the proceeds?

Is short selling safe? Discuss.

Do you believe in legal prohibitions on short selling? Give reasons why you favor or oppose them.

CHAPTER VII

THE WAYS OF WALL STREET (*Continued*)

1. *Puts, calls and straddles.*—There are several other ways in which a man may operate in stocks besides those considered in the last chapter. "Puts," "calls," "straddles" and "spreads" were formerly much used here by stock speculators and are still extensively employed in London. They are forbidden on the New York Stock Exchange, and their use seems to be less popular than formerly. When Jay Gould was in his prime he dealt extensively in "puts" and "calls."

These methods of dealing in stocks are collectively known as "privileges." They are sometimes called "true options" because the buyer has the option of carrying them out or not as he sees fit, but they should not be confused with "buyer's and seller's options" on the stock exchange, which are quite different; or with the use of the same word on the produce exchanges to mean the months, or futures traded in. In principle they correspond to an option on real estate, where an operator pays a few dollars down for the privilege of buying a lot two months later for $5,000.

A "put" may be defined as an option which gives the buyer of the "put" the privilege of making the seller of the "put" take a certain amount of produce or securities at a stated price within a given time stated in the agreement.

A "call" on the other hand is the opposite of the "put." This privilege gives the buyer the right to call upon the other party for a certain amount of produce or securities at a fixed price within a specified time.

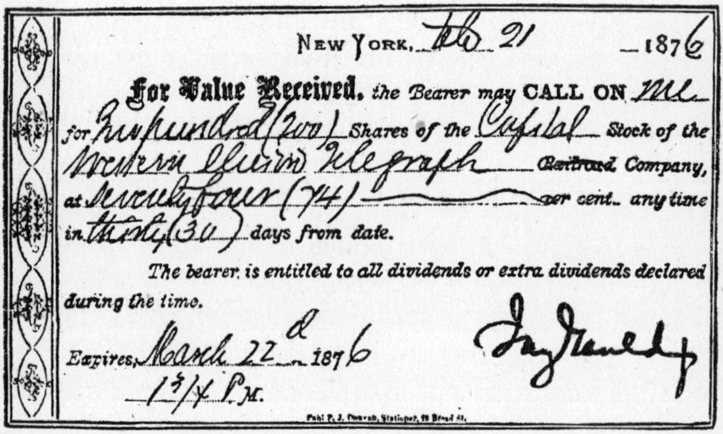

NEW YORK, Feb 21 1876

For Value Received, the Bearer may CALL ON me for Two hundred (200) Shares of the Capital Stock of the Western Union Telegraph Railroad Company, at Seventy four (74) per cent. any time in thirty (30) days from date.

The bearer is entitled to all dividends or extra dividends declared during the time.

Expires, March 22d 1876
1 3/4 P.M.

Jay Gould

FIGURE 1.—A CALL SIGNED BY JAY GOULD.

A "straddle" is a combination of a "put" and a "call." It gives the purchaser the privilege of either putting or calling the produce or securities at the named price within a given period. A "spread" is similar to a straddle, differing only in that the put and call prices are not alike.

2. *Puts.*—These four privileges are used almost entirely in speculative transactions. They are simply

bets upon anticipated changes in the price of the security or product which is traded in. Let us suppose that a man believes that the price of a certain stock will fall owing to some circumstances which he feels reasonably certain will be brought about. He desires to profit by this decline in price. He therefore seeks out some one and purchases a "put," by which he is given the privilege of delivering the stated number of shares of the stock within a given time at a price which is named. Now if his judgment prove to be correct and the price of the stock falls, he can go into the open market and purchase the number of shares mentioned in the "put" at a price much below that at which the seller of the "put" has agreed to buy it. He will then take over the stock, demanding the fulfillment of the contract named in the "put," and will make the difference between the price at which he bought the stock and the price at which he sold it under the "put"—less, of course, the commission on the purchase of the securities and the amount which he paid in order to purchase the privilege. As a matter of fact in most cases this transaction is never carried out, for a "put" is in reality a pure gamble and settlement is made by the payment of the difference in price to the lucky speculator.

3. *Calls.*—A "call" is used largely by short sellers or bears who have sold something which they do not own. Suppose a man has sold a certain stock at seventy which he expects to be able to go into the market and buy later on at a smaller price, thereby

realizing a profit. He desires to protect himself against a sudden rise or against a possible corner. He finds that he can buy a call for 72 which will give him the privilege. In case, for example, the stock goes to 74 he requires the seller of the call to deliver it to him at 72. In such a case the loss to the buyer of the call is limited because he cannot be caught on the wrong side of the market for more than the two points on his stocks, plus, of course, the amount which he has to pay in order to secure the privilege. When used in such transactions the price which he pays for the call is largely an insurance premium which he pays in order to be protected against a heavy loss.

Calls are also used by those who believe that the price of securities will advance above the price named in the call. They do not care to invest in stock but purchase instead this privilege which gives them the right, in case their predictions are verified, of calling for delivery of the stock at a price which is lower than that then prevailing in the open market. This, of course, enables the speculator to make a profit.

4. *Straddles and spreads.*—Double privileges, combining puts and calls, are used by those who desire to be on both sides of the market at once. They believe that the price of the stock will not remain stationary because they find that, for example, there are powerful interests opposing each other—one to advance and the other to cause a decline in the stock. The speculator is not certain which will win or even that he is correct, but knowing that the value of the

stock must move in one direction or the other, he desires to profit by it. He knows, too, that if he can purchase a straddle or spread, it is immaterial which way the stock will move just so long as it moves sufficiently far in either direction for him to attain this end.

The idea in buying a double privilege is to take advantage of the market either way it goes. The spread [1] is the more common of the two privileges. If a speculator buys a spread on a stock, with the price on the put side 120, and on the call side at 125, and during the life of the spread the stock declined to 110 or advanced to 135 there would be a profit of 10 points, less the cost of the privilege itself.

Straddles can only be purchased when those who sell them expect a stagnant market in which the price of securities will not fluctuate sufficiently to force them to redeem the privileges which they sell. If the market fails to move beyond the limits named in the contract, the buyer is out of pocket the amount which he has paid for the privilege, while the seller of the privilege has the total sum which he has received as compensation for the risk which he has taken. The risk is, however, very great because the seller of the right gambled on the market's being stationary, which is very unlikely. The cost of the straddles is therefore usually heavy even when they can be purchased.

5. *Price of privileges.*—As compared with puts and calls, there are many times when a straddle cannot

[1] The term spread also is used in another connection, to describe arbitrage operations in commodities or stocks where there is more than the normal difference in prices between two markets.

be purchased at all. In fact, they are not used to any great extent. The prices paid for privileges depend upon the following factors:

1. Upon the length of time during which the privilege is to run. If the time is long the risk of fluctuation is larger and the price greater.

2. Upon the difference between the prices named in the agreement and those then prevailing in the open market. The greater the difference in the prices, the less likely is the seller of the privilege to be called on to fulfill the contract.

3. Upon the condition of the market. When the market is wild the seller of the privilege is running a greater risk than when the market is steady.

4. In the case of securities the nature of the security must always be taken into consideration.

Possibly $150 is a fair average for a put or call on 100 shares of stock for 30 days.

These privileges, as has been said, are used most extensively at the present time in the grain market. There is usually a regulation charge of perhaps $10 per thousand bushels of grain. This is varied frequently, however, to fit the occasion. But these privileges even in the grain market, are falling into disuse because they are pure gambling, and the exchanges are coming to frown upon them more and more as time passes.

Theoretically the only risk in buying a privilege is the cost, and it is said that an unskilled speculator loses less money in this than in any other way, for he knows exactly what his loss will be. But the difficulty in recent years has been that many irresponsible parties have come to deal in privileges.

6. *Stop orders—or stop-loss orders.* — In theory, privileges may be used only to prevent loss in the market, but in practice they have come to be used largely for betting purposes. Another method of preventing loss which is in better repute is the stop order, or the stop-loss order. This is permitted on the Stock Exchange. It is an ingenious device to limit one's loss to a fixed point or amount. Speculator A has 100 shares of stock which he bought at 103, anticipating its rise. Contrary to his expectations the security begins to decline in price. A then issues a "stop-loss order" to his broker to sell when prices reach 90. He believes the fall is merely temporary and the security will recover its loss and hence he is willing to risk a drop to 90. When general bids begin to hover around 90, the broker will wait until a transaction is made at that price and will then offer the stock for sale at 90 or the next best price.

The expression "many stop orders were uncovered" is often used. This means that the market fell to a point set by many holders of stock as a stopping point for their losses, and consequently orders to sell were filled by brokers.

7. *Averaging.*—Another common practice for mitigating one's losses is averaging. A buys 1,000 shares at 85 which during the day declines to 65. He may then buy another 1,000 shares quoted at 65, in order

to lessen his loss on the first transaction. The average price he has paid is 75. If the stock recovers and goes about 77, a profit can be realized altho the price may never reach the original point of 85.

8. *Pyramiding.*—What is known as pyramiding should really be known as an inverted pyramid, because it indicates a dangerous method of trading, while the pyramid is a symbol of stability. It denotes the use of "paper profits," not yet cashed and therefore not in hand, to extend one's operations. If a man buys 100 shares of stock at $50 a share and it goes to $100 he may buy another 100 shares without either cashing in his profits on the first transaction or having any additional outside resources. The danger is too obvious to need further explanation.

9. *Arbitrage.*—The practice of arbitrage consists in buying a security in one market and selling it in another. The principal arbitrage business is between New York and London, altho the volume of business was much reduced by the war. Transactions of this character are also conducted between New York and Boston, New York and Philadelphia and other exchanges. The basis of the business is the inequalities of prices that exist in the various markets in which securities are sold. A broker buys stock in one market for a low price and sells it almost simultaneously in another market for a price that will yield a net profit. As most of the transactions of this character are made with a view of profiting by the difference between quotations in New York and those in Lon-

don, the mention of the term usually conveys the idea of foreign trading.

The arbitrage business is handled for the most part by the houses engaged in foreign exchange business. This trading rests largely on the difference in time between New York and the European world and in addition there is a difference in the period during which these exchanges are open for business. The difference in time between New York and London is almost five hours, to be exact it is four hours, fifty-five minutes and fifty-nine seconds. Thus it happens that both exchanges are in session at the same time for only one hour and four minutes of the day. When the New York Exchange opens for business at ten o'clock, the clock in London indicates four minutes of three, but as the London Exchange does not close until four o'clock there is still time to transact a great amount of business. The brokers and their customers make a detailed study of the London quotations before the Exchange opens at ten o'clock as they are aware that the prices in London will most likely exert an influence upon opening prices in the New York market.

10. *London and New York prices.*—The London prices of American securities will not always coincide, however, with the prices quoted in New York. Money may be tighter in London than in New York. The foreign prices of stock may suffer a loss thru some local tendency which has a remote bearing upon the New York market. This is the opportunity which

the arbitrageur awaits and out of which he secures his business. Usually between 9:15 and 9:30 the London quotations begin to come in over the ticker and on the news slips. The slips containing the London quotations will usually give the lowest and closing quotations in case the market is closed for the day, and opposite the closing quotation will give the New York equivalent, or the sum in American money which is represented by the New York quotation. This equivalent, however, is not accurate. It is really considerably higher than the New York equivalent and it is necessary, therefore, for the broker to reduce the London quotation to the price prevailing in the American market. The quotations are not on a par because all American stocks are quoted in London on an arbitrary basis—viz., that one pound sterling equals $5; that is to say, $1 equals four British shillings.

The reason for this is that the rate of exchange is constantly changing. If the real quotations were taken there would be continual dispute as to what the rate was at the time the bargain was made. We cannot, however, afford to give the English more than the prevailing rate in exchange for one of their pounds.

When exchange is perfectly normal one pound sterling equals $4.8665, altho the ratio of exchange has varied from $4.50 to $6 and even $7. The rule usually followed is to multiply the London price by the Wall Street price of demand sterling, and then divide this product by five. Such arithmetical calculations if always necessary would prove burdensome, especially in view of the rapidity and promptness with which transactions in the two markets must be carried out in order to reap any advantage resulting from a difference in the price of the same security in the respective markets. In order to lighten this work and eliminate the delay, various tables have been prepared to enable a quick conversion of London quotations to these New York equivalents.

Arbitrage between New York and London requires very quick conversion of London prices into New York equivalents by means of the tables referred to. The expenses of cabling, of shipping the securities and of insurance must all be carefully considered. During the war the prices of insurance especially were exorbitant.

11. *Delivery of stock.*—Each day after the Stock Exchange closes, buyers and sellers "compare" their transactions, that is, they exchange slips of paper on which are noted their operations with one another. In this way any possible error is checked up at once. It will be recalled that when a broker on the floor buys or sells he merely writes down the essential facts on a memorandum pad, and these little sheets he, of course, turns over to his clerical staff as soon as he returns to his office. Deliveries of securities must be made before 2.15 p. m. on the same day if sold for cash, and they must be delivered prior to 2.15 p. m. the following day, if sold in the regular way, except when the transaction takes place on Friday or Saturday in which case delivery occurs on Monday. While

brokers carry stocks for customers on margin, all transactions among themselves are on the basis of full payment and delivery, unless the operations of the Stock Exchange Clearing House be considered an exception.

12. *Stock clearing house.*—In 1892, the New York Stock Exchange adopted a clearing house system, very similar to that used by the banks. Here are effected settlements in certain designated active stocks. Bonds are "cleared" only on special occasions and lots of less than 100 shares do not go thru the clearing house. All members of the Stock Exchange are entitled to its use.

After the close of business each day all members report their transactions in the designated stocks to the clearing house. Suppose broker A sold 10,000 shares of Union Pacific and bought 8,000 shares. He is instructed next morning by the clearing house to deliver 2,000 shares to some particular member or members who are entitled to that amount, and he receives none himself. Or take another case. Suppose broker C sells 500 shares to broker D who in turn sells 500 shares to broker E. C has perhaps never heard of E, and has had no dealings whatever with him. Yet he will be instructed by the clearing house to deliver 500 shares not to D, to whom he sold them, but to E. In other words all parties who are "even" on a stock have nothing to receive or deliver. Those who have a balance to deliver and also those who have a balance to receive are instructed to that effect.

A delivery price is fixed each day for each stock; it is the even price (without fractions) which most closely approximates the last price of the day. Suppose the delivery price of Union Pacific is 132. A has sold Union at 134½, and B had sold at 131¼. All deliveries go thru on the books of the clearing house at 132. To avoid loss, A must receive a check from the clearing house for $2.50 a share and B must send to the clearing house his check for 75 cents a share. The even delivery price greatly facilitates the operations of the clearing house.

13. *Speculation and the clearing house.*—There is much argument pro and con as to whether a clearing house promotes speculation beyond what would exist if delivery of certificates were required for the full number of shares bought or sold. As only active stocks are cleared the possible criticism does not apply to the great number of less active investment stocks, or to bonds. No doubt it is easier for brokers to carry on large operations in speculative stocks thru the clearing house. Its use lessens the strain on the banks and the money supply. It has been estimated that on some days brokers would have had to borrow as much as $300,000,000 more than they did, if no clearing house had been in operation.

The question of the justification of the clearing house hinges entirely on whether the brokers could borrow the money without it. If they could do so no criticism would lie against the clearing system. For if there were no such institution the broker who sold

10,000 and bought 8,000 shares of Union Pacific would merely send a certificate for 10,000 shares out of his office one moment and perhaps, at exactly the same moment, would be taking in a certificate for 8,000 shares, the operation being precisely the same as that now taken care of by the clearing house, except that he would have to borrow more money and that there would be greater danger of loss of stocks by carrying them thru the streets. And the net result would be to leave both brokers exactly where they are with a clearing house.

14. *Transfers.*—Many Wall Street customs become clear, and much of its intricate machinery is explained when the system of transferring stocks is understood. In the first place it is to be noted that the Stock Exchange rules provide in the most minute detail what constitutes a "good delivery," that is, exactly what sort of a stock certificate or bond may be delivered as the result of a "sale" on its floor. The protection which the Stock Exchange provides in respect to the physical safety of securities approaches perfection.

The usual method of transferring ownership in stock from one person to another is for the holder to fill in on the back of the certificate his name and that of the new owner. The certificate then goes to the transfer office, or agent, of the corporation, and a new certificate with the new owner's name on the front is issued, and the old certificate cancelled. But if the first holder sells the certificate to another person and does not write the name of the new owner on the back, then the certificate is transferred, or indorsed *in blank*, and may pass from owner to owner indefinitely until it is worn out, without a new certificate being issued.

In Wall Street the great bulk of speculative business is carried on with these blank certificates, commonly known as "street certificates." The Stock Exchange permits delivery either by transfer or by certificate. Many of these street certificates are made out in the names of clerks, but to be good deliveries they must be indorsed and witnessed by stock exchange firms. Of course the loss, theft or destruction of such a certificate causes more complications than would the loss of one still in the hands of the original owner. When dividends are declared, it is necessary for the last owner to trace his right to it back to the original owner because the corporation knows only one owner, the one whose name is on the certificate.

A vast volume of business is conducted with these street certificates. In fact speculation would hardly be possible without them, for quick operators could not wait for the slow processes of actual transfer on a company's books. Thus every broker has on hand numerous frayed and worn pieces of engraved paper, made out perhaps, in the name of some forgotten clerk that he can use with the same celerity as a ten dollar bill.

15. *When brokers fail.*—Altho failure among stock Exchange members is comparatively rare, when it occurs many legal difficulties arise. The solution of these difficulties depends upon the application of a

principle of equity which provides that persons entitled to specific property or money can recover that property or money as long as they can identify it. In a leading case on this principle the English judge who made the decision said: "Supposing the trust money were 1000 sovereigns, and the trustee put them into a bag, and by mistake, or accident, or otherwise dropped a sovereign of his own into the bag, could anybody suppose that a judge in equity would find any difficulty in saying that the *cestui que trust* (the customer) has a right to take 1000 sovereigns out of the bag?"

With this principle in mind, let us examine a few of the circumstances that might arise when a broker fails. Customers who cannot trace their money or securities into a special fund become general creditors and share with the general creditors in the estate of the insolvent after the specific liens or claims have been satisfied. If a customer has given his broker money to buy securities outright, he will be entitled to the securities or to the money if he can identify the one or prove into which bank account the other has been placed. The same situation arises when a customer sends securities to his broker to be sold. He is entitled to the identical securities if they have not been sold or to a repayment of the proceeds of the sale if he can show into what fund or account they have been deposited.

Where a broker pledges *en bloc* securities, part of which were purchased for some customers on margin and the rest of which were purchased outright, the margin customers have inferior equities to the outright purchasers, since the hypothecation of the margin stock was rightful and the hypothecation of the other stock was wrongful. Securities pledged by a broker cannot be released unless the pledgee has paid his debt. Thus, if a customer owes the broker $1,000 on stock and the broker pledges the stock to a banker for $1200, the banker is entitled to his $1200 before being compelled to give up the stock.

Under the rules of the Exchange, members who are creditors of an insolvent fellow member have a first lien on the value of his seat.

REVIEW

What is the difference between a "put" and a "call"?
When and by whom are "puts," "calls" and "straddles" used?
Name some factors influencing the prices of straddles.
What is the most reputable way of preventing losses on stocks?
What is the object of arbitrage? Where is it practised and upon what basis does it rest?
Why do not prices of American securities sold on New York and London stock exchanges agree? Who benefits by the difference in price and why?
What do you believe to be the service which a clearing house performs?
How is stock transferred?

CHAPTER VIII

USE OF INFORMATION ON THE EXCHANGES

1. *Value of news.*—Wall Street is the world's biggest cash market for news. The quickest and most accurate news is absolutely essential to this vast money whirlpool where men speculate in stocks, grain, cotton and other commodities. Even the uninitiated have some idea how exceedingly delicate and flexible are the great markets and how easily the trend of prices changes in either direction as unfavorable or propitious news becomes known. Thus it is the business of the speculative operator to learn as quickly as possible what is going on in the world. If time is money, so is news.

Thus it comes about that Wall Street is as hungry for news as a famished wolf for a woolly victim. To anyone visiting the financial district this eagerness displays itself immediately. "What do you know?" is the common greeting, and the question does not refer to health or individual affairs but to national and international intercourse.

As the writer stated in the *Saturday Evening Post* of December 25, 1915:

In that central ganglion of the financial nerves of two hemispheres, Wall Street, an obscure man may let loose a paragraph powerful enough to create or demolish fortunes, initiate whole new cycles of national development, and reverberate for decades thru the halls of Congress and state legislatures.

It is a royal battle of wits, this unearthing of big financial news. Once the secrets of high finance reach the light, whether willingly or otherwise, there is no gauge to their momentum. They may roll and thunder on with consequences and after effects that no wizard can foresee.

Less than a year ago it was said that big news, inside news, "beats," as the newspaper reporters say, were no longer obtainable in Wall Street; that not until another J. P. Morgan or E. H. Harriman appeared upon the scene, and another era of great mergers got under way, would financial news again become supreme. Also it was said that speculation had died peacefully of old age. Both assertions were wrong. Never was there more big news than now; never was inside news of high financial import more eagerly sought after.

Today the air is filled with rumors of mergers and new exploitations. With several billion dollars of war orders, the very spirit of 1901 lives again, and the machinery for blazing forth to a money-crazed public every step in the new era of industrial promotion is more complete than ever before.

What are the sources of information upon which the speculator relies? They are by no means haphazard or occasional, but on the contrary, are as accurate and regular as the ingenuity and intelligence of man can make them.

2. *The ticker.*—The most important single agency engaged in the spreading of news in and about the exchanges is the ticker. It is a marvelous electrical typewriter worked from the headquarters of the companies that rent the tickers to subscribers. It prints a narrow strip or ribbon of paper known colloquially

as the "tape." The tape is not confined to the Stock Exchange nor to the Wall Street district. It is used both by members of the Exchange and by outsiders. The New York Produce Exchange, the Chicago Board of Trade, the New York Coffee Exchange and the New York Cotton Exchange each have tickers of their own, giving the actual prices or "quotations" made in these exchanges and distributed thru the country. Each system is operated by separate companies but all are conducted on a similar plan and with a common purpose. There are twenty cities outside New York that have their own ticker services. About a century ago doves were used in England to carry news and reports, but their usefulness ceased with the development of the cable, telegraph, telephone and, finally, the ticker for price movements.

The ticker seen in banks, in brokers' offices, in hotel lobbies is a machine about four feet high, resembling somewhat in shape and size a subway or theatre ticket receiver. Within is a spool of narrow paper ribbon which feeds itself into the printer, and upon which the machine operates like a visible typewriter. After the printing by telegraphic conveyance of the first quotation the spool slowly revolves to make room for the printing of the next quotation. Near the ticker is placed a basket into which the ribbon gradually falls as the price quotations continue to come in.

3. *Stock abbreviations.*—As there are over 1500 bonds and stocks listed on the Stock Exchange, it is inadvisable from the financial point of view as well as

USE OF INFORMATION

practically impossible, to spell out in full the name of the security dealt in. Abbreviations, often one letter in length, are employed and the number of stocks sold, together with the price are given. The following are sample abbreviations:

U—Union Pacific.

UB—Utica and Black River.

UC—United Cigar Manufacturing Company.

UCS—United Cigar Stores.

The sale of 100 shares of Union Pacific common stock at 132 would read 100 U 132. Many of the nicknames for stocks arise from these abbreviations, for example "Mop" for Missouri Pacific, from M. P.

Other abbreviations beside those for the stocks themselves are used for the correction of errors, for offers without bids, or bids without offers, also when a sale is not reported in its proper order, to distinguish the amount sold and the price paid when they are so nearly alike as to cause confusion, to indicate three-day contracts, options and so forth. A word and phrase book and a complete list of abbreviations is sometimes fastened to the stand upon which the ticker rests.

4. *Use of the ticker.*—Men gather round the ticker in the various offices and follow its story with keen interest. Except when the market is very dull the ticker never quite keeps up with it, being from one to ten minutes behind according to the activity of the market. Only in an extremely busy market would

it be ten minutes behind. Mistakes tho rarely made are quickly corrected.

The louder the sound of ticking the more notice the machine attracts because loud ticking is a sign that the market is active. From the activity of the ticker, the character of stocks appearing upon it, the amount and units of the deals, the prices, the variety or lack of variety of stocks dealt in, the order of their appearance and other ticker signs which are soon learned, one may get an almost complete picture of the market, indeed the nearest approach to it that anyone who is not on the floor, newspaper reporters not excepted, ever gets. Tickers are used even on the ground floor of the Stock Exchange itself and brokers cluster about them, and then rush to the various posts again to make more deals, the quotations for which they read in the ticker a few minutes later.

5. *Quotation companies.*—How is the rapid printing of price quotations made possible? On the floor of the exchange brokers are buying and selling continually. Official uniformed reporters engaged by the exchange, fly hither and thither to secure information as to the sales made, the stocks involved, the quantities sold and the price obtained. Upon getting the information the reporter immediately rushes to one of the four telegraph stations placed at convenient intervals on the floor, from which the message is sent to a gallery where there are employes of the ticker companies. These are two companies only; the New York Quotation Company is owned and managed by

the Exchange itself primarily for the purpose of benefitting its own members. It gives out its figures to about 1100 tickers, located in the Wall Street district, which in this case means south of Chambers Street. The other company is a subsidiary of the Western Union Telegraph Company, known as the Gold and Stock Company. It pays a large sum, formerly $100,000 a year, for the quotations which it gets simultaneously with the company first named and supplies them to persons all over the country not members of the Exchange. The Exchange attempts to determine who shall and who shall not receive these quotations, in order to prevent their falling into the hands of bucket shop keepers and other undesirable persons, but the whole subject of its right to control their sale is constantly being fought out in the courts.

Another function the ticker performs is that of acting as time keeper. A minute before the limit is reached the words "Hammonds Time" appear on the tape, followed by fifteen distinct clicks. At the end of the fifteenth beat it is 2.15. The ticker thus serves as a valuable reminder and regulator to those who are continually in a state of mental excitement and worry and who are apt, thru their preoccupation, to forget their obligations. On the surface this may seem unimportant to the novice, but it requires years of experience to appreciate the value of minor details of which this is an illustration.

Another interesting detail regarding the tickers is that while the Stock Exchange collects the quotations and puts them out on the tickers, it assumes no responsibility for them. They are neither official nor guaranteed. If they were "official," the officers of the Stock Exchange would hardly have a moment free from testifying in court in disputes over stock deals.

6. *News tickers.*—Somewhat similar to stock quotation tickers are the news tickers which are owned and controlled entirely by different private companies. As the title indicates, news is the primary consideration with these tickers. Declaration of dividends, amalgamations, and mergers, election of directors and officers, financial conditions, internal and external, and a myriad other facts are disseminated by this system. The news tickers are located in most of the larger cities including New York, Chicago, St. Louis, Boston, Philadelphia, Baltimore, Cincinnati, Cleveland, Washington and Buffalo. The paper used in them is for obvious reasons considerably wider than that used in the stock ticker, so that the news ticker is known as the "broad" or "page" ticker. Its work is rapid and accurate and it is a practically indispensable instrument to brokers and speculators, for not only must current prices be known, but the circumstances which exert a powerful influence on the movement of prices must be taken into account.

7. *Bulletin service.*—Hardly less rapid is the dissemination of news by means of the bulletin service. Only a limited number of cities have this facility. In New York City there are two, Boston has two and Philadelphia, one. About every half hour during the

period of business activity, from 9 a. m. to 3 p. m. these bulletins come out with extensive information on the many subjects treated.

Page tickers, bulletins, and certain evening and morning financial newspapers are all published by the same companies known as "news bureaus." Thus the same news is used in all three forms of publication, appearing as a mere flash of the essential facts on the ticker, in fuller detail in the bulletins and naturally most complete of all, in the papers.

These reporting companies operate with great rapidity thru the employment of many reporters on a single detail. If directors of a certain railroad company are to meet at noon to declare an important dividend, the financial news bureaus will detail several men to the job. One man stands outside the meeting room, another at the end of the hall and another at the nearest available telephone. Days beforehand arrangements are made to obtain the use of a telephone close to the directors' meeting room and this is held open to the news bureau's office from perhaps ten or eleven o'clock on. By this practice and by the use of relays of men it is possible to get out on the tickers the news of some event or action within sixty seconds of its actual announcement.

It is difficult to conceive of the consummate perfection reached by the news service of Wall Street. On a certain day of each month on the dot of noon, Western Union time, a clerk in the offices of the United States Steel Corporation hands to reporters on the other side of a railing a statement of the amount of the company's unfilled orders. When this is done the news tickers which stand in the offices of hundreds of bankers and brokers thruout New York City print the figures anywhere from one to two minutes after twelve. The directors of the Standard Oil Company of California met one day in San Francisco and declared a dividend. Their action was wired to New York by the San Francisco representative of a Wall Street news agency and wired back to a broker's office in San Francisco within fifteen minutes.

8. *Newspapers.*—Naturally the cheapest and most widely used sources of Wall Street information are the financial pages of the daily newspapers. Much of the financial news that appears therein is adapted from the news bureaus, while on the other hand the agencies get many of their suggestions from the general daily press. In the same way the morning and evening papers get many suggestions from each other. Each paper has its own clientele and its own method of treating the news.

This is not the place to describe in detail all the papers which give news of interest to persons who trade in stocks or commodities. In New York, in addition to the extensive departments in the general press, there are four dailies which contain little else; the *Wall Street Journal, Financial America, Journal of Commerce,* and the *Commercial.* There are also numerous weekly and monthly publications as well as the so-called "manuals," containing information

USE OF INFORMATION

about the leading corporations, and many "services" and card systems along the same lines.

Further, there is the enormous output of "literature," booklets, circulars and letters from brokers and investment bankers, nearly all of whom maintain so-called "statistical" departments. The mass of facts, rumors, information, "tips," advice, "write-ups" and miscellaneous printed matter concerning stocks and commodities traded in on the exchanges is beyond all belief and calculation. In his "Work of Wall Street," S. S. Pratt declared that one-fifth of everything published relates to business, and it may be added that most of it has some bearing upon the movement of prices on the exchanges. One estimate places the commercial and financial articles and reports in the daily, weekly and monthly press at the annual equivalent of 275,000,000 medium sized books.

9. *Reading the financial page.*—Ability to read the financial page depends entirely upon one's knowledge of business and financial subjects. It is not a subject in itself. It is no closed book, no secret, to one who has pursued the Modern Business Course. Aside from certain technical aspects which are explained in this Text and in those on Investment, Corporation Finance and Banking, knowledge of the various branches of business itself is needed. The stock and produce exchanges are delicate barometers which instead of reflecting atmospheric conditions are influenced by conditions in the business world.

Without attempting therefore to analyze all the

news on the financial pages it may be well only to dissect a portion of the daily stock and bond tables. The table shows the form in which the *New York Times* prints these quotations. After giving the total sales of stocks for the day, for the same day the year before and two years before, for the year to date and for the year to date two years ago, a table is given of which a few entries follow:

Sales		First	High	Low	Last	Net Change
12,000	Am. Beet Sugar	87⅞	87⅞	85⅛	86½	—1¼
100	Am. Br. S. & F'dry..	103½	103½	103½	103½	+2½
1,700	American Can.	54¾	54¾	54	54¾	.....
200	American Can. pf.....	110	110	110	110	.....

Now it is apparent that 12,000 shares of American Beet Sugar, common, were sold. The first or opening price was $87⅞ which was also the highest of the day. At some time the stock fell to $85⅛ but when the market closed the last sale was made at $86½, which is evidently 1¼ points below the figure at which it closed the day before, the difference being known as "net change." Evidently none of the preferred stock of the same company was sold because it is not quoted. There is only one other point to note about these selected quotations. In the case of American Can and American Can preferred it will be seen that no "net change" took place, the closing prices being the same as those of the day before.

We will now take a selected portion of the sales of the bond table.

USE OF INFORMATION

Armour & Co. 4½s
　1,000 ....93⅜
　3,000 ....93⅝
　1,000 ....93⅜

A, T & S F gen 4s
　5,000 ....92¾
　1,000 ....92⅝
　5,000 ....92¾
　4,000 adjust 4s, stpd.......84⅛

Here the method of quotation is entirely different. It will be seen that $1,000 of Armour & Co. 4½ per cent bonds were sold at 93⅜ per cent, $3,000 at 93⅝ per cent and $1,000 at 93⅜ per cent. Also $5,000 Atchison, Topeka & Santa Fé general 4 per cent bonds at 92¾ per cent, $1,000 at 92⅝ per cent, $5,000 at 92¾ per cent and $4,000 of the adjustment 4 per cent stamped bonds of the same company at 84⅛ per cent.

REVIEW

Why do you think the broker needs up-to-the-minute news of financial operations?

Describe the mechanical working of the ticker. What is its functions?

What would you need to know to read the ticker intelligently?

Do you consider unofficial figures such as are issued on the tickers valuable?

Who collects the material printed on the tape and how is such material collected?

What do you consider the value of news bureaus?

CHAPTER IX

THE CURB MARKET

1. *Physical characteristics.*—One of the most picturesque and instructive sights for a visitor to the metropolis is the New York Curb Market. There is also a curb market in Exchange Place, Boston, which does a large business, but it is not of such national importance as is the one in New York. This market takes its name from the fact that it does business in the open street and overflows, in periods of activity, the curbs and sidewalks. It has no building and therefore none of the external manifestations or ornaments of an "exchange." This peculiar circumstance distinguishes the curb from all other markets.

The New York Curb Market meets daily at the same hours as the Stock Exchange. Its present location is on Broad Street between Exchange Place and Beaver Street, just south of the Broad Exchange Building. An area is marked off by means of iron standards and ropes, but the curb constantly overflows its supposed area. It has no legal rights upon the street, except upon police suffrance, but its economic function is so great that the police overlook the fact that it technically constitutes a public nuisance by blocking traffic of all kinds on a very important street.

Curb markets are among the oldest of financial in-

© *Broun Bros., N.Y.*

OFFICE OF A CURB BROKER

Note the signalling to the crowd in the street, dimly seen thru the large panes of glass

THE CURB MARKET

stitutions. A curb existed in London on Change Alley for nearly a century. Paris had a roped off curb as early as 1720. The New York Stock Exchange dates from a meeting of brokers under a tree at what is now 68 Wall Street. During the Civil War the center of gravity was shifted from the shade of the old tree to William Street, the hours of business extending from early in the morning, usually eight o'clock, to nightfall. Often darkness did not terminate the activity and traders resorted to the Fifth Avenue Hotel when natural light was no longer available.

2. *The great open market.*—To those unacquainted with its ways the curb market appears to be an angry, shouting, howling mob. But there is almost as much system on the curb as on the Stock Exchange. Being in the open street, subject to the weather and often to the traffic, there can be no mechanical devices for recording transactions or even for transmitting orders to the brokers. This end is effected by a deaf-and-dumb sign or wig-wag system between the brokers and clerks who sit in the open windows of surrounding buildings. Of course the noise is too great for vocal communication. The nearby windows are filled with hundreds of boys transmitting orders. Just behind them are the telephone and telegraph instruments by means of which communication is had with other parts of the city and country.

Only severe rainstorms drive the curb off the street. Any ordinary bad weather affects it not at all. There is no ticker service or any such complete system for gathering quotations as on the Stock Exchange. The curb derives great advantages from being on the street. This peculiar location serves as a sort of free advertisement which makes the curb a distinctive market, and without doubt appeals to persons of small means, who cannot gain admission to the Stock Exchange, even as spectators.

Altho the curb has an organization and regular membership, and also has a regular "listing" process, it is an "open" market. All stocks, except those listed on the Stock Exchange, can be bought and sold on the curb, and all persons have the right to trade there. In these respects the curb differs radically from the Stock Exchange. Another important point of difference is that a broker on the curb is not obliged to take the first contract offered to him. In fact he can refuse any contract he cares to, and can pick and choose as much as he likes.

3. *Organization and membership.*—Until about ten years ago the curb had little if any organization. Frauds were constantly being perpetrated, and evils of every kind were rampant. Brokers frequently "lay down" on their contracts. But beginning with the work of the late E. S. Mendels, who was first merely known as the "dean" of the curb fraternity, then as "curb agent" and finally as Chairman of the New York Curb Market Association, the better element of brokers has gradually taken more and more control and built up an organization.

The curb now possesses a staff of officers, corresponding to those in control of any institution or corporation,—chairman, secretary and treasurer and in addition a governing committee, and committees on arbitration, listing, complaints, commissions, memberships, etc. The rules and regulations adopted since its reorganization are rigidly enforced, resembling as they do in essence those of the other exchanges.

The membership of the curb registered a total of 334 in January, 1916, which is the largest in its history. There seems to be a tendency toward expansion which bids fair to make the market second only to the New York Stock Exchange.

4. *Present importance.*—The present war has greatly stimulated trade on the curb and some brokers maintain that now it is the second largest center of stock market activity in the whole world. At times during 1915 and 1916, dealings on the curb were larger than on any stock exchange in the world excepting only New York Stock Exchange. The fee for membership is $250. The committee is seriously considering raising this fee because of inability to accommodate all applicants and because limitation of membership is a policy contemplated for the near future.

Owing partly to its increased prosperity and also to the desire of the better element to rid itself of the evils inherent in any free-for-all stock market, the curb was anxious, in 1916, to "go indoors." At various times two smaller exchanges in New York, the Produce and Consolidated, have both tried to appropriate curb stocks. "Calls" were held on the floor of the regular exchanges, but the real market stayed right out on the street where it had always been. One influential reformer connected with the Stock Exchange suggested a combination of the better element of the curb brokers with the Consolidated Exchange brokers allowing them to become a junior department of the Stock Exchange and to meet in its New Street lobby. His idea was to bring into the august "board," but only as far as its lobby, the sheep on the curb and leave the goats outside. But the difficulty with this and all other separatist schemes is that the goats left outside would, in time, form a new market of their own which might become as powerful as the old curb.

5. *Relation of the Stock Exchange to the curb.*—Altho the Stock Exchange has no direct or official authority over the curb, more than three-fourths of all the business on the curb is transacted by clerks or members of stock exchange firms, or originates with them in behalf of themselves or their customers. But in every city, members of the organized stock exchanges are forbidden to belong to any other exchange in that city and if the curb should leave the open and go into a building, another exchange would be created. The New York Stock Exchange, for example, prohibits its members from trading on, or in any way affiliating with, other stock exchanges in the City of New York. Article XX, Section 4 reads thus:

Dealing upon any other exchange in the City of New York or publicly outside of the Exchange, directly or indirectly, in securities listed or quoted on the Exchange, is forbidden; any violation of this rule shall be deemed to be an act detrimental to the interest and welfare of the Exchange.

The curb members have been considering the advisability of doing their trading indoors. This will probably be effected within a very short time.

6. *Functions of the curb.*—Indeed it is distinctly in the public interest that a great semi-organized street market should be kept up. It affords the public a place to obtain markets and quotations for thousands of cheap shares, which are not listed on the stock exchanges or on the curb for that matter, and which would otherwise have no market except that made by brokers over the telephone, at such prices as the brokers chose to make. There are said to be as many as 5,000 different securities which find quotation on the curb, altho hardly more than 250 are noted in the regular quotation sheets and only about 300 are "listed."

The functions of the curb market may be considered from several angles. First, it is a well known fact that the curb serves a ready and embracing market for security issues of a great many industrial, mining and miscellaneous enterprises, which constantly make their appearance as capital expands into newer channels.

The curb is very quick in obtaining new classes and groups of securities. Hardly has the public realized that a new industry is becoming important, such as a motor accessory manufacture, before the curb is madly trading in motor accessory stocks by the dozen, as if it had never heard of any other kind of shares. Fashions change rapidly on the curb.

Corporations and undertakings that are passing thru a period of preliminary organization, and have not as yet transacted business, find a market on the curb. In such cases "when issued" securities are dealt in and the deliveries are made when the certificates are ready to be distributed. All members of the Curb Association as well as outsiders who, altho not members, are of good financial standing and responsible business men, are permitted to participate in these transactions.

Information concerning the amount of capital, the purpose and place of the business, management and other similar facts must be given for listing. In addition, after the security is recommended for listing by the proper committee, a fee of $100 is exacted. This safeguards the public from many fraudulent and get-rich-quick schemes and contrivances of the more obvious sort. But it must not be supposed that listed securities on the curb necessarily have value. The curb admits to the list what it calls "prospects," a designation which is fair warning to all the untried character of the enterprise.

On the other hand, before official admission is secured speculation in risky ventures is fostered. This circumstance is inevitable since there must be some center where trading in short-lived enterprises may be carried on. The large exchanges usually require a period of at least a year's business activity and proof of profit-making, before stocks may be listed. During this period of development a market is open on the curb to aid these enterprises to pass thru a somewhat checkered career.

If one wants to assume risks and enter into a highly speculative and dangerous territory, he is free to do so, with a vengeance, on the curb. But the curb has gone out of its way to mark off the boundary line and "he who runs may read."

The curb serves an excellent purpose in that it makes possible trading in securities the par value of which are as low as ten cents. Mining corporations especially issue stocks ranging from ten cents per share to twenty-five dollars. At present there are many corporations as meritorious as those listed on the larger exchanges, which could find no market if it were not for the curb.

There are many well known and exceedingly valuable stocks that are not listed on any exchange, the liquidation of which could never be effected with the facility that only a central market affords, were it not for the curb. The Standard Oil Company's stocks offer a splendid illustration of this class. This corporation has never applied to the New York Stock Exchange or to any other exchange to have its shares listed until recently, simply because the few men in control did not care to have a market. There are many other stocks of similar character which are tightly held and have no market, or at most a narrow one, because the chief owners do not care for one. The facilities which the curb offers make it possible for the smaller holder to turn such stock into cash, whenever he likes and to record reasonably accurate quotations on these transactions.

Still another function of the curb may be inferred readily enough from those that have already been mentioned. It is a place of preparation and trying out for the Stock Exchange. If it had no other importance it would constitute an exceedingly large cog in the financial machine, because it has housed at one time or another a great number of the best known securities, investment and speculative alike, whose ownership has later become widely diffused thru the Stock Exchange.

A definite schedule of commission rates, which members may charge on transactions taking place on the curb, has been adopted. This schedule is an increase over the former rates. For securities selling under $1 the minimum rate is 2% of the amount involved in the trade; from $1 to $3 the rate rises to $4 per 100 shares; from $3 to $5—$5.50; from $5 to $10—$7.50; from $10 to $125—$15; from $125 and over, $20 per 100 shares. As is the case in all organized markets the rates that are enforceable, at the penalty of expulsion or similar drastic punishment are the minima. Usually brokers who trade on the curb raise the commission charges above this level on the lowest and highest stages in the scale; that is to say, on securities selling for less than $1 and above $200. On intermediate values the rates are usually uniform because of keen competition between broker and broker. The minimum commission on any transaction is $1.

REVIEW

How does the curb market differ from the Stock Exchange?
What is the relationship between the two markets?
In your opinion what functions does the curb market perform?
In what sort of stocks does the curb market trade?

CHAPTER X

OTHER AMERICAN STOCK EXCHANGES

1. *Consolidated Stock Exchange of New York.*—
One must be careful not to confuse the Consolidated Stock Exchange of New York with the New York Stock Exchange, altho both deal, for the most part, in the same securities. The Consolidated Exchange carries on small operations in a few mining shares and in some others not listed on the Stock Exchange, but it is essentially a secondary market for some of the more active and popular securities on the big Board. It is said that the Consolidated is the third largest market for securities in the country, ranking next to the New York Curb. The assertion is even made that, at times, its total sales equal the combined total of all the stock exchanges outside of New York City. At other times, however, its dealings do not much exceed those on the Boston Stock Exchange. It is rarely that the dealings on the Consolidated exceed one-fifth of those on the New York Stock Exchange.

The unit of trading on the Consolidated is ten shares, as on the London Stock Exchange, and it is a fractional or odd-lot market of no small proportions and importance. Of course, large transactions are often effected, but the exchange is essentially a market for small operations. In times of panic or of unusual stress it often assumes increased importance, but for the most part this exchange does not initiate movements in stocks, and the prices on its floor tend to follow rather than to lead those on the New York Stock Exchange for the same securities.

While there are a number of very active commission brokers in the Consolidated, this exchange is noted for the fact that with a comparatively limited outlay, a man may become a member and trade on his own account. The Consolidated maintains a ticker service of its own. A form of listing requirements is prescribed, but original listings are rare; this exchange merely trades, for the most part, in stocks already admitted to the Stock Exchange.

2. *History and description.*—The present exchange is an outgrowth of what was known, about four decades ago, as the New York Mining Stock Exchange, which was organized because of the necessity that arose of having separate quarters for the growing business done in mining shares. Two years later it absorbed its fifteen-months-old rival, the American Mining and Stock Exchange and, in 1886, it added three more exchanges, the National Petroleum, the Miscellaneous Security Board and the New York Petroleum Exchange and Stock Board. At first the Consolidated conducted no business except that in mining stocks and petroleum pipe-line certificates, but it has long since ceased to deal in the latter and deals now only slightly in the former. The Consolidated has moved several times, and now has a large build-

ing of its own at Broad and Beaver Streets. It has a slightly larger membership than the New York Stock Exchange. The present cost of membership is about $500.

The Consolidated broker charges $7.50 for 100 shares on stocks selling under $10 per share, and $15 for 100 shares of stock selling at or above $10. If the trading is done thru fellow members, the commission is 1/32 of one per cent. The Consolidated has a clearing house, where the monetary balances come up for settlement each day, but clearances in stock balances are made semi-weekly only, instead of daily, as on the New York Stock Exchange.

3. *Stock exchanges outside New York.*—Outside of New York City there are a number of stock exchanges, but for the most part they are of relatively small importance. Among the first twenty cities of the country there are six, Buffalo, Milwaukee, Newark, Minneapolis, Jersey City and Kansas City which have no stock exchange. In the case of two of the cities the absence of a stock exchange is readily explained by the proximity to New York City; in the other cities the interest in grain and other produce overshadows that in securities.

Stock sales on the exchanges of the other cities for 1916 and 1917, the cities being named in the order of their population, were as follows:[1]

[1] This information was courteously furnished to the Alexander Hamilton Institute by the secretaries of the respective exchanges.

OTHER AMERICAN STOCK EXCHANGES 143

	Shares (Thousands)			Shares (Thousands)	
	1916	1917		1916	1917
Chicago	1,610	1,701	Detroit	1,488	488
Philadelphia	5,382	3,721	San Francisco	64,053	78,017
St. Louis	100	128	Cincinnati	232	74
Boston	12,907	5,102	New Orleans	30	11
Cleveland	400	329	*Washington	....	....
Baltimore	2,534	1,120	Los Angeles	19,420	11,578
Pittsburgh	9,373	7,639			

*Not compiled

In forming any judgment as to the significance of these figures regard must be had for the stocks represented. In San Francisco and Los Angeles the stocks traded in, for the most part mining stocks, have a very low value. The total sales in San Francisco in 1917, for instance, represented a value of $17,124,927.

The principal stock exchanges in the Dominion of Canada are those of Montreal and Toronto. Sales on the former exchange in the year 1916 amounted to 3,396,000 shares, in 1917 to 1,131,000 shares, while the sales of the Toronto Exchange for 1916 aggregated 1,300,000 shares and 1917, 513,000 shares.

Not only is the volume of business slight on the markets of most of the large cities in the interior, and the character of the securities almost wholly local, but in such cities so large a part of the total volume of business is transacted over the counter of investment dealers, rather than on the floor of the exchanges, that the latter are reduced to a minor position.

4. *Services of the smaller exchanges.*—In general the exchanges outside of New York City deal in local securities. In a sense they serve the New York Stock Exchange somewhat in the same manner as does the

curb in trying out new securities. Enterprises which at the outset appear as local in scope expand to national proportions and when they do so they gravitate naturally to New York.

It is a fact which in no way minimizes the importance of other financial centers, that when investors desire a broad, active, national market, for their securities, they usually send them to New York. Thus Philadelphia has long since ceased to be the primary market for Pennsylvania, Lehigh Valley and Reading, three railroad stocks in which at various times the Philadelphia market had an important "say." Altho all the directors of the Pennsylvania Railroad live in the state of Pennsylvania and the company is absolutely ruled from its headquarters in Philadelphia, the only market of any importance for its stock is on the New York Stock Exchange. For a long time Lehigh Valley enjoyed an active market in Philadelphia, but New York was finally able to absorb that also.

5. *Boston Stock Exchange.*—The Boston Stock Exchange occupies a prominent position because of the fact that Boston has long been the center of a very rich section. New England has supplied capital to the newer parts of the country from the earliest days of the railroad business. In other words, Boston has financed many of the country's largest enterprises, including many of the richest copper and zinc mining industries. But the New York Stock Exchange

has already absorbed a large number of these companies, and is constantly absorbing more and more of them as time goes on.

The Boston Exchange dates from 1834, when it was established as a market for the stock of New England railroads. Among the important stocks in which this exchange deals, and which have been largely financed by New England capital, are American Telephone, American Sugar, American Woolen, General Electric, Swift and Company, United Fruit and United Shoe. The primary market for most of these stocks, however, is now New York.

The Exchange has on its lists at present the stocks of about two hundred different companies, but by far the most active of these are the copper mining shares. In many cases they sell at very high prices, far above their par value. Calumet and Hecla, with a par value of $25, sold up to December, 1917, as high as $580.

The membership of the Boston Stock Exchange is limited to 150. The price of seats has varied from $15,000 to $38,000, but the lower figure is the more normal one. The listing requirements are of the same strict nature as those that prevail generally in the larger exchanges of the country.

Because the rates of commission differ from those on the New York Stock Exchange it may be well to give them in some detail.

Bonds, on the par value ⅛ of 1 per cent (Government bonds are exempt from the regular rates); bank and trust company stocks, 25 cents per share; insurance stocks, 25 cents; textile manufacturing and real estate trust stocks, $\frac{1}{4}$ of 1 per cent on the par value (when stocks are selling double their par value, the commission on them is doubled); mining stocks selling at $300 or above, 25 cents per share; selling between $300 and $10, $12\frac{1}{2}$ cents; selling between $10 and $1, $6\frac{1}{4}$ cents; for mining stocks selling below $1 the rate is $1 per 100 shares or any fraction thereof. All other stocks selling at $300 or over, 50 cents per share; selling between $300 and $125, 20 cents; selling between $125 and $10, 15 cents; selling between $10 and $1, $7\frac{1}{2}$ cents; and for those selling below $1, the rate is $1\frac{1}{2}$ cents with a minimum charge of $1. Commissions to members of the exchange are much smaller.

6. *Chicago Stock Exchange.*—The exchanges of Chicago and Philadelphia rank next to Boston in importance, altho since the war, the Baltimore and Pittsburgh exchanges have come into greater prominence.

The Chicago Stock Exchange has about 250 members, and carries on a very active business. Several corporations which formerly permitted dealings in their securities in New York alone, now allow them to be traded in, on the Chicago Exchange. Many important local stocks are dealt in there, such as Booth Fisheries, Chicago Railway, Chicago Telephone, Commonwealth Edison, Chicago Pneumatic Tool, Chicago Edison, Illinois Brick, Quaker Oats, National Carbon, People's Gas, Pullman, Sears-Roebuck, Swift and Company and Union Carbide. Considerable sales in bonds of local companies also take place on the Chicago Exchange, but it is noteworthy that even of these local Chicago companies many enjoy a much more active market on the New York Stock Exchange. The American Can, National Biscuit and Diamond Match, which were originally promoted by Chicago operators, find their chief market in New York.

7. *Philadelphia Stock Exchange.*—The oldest stock exchange in the United States is the Philadelphia Exchange. Brokers and merchants who later formed the nucleus of the exchange at first met in the "London Coffee House," established in 1754. It was a "licensed place to which will come and be centered the news from all parts of the world. An exchange upon which our merchants may walk, and a place of resort where our chief citizens in every department of life can meet each other and converse upon subjects which concern the City and the State."

In its first roster are recorded the names of only ten members. This number was increased by eight in 1818. Since then expansion has been fairly rapid, and now the maximum membership permitted by the constitution—230 members—has been reached. The price of a seat is about $10,000 and listing requirements are very strict. With the exception of moderate quantities of railroad stocks, most of the business is done in bonds and public utility shares.

8. *Pittsburgh Stock Exchange.*—On the Pitts-

burgh Exchange many local steel, oil, iron, natural gas and miscellaneous manufacturing stocks, together with a few local railroad and brewery shares, are traded in. As on the Philadelphia, Boston and Chicago Exchanges, small quantities of United States Steel are bought and sold, but the big market for this stock is New York. Like the other exchanges, Pittsburgh has lost many stocks to New York, such as the Westinghouse issues, Crucible Steel, Pittsburgh Steel, Pressed Steel Car, Harbison-Walker Refractories and Pittsburgh Coal.

REVIEW

What kinds of stocks are traded in on the Consolidated Stock Exchange? How does it differ from the New York Stock Exchange?

What is the nature of the stock exchanges outside of New York, and what are the kinds of securities in which they deal?

CHAPTER XI

THE LONDON STOCK EXCHANGE

1. *Importance of the London Stock Exchange.*—
As with so many other institutions, a thoro knowledge
of the American stock exchanges depends upon having a clear idea of how the same organizations operate
in England and upon the Continent. Americans
have just reason to be proud of the elaborate and easy
running machinery of the New York Stock Exchange.
In some respects it is superior to any in the world.
But it is not so large as the London Stock Exchange
and in many respects it is not so important. The
more closely an American investigates the London
market for securities the less boastful does he become
of his own institutions.

In many points the London and New York stock
exchanges are similar and are in sharp contrast to
those on the continent of Europe. But then again it
will be found that London, Paris, Berlin and Amsterdam have much in common that is wholly unfamiliar to the practice of brokers on this side of the
water.

2. *Effect of the war.*—The war has wrought great
changes in the European exchanges, or bourses as they
are more commonly called on the Continent. Only
one of the neutral European countries, Holland, had

a bourse of any importance when the war began and naturally its business has grown. But upon the three great markets of Europe, those of London, Paris and Berlin, the war has placed innumerable restrictions. For a long period they were entirely closed, and early in 1918, the publication of stock quotations was still forbidden in Germany. The Paris Bourse, too, has not yet recovered its former greatness.

On the London Exchange the alterations due to war are far too numerous to be even mentioned. For the purposes of this Text what is needed is a working knowledge of the great London market in normal times, rather than a description of war-time developments, in order to compare conditions with those of this country. Among the changes which have taken place are these: Expulsion of a great number of members of German origin; enlistment of several thousand members; the passage of complicated rules forbidding all trading in securities issued in enemy countries or even in the issues of neutral and allied countries when they are owned by citizens of countries with whom Great Britain is at war, and the enactment of measures to force Britishers to sell foreign securities and to buy only British securities, chiefly government bonds. The restrictions placed upon the London Stock Exchange quickly forced its New York cousin into the world's first place. Just how far the London market will resume its former premier position after the war it is now impossible to predict. But certainly normal conditions will be restored to a large degree; and a brief study of them is essential to this Text.

3. *International scope of the London Exchange.*—Since the war, the New York Stock Exchange has taken on many foreign securities, but normally the London Exchange carries on incomparably more international transactions. Dealings in foreign government bonds, railways and countless other enterprises play an exceedingly important rôle on the London Stock Exchange. One may gather an idea as to the variety of foreign trading done by reading the names of a few securities gathered from the London Daily List, the official register of the London Stock Exchange: Cape of Good Hope debentures; Municipal Stocks of Pernambuco; Harbor Board Mortgages of Oaman and Wangamii, Honduras loans, loans to Brazil, Argentine, Siam, Costa Rica, Portugal, Straits Settlement, etc.; Malacca Rubbers, Singapore Electrics, Amazon Telegraphs, Sao Paulo Match Factories, etc. Until the war England always had an available supply of loanable capital at her disposal to lend to undertakings carried on in distant parts of the world.

The London Stock Exchange has four or five times as many members as its New York rival and quotes nearly 10,000 securities, altho those actually listed are about 5,000 as compared with 1,600 in New York. While in certain respects the London market is far broader and vaster than that of the New York Exchange, in other matters its machinery seems more antiquated and clumsy. Speculation is more active and sustained in New York but curiously enough the Britishers are more inclined to occasional excesses or manias of speculation.

4. *Lombard Street.*—The London Stock Exchange is but one institution among many that make London so powerful as a financial center, just as the New York Stock Exchange is but one element in Wall Street. "Lombard Street" has much the same general significance as the term "Wall Street" with us and includes the Bank of England, the joint-stock banks, the bill brokers and other moneyed institutions that go to make up what Walter Bagehot, the famous English financial writer, described as "by far the greatest combination of economical power and economical delicacy that the world has ever seen. . . . Money is economical power." But there are other terms in London that correspond more or less with Wall Street. Thus Capel Court is most closely associated with the Stock Exchange, and Threadneedle Street with the Bank of England. However Lombard Street is the more general term.

With the founding of the Bank of Venice about 1157, banks began to flourish among the Italian cities and by the end of the fourteenth century they began to spread to other lands. Banking houses were established in foreign countries particularly by merchants of Lombardy, who were called Lombards. Accordingly some traveled to England and established a center in London which accounts for the name of Lombard Street. Gradually the Italian cities lost their influence and supremacy in financial matters passed to the Dutch. A century after the Bank of England made its appearance in 1694, the British Isles had become the world's leading financial power, a distinction which they enjoyed without question till the beginning of the present war.

The first home of the London Stock Exchange was in the rotunda of the Bank of England. Later it moved to Lombard Street, then Change Alley, Sweetings Alley and Old Jonathan's Coffee House. The latter place burned down in 1748 and in its place arose New Jonathan's Coffee House, which twenty-five years later was given the title of "The Stock Exchange." The record of this transaction reads "the brokers and others at New Jonathan's came to the resolution that, instead of its being called New Jonathan's, it should be called the Stock Exchange which is to be wrote over the door."

British government bonds, "consols," fluctuated so widely in price during the Napoleonic Wars that the growth in wealth and membership of the Exchange warranted a new building. So, in 1801, a building was constructed in Capel Court with a membership of five hundred. The Constitution of the Exchange as then amended and adopted remains to this very day in essence, altho new rules and regulations have been added to meet new conditions.

5. *Organization and machinery.*—The management

of the London Stock Exchange rests in the hands of two bodies, the Board of Managers and the Committee. The Board of Managers consists of nine members who represent the "shareholders" or "proprietors" of the Exchange. Fees for admission, appointment of practically all the officials and the supervision of the real property of the Exchange are left to their care. On the other hand, the Committee, comprising thirty members, looks after the technical details involved in the management and trading of the Exchange, and corresponds somewhat to the Governing Committee of the New York Stock Exchange.

Before going into detail regarding the membership, it may be well to explain the terms "shareholders" and "proprietors." When, in the year 1801, the "new" structure was built in Capel Court not all the members subscribed to the building. The wealthier individuals who provided the capital demanded in return that to insure the safety of their investment, they be permitted to control the finances of the Exchange. In this way, two classes of members made their appearance, proprietors and members.

In order to become a member four conditions must usually be met by the candidate. First, he must pay an entrance fee of 500 guineas. Second, he must secure three individuals, who are already members of the exchange, to vouch for him. This procedure is quite different from that of the American exchanges and has a peculiar significance. These sponsors must agree to be responsible for the sum of 500 guineas each for four years. In case their protégé becomes bankrupt and is unable to pay his obligations, the sums for which they stand security are forfeited. Third, the candidate must purchase three shares of the Stock Exchange. In 1913, each share was worth £190, but in April 1914, the average price was £165. The Exchange has issued 20,000 shares each £12 paid in. Dividends amounting to £10 annually are declared on each share as a rule. Finally, a candidate must buy a nomination from a retiring member which costs from £40 to several hundred pounds according to the demand and condition of the market.

A less expensive and easier way of entering the Exchange is also provided. If a man serves four years as a clerk in the Stock Exchange, special concessions are granted to him. Instead of three sources of surety only two need be secured and he is required to buy but one share of stock of the Exchange.

Membership is not limited as in most other exchanges. In 1910, there were 5019 members and at present there are about 5200. However, this statement requires some modification. It is obvious since there are only 20,000 shares and each member gets one and in some cases three shares, the maximum number of members will range about 7000.

A peculiar feature of the Exchange is the requirement that members must be re-elected yearly, the understanding being that members are elected for one year only Often 150 brokers drop out at the end of a year. In addition, the committee may elect a few members each year without nomination. The founders of the Exchange devised this scheme in order to prevent the raising of objections that it was or ever will tend to be a monopoly.

6. *Brokers and jobbers.*—A very important feature of the London Stock Exchange is the distinction between brokers and jobbers. When a man becomes a member he must indicate whether he will be one or the other. The broker, that is a commission broker or retailer, is an agent for the public. He buys from and sells to the jobber, who has no relations whatever with the public. The jobber is a middleman, a trader, a dealer, a specialist and a wholesaler. The jobbers trade among themselves and with brokers, but brokers do not trade with other brokers.

It is difficult for an American to appreciate how different this system is from ours. We may compare the jobbers to our specialists, to our odd-lot brokers and to our room traders. But the London jobber is much more than all these. He is the market itself. He makes the market. He is the only one who furnishes quotations for the inadequate ticker service. He is the only one in fact who knows much of anything about prices.

The jobbers are of all degrees of importance. Competition among them is severe. Many are merely small speculators, and it is not uncommon for dozens of them to fail every few months. On the other hand the larger jobbers are great capitalists, dealers in stocks on a gigantic scale. A single jobber has been known to handle more than 200,000 shares a day.

The jobbers in any given class or group of stocks, such as Americans, Canadians, English rails, South Africans or whatever it may be, stand in a row. A broker with a buying order to execute comes along and the jobber asks him: "What do you want to do?" It may expedite matters for the broker to say whether he wants to buy or to sell, but he is not compelled to do so. On the other hand the jobber is expected to name two prices, one at which he will sell and the other at which he will buy. Then he is obliged to buy or sell at the price named up to a certain amount, known as the "jobber's limit," which varies with the price of the stock, but never exceeds a few thousand dollars.

7. *How jobbers operate.*—If the jobber is shrewd he will guess what the broker wants to do, buy or sell, and name his prices accordingly. Or he may wheedle the broker into telling. Or the broker may beat him down by insisting: "Come closer." If the jobber names two figures, the buying price being 50¼ and the selling price 50⅝, the broker may insist on a closer price, and the jobber may make it ⅜ and ½ or even closer, because variations in price of sixteenths are permitted. If the broker still insists upon a closer fraction he may go on to the next jobber. The jobber makes his profit from what is called the "jobber's turn," which is merely the profitable difference between his buying and selling price.

The great point is that having once named two prices, the jobber must live up to them and do business at those prices.

If jobbers are afraid to do business they "go to lunch all day," as during the slump in the rubber boom in 1910, or they name prices so wide that no broker can afford to buy or sell for his customers at such figures, as at the beginning of the war when jobbers' prices for Montenegrin bonds were 70–80.

To the American the London system of brokers and jobbers seems roundabout, typical of English conservatism, antagonistic to direct methods. It is like the old fashioned division of lawyers into barristers and solicitors. But it is claimed that the division of functions between brokers and jobbers makes for a free market and closer prices. There are so many little known foreign stocks on the London Exchange and so many more shares of small domestic companies than on the New York Exchange, that a complete system of specialists rather than the more open and general system of New York may be necessary. W. P. Hamilton, Editor of the *Wall Street Journal* and a Britisher by birth and training, is quoted in the "Work of Wall Street" as saying:

> The London system has its advantages and its disadvantages. In our market the jobber's turn is saved, but, in an excited and feverish market, the broker may be hours before he can trade at all. In London, he is always sure of being able to sell at some price or buy at some price—both very important conditions in a panicky market, when it often happens here that the broker has to offer the stock down

THE LONDON STOCK EXCHANGE

indefinitely until he finds a purchaser. In the May panic of 1901, Jersey Central was offered down here from 153 to 102 without a single transaction. The stock was sold at 102 and the next transaction was 148. This would have been impossible in London. The jobber might have made a very wide price, but the broker would have been able to sell for his customer at worst within five points of the previous quotation.

8. *Publicity.*—One great fundamental difference between American exchanges and the London Stock Exchange is in respect to publicity. In London the telephone is rarely used, partly because of the poor service. The business of the jobber is done with secrecy and none but himself and the other party to the transaction knows the terms of sale. Consequently no ticker service that is in any way comparable to our own exists, and no summary of the transactions or volume of sales during the day is published. No record of sales is made, only the prices at which stocks are sold. A customer can not give an order one moment and see it on the tape a few minutes later, as in New York.

Everything takes longer in London, partly because so much business is done with distant parts of the Empire. Stocks do not pass from hand to hand as much as in New York. There is less scalping for small profits, less miscellaneous speculation in fact, altho Britishers go to greater excess than Americans when they really do speculate. Probably there is more outright cash buying in England relatively than in this country.

There are evils and advantages in both systems. The secrecy of the London system is bad, but the larger proportion of cash investment is a desirable feature.

9. *Settlements.*—Unlike the method of the New York Stock Exchange settlements are effected in London only twice a month, these being known as the "fortnightly settlements." As explained in a previous chapter our exchanges have clearing houses some of which are incorporated separately, where balances are settled up by cash the day after transaction. This procedure is practically impossible in London. Clearings there are vastly larger than here, owing to the volume of international trade, and consequently a daily settlement would entail unnecessary hardship. One great advantage accruing from the American system of settlement is that failures are rarer than in London. The postponement of settlements to two weeks (to be exact 19 times a year), involves serious risks to creditors because during this whole period the actual situation of the debtor is unknown. Thus, if a speculator loses one day, he expects to make up his loss the next day. He is thus able to delve into all sorts of speculation for two weeks without any reckoning, which may result disastrously for him and others. This is why so many small jobbers fail. However, to lessen the evil and because their system is based primarily on credit, London brokers must and do exercise great caution in trusting their customers.

No definite system of margins has been worked out

in London and consequently no generalization is possible. Each broker decides for himself and after making very careful inquiries concerning the credit of his prospective customer, he "carries" the customer on such terms as seem proper. The unit used on the floor of the exchange is ten shares instead of 100, as on the American exchanges. If the customer is a mere speculator who desires to realize the difference between cost and selling price before the day of settlement, the process that the broker resorts to is called "contango," "carry-over" or "give-on." The broker goes to the jobber and says that the customer wants to defer the payment of his obligation till the next settlement day. The jobber agrees to "take in" the shares, charging the prevailing rate of interest which is in this connection called "contango." The broker adds to his rate a fraction as compensation for his services and the matter is complete. "Contango days" are the two days during the settlement time when the agreement goes into operation.

If the speculator is short and the broker finds it difficult to borrow stocks, he charges what is called "backwardation," or "back." If too many jobbers, with their allied brokers and customers of brokers, are carrying over stocks from one settlement to another, the banks call loans, just as they do here, and force the speculators to pay for their stocks or drop out of the "game."

Those who wait until the fortnightly settlement to pay up are said to buy or sell "for the account." But of course payment and delivery may be made immediately in which case one buys or sells "for money." This corresponds to "cash" transactions in New York.

10. *Commissions.*—Until May, 1912, the English broker was at a great disadvantage compared to his American cousin in regard to commission charges. Here a definite minimum rate is established which must be collected by the broker. The British broker, on the other hand, was not assured any minimum charge. Individual members could cut prices to any extent. Competition reigned supreme and hundreds of brokers earned little if anything. In order to make both ends meet a broker had to transact an immense amount of business and the great number of brokers made this difficult.

Accordingly, in 1912, a new tariff was adopted regulating the rates of commissions. The charges are as follows: one-eighth per cent on British government securities, Indian government stocks and foreign government bonds; one-fourth per cent on certain securities; one-eighth per cent on railroad stocks of £50 or under and sliding scale ranging from $1\frac{1}{2}$d. to 2s. 6d. per share on shares transferable "by deed." In the case of American securities on prices of $25 or less the commission rate is 6d. per share; $25 to $50, 9d.; $50 to $100, 1 shilling; $100 to $150, 1s. 6d. and over $200, 2 shillings. Reduction of the commission rates is permitted in the case of large orders covering high and low priced securities when a general rate of one-eighth per cent may be applied.

THE LONDON STOCK EXCHANGE

11. *Listing securities.*—A complete list of securities dealt in on the London Stock Exchange is published daily and fills in small type, sixteen full pages as large as an ordinary newspaper. Listing requirements are far less strict than on the New York Stock Exchange. This is largely to be explained by the operation of the British Companies Act, which makes it much more difficult to float worthless securities in England than in the United States. The existence of different incorporation laws in forty-eight states, some of the laws being very lax, makes it necessary for the American stock exchanges to be especially careful what they admit. In England, of course, there is one uniform law. Another fact to be considered is that London has no preparatory market like the New York curb where new securities become seasoned. The theory in London seems to be that everything should be admitted to the Stock Exchange.

Before the Listing Committee admits a stock, it sees that a certain portion of the shares are sold to the public at large. In addition, the shares that the seller receives for the property cannot be listed until six months have elapsed after the remaining securities were offered for public subscription. This prevents "insiders" from dumping their stock on the public.

REVIEW

What do you consider the most important stock exchange in the world?

What is the size of the London Stock Exchange as compared with the New York Exchange?

How is membership in the London exchange granted?

Do you consider the English method of doing business on the exchange applicable to the United States?

What do you consider the importance of the jobber?

What advantage do you see in the system of fortnightly settlements over the system employed in the United States?

CHAPTER XII

THE CONTINENTAL BOURSES

1. *How they differ from American exchanges.*—
The Paris Bourse has long been by far the most important of the Continental stock markets, and is the second most important international stock market in the world, with total listed securities equalling those of New York. The bourse will be considered later in detail but first it may be well to note the common characteristics of all the continental stock markets.

On all European stock exchanges the unit of trading is less than in New York. The common unit abroad is 10 rather than 100 shares. Cash transactions are more common, and the margin system is worked out less completely. Marginal speculative operations on all the European exchanges are "for the account," which means, as we have seen in the case of London, that they are to be paid for, if at all, at the end of a given period, usually about two weeks, or else carried over for another period. On some of the bourses the word "futures" has the same meaning as "for the account."

Speculative accounts are rare in Europe. The people buy government securities or other investments recommended by their banks, and their speculative instincts are catered to by lotteries, and occasionally by irresponsible, ungovernable gambling in wildcat shares. Organized speculation is confined far more to a few capitalists and professionals than it is here. Dealings for future delivery have been permitted on the Paris Bourse only since 1885.

The volume of sales in individual stocks and the total for the entire day are not reported abroad. Yearly reports of total sales are made by the Departments of Finance in Germany and France. In both countries the bourses are more under the control of the large banks and the government than either in England or in the United States. In a single year the Bank of France deals in scores of millions of dollars of securities on the Bourse. Speculators also borrow more directly from the banks and less from brokers than in New York. In London and Paris, brokers are forbidden to speculate on their own account, altho the London jobber is nothing but a speculator. Hours are uniformly shorter on the foreign bourses, an extreme case being that of the Amsterdam bourse which is open only from 1.30 to 2.45 p. m.

But the most important respect in which all the European stock exchanges, including London, differ from those in the United States is in regard to settlement periods. The essential characteristic of the New York and most other American stock exchanges is the daily settlement for securities. In Europe settlements are usually made twice a month and in some instances only once a month.

2. *Berlin Bourse.*—The Berlin Bourse has never

THE CONTINENTAL BOURSES

been of much importance in itself, largely because the great banks of Germany have absorbed practically all dealings in stocks as well as many other economic functions. There is a horde of small brokers on the Bourse who pay a license fee, but the important men in the institution are the eighty official brokers who make the quotations and are closely related to the Government. Most of these official brokers do business for the banks. Unlike France, England and Holland, Germany has never encouraged the investment of its citizens' funds in foreign enterprises, altho at various times considerable quantities of American railroad and industrial stocks have been held in Germany, especially Baltimore & Ohio, and Canadian Pacific. But in the main, Germany has needed all her spare money at home so that Berlin has never become an international financial center.

Possibly the most interesting feature of the Berlin Bourse is a chapter in its past history, namely, the attempt made some years ago to regulate speculation. This is described in a later chapter. When the war started in 1914 no government was more ruthless in suppressing tell-tale speculation than the German. It believed that dealings in stocks at such a time were opposed to public interest. But so prosperous did some of the war munition makers grow that it became very difficult to stop operations in these stocks, as the following dispatch from Frankfort on July 10, 1916, indicated:

Altho no stock quotations are published in Germany at

present, speculation at the different stock exchanges in Germany had lately attained such dimensions that conservative circles became alarmed and cast about for means to restrict dealing in stocks. The Chamber of Commerce in Berlin, supported by the "Board of Elders of the Stock Exchange," submitted to the government certain new regulations, which now have been adopted. They prohibit all transactions involving deliveries at some future date, permitting only the so-called cash business, which provides the fulfilment of every contract within three days. In order to prevent manipulation within this limited period all contracts are to be submitted to a commission appointed by the "Board of Elders of the Stock Exchange," which is authorized to determine the amount of damages due to the non-performance of a stipulation in the deals.

The calling out of quotations in a loud voice is forbidden; also advertising which would stimulate stock exchange business. Bankers and brokers are not to forward to their customers regular market reports; they are empowered, however, to reply to requests for information. The punishment for infraction of these rules is to be meted out by the "Board of Elders," who may exclude members till the end of the war, when all these new rules will automatically become void.

3. *Paris Bourse.*—In essence the Paris Bourse is a private monopoly under government control. The brokers are practically government officials, appointed thru and under the supervision of the French Department of Finance by the President of the Republic. In some respects it is a primitive institution, without the facility for swift transfer of stocks and the enormous speculation coupled with the utmost publicity of the New York Stock Exchange, or the efficiency and international scope of the London Stock Exchange. But it is far safer than either. Failures rarely take place. The brokers are among the most respected and leading financiers of the Republic.

The Paris Bourse was the result of spontaneous growth and has survived all the political and economic turbulence thru which so many French institutions have passed. Originally merchants had wares to sell and they sold them in markets. At first the bourses were given free play without government control, but there was fleecing and dishonesty. The Mississippi Bubble led to restrictions. It was then decided to turn the business of trading on the Bourse into a monopoly and to hold the traders responsible not only for their individual acts but collectively for all the business transacted. In the period from 1720 to 1750, the Bourse assumed practically the form it has today.

In France there are two distinct kinds of exchanges, stock exchanges (*bourses des valeurs*) and commercial exchanges (*bourses de commerce*). According to this classification the names assigned to operators are *agents de change* and *courtiers en marchandises*. It is the first class that interests us at this point, as the Paris Bourse is a "bourse de valeur."

4. *Membership and government.*—Altho the total of securities listed on the Paris Bourse about equals that in New York and is half that in London, the membership is limited to 70, as compared with 1100 in New York and about 7000 in London.

When a stock broker who is a member of the Bourse wishes to retire, he does not sell his membership but merely disposes of "the right of introduction." The price of the latter fluctuates between $300,000 and $400,000. After the candidate, who must be a French citizen, has satisfied the requirements of the government as to character and fitness, he is nominated and elected as an official of the Department of Finance. In addition to the cost of the membership itself, a deposit of 250,000 francs or $50,000 is required as a security upon which an interest rate of four per cent is paid, and a fee of 120,000 francs ($24,000) is exacted which goes into the treasury of the Bourse. The combined memberships are now worth about twenty million dollars and there is no doubt that with the lapse of time the membership will become still more valuable. The dean of the Paris stock brokers died in 1913 leaving an estate of $16,000,000.

The government of the Paris Bourse lies in the hands of a Syndical Chamber, consisting of a syndic and eight members chosen from the seventy. This body corresponds to the Board of Governors on the New York Stock Exchange and the Committee on the London Stock Exchange, except that the Syndical Chamber is under the control of the Finance Department.

5. *Prerogatives of stock brokers.*—Members of the Paris Bourse have the following rights and duties: (1) the exclusive right of trading in government bonds, with exceptions shortly to be noted; (2) the exclusive right of trading in negotiable bills of exchange, notes and all instruments of a similar character; (3) the exclusive right of making quotations

for the securities they deal in with the inclusion of the quotation of metals; (4) the granting of the necessary certificates for the transfer of rentes (French Government bonds); (5) with the permission of the courts, the negotiation of loans and the liquidation of securities that have been pledged; (6) and, finally, when called upon by the courts, the disposal of the property of minors.

The exclusive right to negotiate bills of exchange and similar instruments means that the important banking houses of France must be members of the Bourse, and it is partly for that reason that membership is so valuable. It will also be seen from the foregoing enumeration of their powers that the *agents de change* perform many of the functions of trust companies in this country, such as acting as transfer agents and caring for the property of minors.

Settlement of accounts, as in the case of the London Stock Exchange, is made twice a month but in the case of government securities the period is still further prolonged to one month. The clearing period in the middle of the month continues for four days and the one at the end of the month for five days.

Stock brokers must under no circumstances permit the names of their customers to be made known. In addition they are strictly forbidden to carry on business operations for their own account. If a stock broker forms a partnership he may act as the firm's representative on the Bourse. But the fact that he is their associate does not permit the other members of the firm to trade on the Exchange any more than it does in New York. His co-partners may advance the sum necessary for the purchase of his membership on the Bourse but in no case must this exceed three-fourths of the total price.

In the rare case of the bankruptcy of a stockholder, the penalty is much more severe than the one inflicted upon private brokers. It is the custom in the bourse for the governing board (the Chambre Syndicale) when members are in a position of financial stringency and cannot settle their obligations, to meet their liabilities out of the general fund. This is not compulsory but the practice has been established. The solvency of stock brokers is therefore a rather assured circumstance which generates a feeling of mutual confidence on the part of the public and the brokers.

6. *Kinds of dealings.*—When a client gives an order to his stock broker to buy or sell, there are three methods by which it can be executed: at a fixed price, at the best price or at the average price. The first is called a *"cours fixe."* A says to his broker, "Buy me so much French Rentes 3 per cent at 101 francs." The price is definite and the broker complies with his instructions if possible.

The order at best (*au mieux*) simply means that the broker is to secure the best quotations that the conditions of the market permit. It is merely assumed that the stock broker will have the interests of his customer at heart and will do the best he can.

The third method of trading an order at the average price, *"cours moyen"* or, as it is abbreviated "C.M." is the most customary. The average price is the one that is half-way between the lowest and highest quotations for the day. Before the Bourse opens, the stock brokers and their clerks come together in a special room set aside for this purpose and state the number of securities they want to buy or sell. Transactions as to the volume of sales is thus completed altho the price has not been agreed upon. At the end of the day the average of the lowest and highest prices is the price the customer must pay. This figure in other words is based on the prices existing in the other two forms of trading. If there is only one quotation this single price is declared the average and if no quotation is made the orders are not executed.

7. *Margins and commissions.*—No definite margin on transactions conducted by a stock broker is stipulated. "The broker makes inquiries concerning his customer's father and grandfather, his financial connections and whether he is a man of honor." Then he uses his knowledge of the individual, with his financial standing and character, as a basis upon which to determine the amount he should advance. The higher the standing the smaller the margin.

Brokerage commissions in France are lower than in the United States. If the price is above 500 francs the rate is one-tenth per cent on the net amount of the entire transaction, if between 250 and 500 francs the rate is 50 centimes for each security and if less than 250 francs, 25 centimes. Brokerage for the smallest amount dealt in for future delivery on a foreign security is 25 centimes and one eighth of one per cent if securities are worth more than 400 francs ($80). Special rates apply to government securities.

8. *Clearings and deliveries.*—There is no clearing house on the Paris Bourse. After the business day is closed the brokers return to their offices and check up their sales and purchases. They immediately send to each other confirmation of the day's business. If there is any difference of opinion as to the price or the quantity of stock sold during the day, the Chambre Syndicale is called in for the final decision. Cash deliveries are made the next day and "future" deliveries before the tenth session following the sale.

9. *The "coulisse."*—This is the name applied to the "curb" market of Paris, an extra-legal body in contradistinction to the official "parquet" or floor. Here no limitation as to numbers is set. Any French subject can join the coulisse. It is governed by two Chambres Syndicales, one for the account or future market, and the other for the cash or *comptant* market. Altho, according to the French law only stock brokers are permitted to deal in French Rentes, curb brokers compete with the others in transacting business of this character. Suits are never brought against them altho in court their operations are considered void. The theory underlying this apparently curious and illogical attitude is the belief that the gov-

ernment will ultimately derive greater advantages by having the market for its obligations free and extensive.

Altho the coulisse has no official or logical recognition it has met for years under the colonnade of the Bourse building, and is a firmly intrenched body. Its name comes from its place of meeting, the word coulisse meaning side issues, wings of a theatre, passageway. There have been generations of conflict between the parquet and the coulisse, but their interests are by no means wholly opposed, because in the end the outside brokers must come to the agents de change for the transfer of securities. The number of small cash transactions on the coulisse is enormous.

In times of great speculative excitement a body of street brokers springs up in Paris. They meet in the open street near the Bourse and are known as *pieds humides* (wet feet).

The period of trading on the bourse is 12 a. m. to 3 p. m. whereas the coulisse opens at 11.45 a. m. and closes at 4 p. m. Each exchange issues daily its official lists with the names of all the securities admitted, prices, rates of exchange, prices of gold and silver bullion, etc.

REVIEW

Point out some of the common characteristics of European stock exchanges, showing how they differ from those in the United States.

What are the two kinds of stock exchanges in France?

What are the rights and duties of a member of the Paris Bourse?

How are orders executed by French stock brokers?

How does the French exchange differ from those of the United States in settling margins, commissions, clearings and deliveries?

What is the coulisse and in what kinds of business does it trade?

CHAPTER XIII

THE PRODUCE EXCHANGES

1. *Importance of the exchanges and of their speculative activity.*—In one respect the commodity exchanges, or as we shall hereafter call them, the produce exchanges are more important than the markets where securities are traded in. Wheat, corn, oats, flour, lard and other similar foodstuffs are more essential to human life than the corporations whose shares form the basis of stock exchange speculation. The relations of the produce exchanges with foreign affairs are fully as close as, if not more so than, those of the stock markets; their use of statistics, information, reports and rumors of every variety is fully as extensive; and the whole question of the benefits and evils of speculation is, if anything more insistent in the "pits" of the produce markets than on the floors of the security exchanges.

In the first chapter of this Text it was explained why the marketing of securities and agricultural produce had been developed by organized exchanges. We have seen how large a part speculation plays in the volume of exchange business, and the subject will be further discussed in later chapters. Obviously speculation can hardly be conducted on a gigantic scale except in competitive industries, because monopoly means control of the supply. There can be no monopoly, of course, in agricultural products of the staple variety, except for brief periods of time. Then, too, these staples are produced in such variable quantities that fluctuations in the price naturally follow those in the supply.

Speculation is difficult where the demand for goods is small or fixed, but the demand for wheat, corn, cotton and the like is both extensive and elastic. Thus speculation is fully as active in grain and cotton as it is in stocks. An idea of how extensive are the opportunities for speculation in wheat may be gathered from the fact that it sold as high at $2 in September 1888, and as low as 50 cents in September, 1894. In 1914, wheat sold as low as 77¾ cents, and as high as $1.31. In 1915, the price varied from 98 cents to $1.68.

2. *Types of produce exchanges.*—Organized produce exchanges have existed in this country since about 1850. They are variously known as exchanges, boards of trade, and chambers of commerce. In Europe, where they are sometimes called bourses, the Liverpool Corn Trade Association and the Liverpool Cotton Exchange are of prime importance, altho there are big wheat markets in Paris, Berlin and Budapest. Other markets are the London Corn Exchange, the Manchester Cotton Exchange, and the bourses of Hamburg, Amsterdam and Antwerp. The Argentine Exchange also forms a large market. Besides the all-important Chicago Board of Trade and the

New York Cotton Exchange, the prominent produce markets in this country are the following: New Orleans Cotton Exchange, New York Coffee Exchange (where sugar "futures," also, are dealt in), Minneapolis Chamber of Commerce, which as a wheat market ranks second to Chicago, Winnipeg Grain Exchange, St. Louis Merchants' Exchange, Duluth Board of Trade, Kansas City Board of Trade, Omaha Grain Exchange, Milwaukee Chamber of Commerce, Toledo Produce Exchange, Buffalo Commercial Exchange, Baltimore Chamber of Commerce, Philadelphia Commercial Exchange and New York Produce Exchange.

The New York and New Orleans Cotton Exchanges are the leading examples of markets where only one staple is traded in, altho the exchanges of Duluth, Minneapolis and Kansas City confine their operations almost wholly to grain. On the Chicago Board of Trade a variety of products are quoted, including wheat, corn, oats, live stock, lard, ribs and pork. The same is true of the New York Produce Exchange. The great media of general speculation, however, are wheat and cotton, with corn a poor third, altho the production of corn exceeds that of wheat. Wheat is subject to more speculation than the other grains because its production and consumption are more international in character. Corn is largely consumed where it grows.

The produce exchanges are strikingly similar to the stock exchanges. The points of resemblance will appear one by one as we examine the operations and methods of the produce markets. In general organization they are almost identical. They represent the highest development in marketing efficiency.

3. *"Spots" and "futures."*—Perhaps the most important feature of the produce exchanges is the prevalence of "future" trading. In the case of the European stock exchanges, or bourses, we have seen that securities may be bought for "cash," or "money," that is, immediate payment and delivery, or "for the account," or "futures," in which case neither immediate payment nor delivery is contemplated. Much the same system prevails on the produce markets. We have, on the one hand, "spot" wheat or "spot" cotton, which involves a sale for cash for immediate delivery, and we have "futures" in wheat, corn, oats, cotton, coffee and sugar. The great majority of speculative operations are conducted in "futures."

Spot transactions not only call for immediate fulfilment and delivery, but their very nature implies the present existence of the commodity in question. Not so with futures. Grain and cotton, of course, can be had several months after the contract is made—that is, whenever the crop matures. Hence the term "future." The United States Bureau of Corporations thus defines futures:

The system of future trading is based on contracts on the part of the seller to deliver, and consequently on the part of the buyer to receive, at a time subsequent to the making of the contract, a certain quantity of the produce at a stipulated price. . . . A future transaction differs from a spot transaction in that the latter invariably represents goods actually on hand or instantly available at the time the contract is made, and moreover contemplates an immediate or an approximately immediate delivery.

4. *Future trading illustrated.*—The process involved may be explained by the following simple illustration. A is a farmer who has grain in the process of growth—wheat, rye, corn, oats or other cereal. B is a merchant who approaches A and makes a contract requiring A to sell B a certain portion of his crop at a definite price. Let us assume, further, that the bargain was made in July, and that the produce will be harvested in September. Meanwhile B is the legal and practical owner of that portion of the final yield that he has purchased, and he is bound by contract to keep the terms of sale. Several weeks later, B sees an opportunity to sell his September crop to C at an advanced price, and he unloads as a consequence. This process may continue indefinitely, the future crop passing successively into the possession of many persons, and each owner, in turn, selling it to another person to take advantage of a rise in price. When the month of September arrives, the harvesting of the grain that has been sold begins, and that portion which was sold to A is shipped, not to him but to the last buyer in the series, say M.

5. *"Contract" trade, another name for future trading.*—Future trading is also known as "contract" trading, because the broker contracts to deliver in the

future a specified amount of a specified grade of wheat or cotton. The word contract comes to have the same meaning as unit, and is used accordingly. The standard unit for speculation in future grain dealings is 5,000 bushels. If a man wants more he calls out the number of thousands desired. Thus, when a broker wishes to bid on the exchange for 50,-000 bushels, he merely shouts, "Fifty." If he does not mention any amount, it is assumed that he wants 5,000 bushels. For purposes of comparison, it might be noted that if wheat is selling at $1 a bushel, 5,000 bushels are approximately equivalent to 50 shares at $100 a share; 10,000 bushels are equivalent to 100 shares at $100 a share, etc. Wheat can be bought and sold in 1,000 bushel lots, but dealings in corn and oats are confined to full lots of 5,000 bushels or more. Wheat fluctuates by eighths of a cent per bushel. Thus, wheat at 1.45⅜, means wheat at $1.45⅜ per bushel. Each eighth of a point is equivalent to $6.25 on a contract of 5,000 bushels.

Futures are classified according to months. In other words, the trader always buys or sells wheat or cotton bearing the name of the month. In fact the term, month, is often used as a synonym for the word, future. Other words that have the same meaning are delivery and option.

Wheat is of two kinds, winter and spring. Winter wheat is sown in the Southern belt during September and October, and harvesting is begun in Texas as early as the latter part of May. Spring wheat is sown in April and the harvesting begins in the Dakotas about August.

Market quotations are usually made in May, July, September and December wheat, because these are the months in which most of this grain is actually delivered. Cash purchases are made with equal facility on every day of the year, but for trading in futures the four-month delivery system is more convenient.

At the beginning of the year, active business in futures is carried on in connection with the May and July delivery. About April some traders begin negotiations for September wheat; and about June 1st, December wheat figures on the market. After May has passed, only July, September and December deliveries are in favor, and in June deliveries for the following May again receive attention. In August —the September, December and May futures are being dealt in.

For whatever month a person buys wheat, the first day of that month is the day on which he must be ready to accept delivery of his purchase, altho it may not be offered until the last day of the month. The seller has the option of delivering the wheat at any time during the month, and altho future trades are often called "options," the only accurate use of the term is that which has just been explained. If a buyer does not wish actually to receive the wheat in the form of a warehouse receipt, he sells in the pit an amount equivalent to what he has purchased—a transaction which may also be made long before the delivery month.

6. *Terms of sale.*—In every trade the seller has the privilege of making delivery on any day of the delivery month. Should the trader wish to stay in the market after the date set for the delivery of his commitment, because he believes that prices will rise and will yield him a larger profit later, he can accomplish his object by buying or selling an amount equal to his previous trade, but for a future month. It is as a rule cheaper for a trader to sell a current delivery and repurchase a future, than to hold grain during the interim and pay the charges which accrue; that is, if he holds 10,000 bushels of May wheat about May 30th, and desires to stay in the market for six months or more, it will be more profitable for him to sell his May holdings and buy December instead. Brokerage commissions and price difference will be perhaps 6 cents a bushel, whereas storage charges and insurance would be 10 cents. Of course, these figures are subject to constant change; on rare occasions they may even be reversed.

If a trader wishes to withdraw at any time, he merely sells the contract, which "passes on" to the next buyer. A contract may change hands hundreds and even thousands of time before the final settlement is made.

It is this constant buying and selling that makes the "continuous" market which is such a remarkable and in many respects valuable feature of grain exchanges. The total volume of future trading is so enormous compared with the actual amount of the commodity marketed, that the actual figures are almost incredible to those who have not been able to grasp the workings and functions of a speculative market. Whether the total volume of future trading is ten or one hundred times the actual amount of grain, makes very little difference, except that it may be said in general that the larger the volume of future trading in any one market, the more frequent the bids and offers of traders, and the more delicate the adjustment of price to every news item or rumor affecting supply and demand.

The facts in regard to wheat have already been discussed. The active months in some of the other grains and provisions are:

Corn.—May, July, September and December.
Oats.—May, July, September and December.
Pork.—January, May, July and September.
Lard.—January, May, July and September.
Short Ribs.—January, May, July and September.

7. *Legal status of futures.*—All contracts for future delivery are binding. The statement of the Bureau of Corporations in regard to the subject is this:

The seller of such a contract is absolutely liable for delivery, and if called upon for such a delivery by the buyer he can in no way avoid compliance with the terms of his contract, except under unusual conditions especially provided for. . . . When the time for making delivery has expired, he cannot sell out his contract. This fact, and the fact that any buyer from the first to the last, can, if he chooses, hold his contract and compel the seller to deliver actual cotton (grain, etc., as the case may be) when the date of a maturity arrives, give trading in futures a character entirely different, in principle at least, from that of a mere wager or bet.

Future contracts are absolutely legal in and of themselves. The sale of property, even tho the property is not in the actual possession of the vendor at the time of sale, is in accordance with all legal requirements. If, however, it was not the intention of the two parties to the contract to deliver or receive the commodities dealt in, but merely to adjust the differences in the price by the exchange of sums, then the process is no longer held to be a business transaction. It is in that case merely one form of gambling, and the courts, viewing it as such, declare it illegal and therefore null and void.

8. *Warehouse receipts.*—Because of the enormous volume of future trading that is done in both wheat and cotton, the question of the quality of the product delivered on a future contract is of the utmost importance. Future contracts are satisfied by warehouse receipts, which are statements issued by storage-warehouse, or elevator companies, showing that a certain quantity of a commodity has been stored with them. These receipts must represent one or more basic or standard grades—"contract" grades, as they are commonly called.

The work of the elevators is an important part of the process whereby wheat becomes flour and bread, for here the vast quantities of grain are stored, and it is the elevator that to a large extent finances the purchase of grain from the farmer. There are country elevators and terminal elevators, the latter in cities like Minneapolis, Chicago, Duluth, Kansas City and St. Louis. First the grain passes thru a country elevator. Of these there are three kinds: (1) independent, which are owned by local interests; (2) farmers', usually cooperative; (3) line, which are owned by corporations that have a system or chain of elevators extending thru several different states along the line of the railroad. The terminal elevators buy from the country elevators and from commission merchants, and sell to the mills.

The warehouse, or elevator, receipts issued by these companies are what makes futures possible, for the care with which they are issued makes them not only easily negotiable, but readily available as collateral security for bank loans, since the bankers have the assurances of recognized companies that the specified commodity is on hand. If this were not so, it would be impossible to finance the crops, for the farmers require huge sums of cash every fall.

9. *Inspection and grading.*—Originally all wheat and cotton was sold upon sight. In other words, the buyer, after examining the goods, would take them away. But in this country especially, such a system soon became cumbersome owing to the vast area on which these products were grown. Later, business was done by sample. Altho large quantities are still sold by sample on the produce exchanges, and still

greater quantities outside the exchanges, the grain and cotton industries could not be conducted on the present vast scale without the use of the grading method, with its system of inspection, weighing, warehouse receipts and state supervision. Certainly future trading is entirely dependent upon these aids.

Inspection and grading on the produce exchanges correspond roughly to the engraving requirements on the stock exchanges. In general, the object in any case is to separate grain and cotton into grades, and to make it possible for any one of several grades to serve as a contract which may be delivered upon the exchanges. The idea is, that, once inspection and grading has been properly attended to, any lot, rather than only a specific lot, will do. Of course, if each lot had to be viewed by both buyer and seller, it would be impossible to carry on future dealings on a large scale.

It is essential that a grade contain grain of as nearly uniform quality as possible, and that there should be a great deal of grain in each grade. Otherwise corners will occur. If it is necessary to have many different grades, the problem of furnishing premiums for the better classes of grain, and discounts for the poorer, becomes a vexing question. The Duluth and Minneapolis markets are said to give the greatest satisfaction in this respect.

The inspection and grading system gives to grain and cotton much the same mobility that stocks possess. Of course it is this system that makes speculation on a large scale possible. To abolish it would produce most serious consequences. Doctor Grover G. Huebner, in his "Agricultural Commerce," gives the following arguments in favor of this system:

Tho much spot produce is sold by actual examination of the commodities, it is a common practice to buy and sell on the basis of samples, or a combination of samples and grades, and sometimes on the basis of grades exclusively. It greatly facilitates the quotation and publication of spot as well as of future prices.

It facilitates the storing and handling of commodities. East of the Rocky Mountains, for example, grain is commonly stored and handled in bulk, all grain of a particular grade being stored and handled in the same bins. Without inspection and grading, the operation of the modern grain elevator system would be greatly hampered.

It makes possible the general warrant or negotiable warehouse receipt system. Without systematic grading, all grain elevator receipts would have to represent specific lots of grain stored in special bins; or, otherwise, all of the same variety would have to be indiscriminately mixed to the great detriment alike of growers, dealers and millers.

It tends in a measure to protect buyers and sellers from unscrupulous and dishonest practices. Inspection and grading services, particularly in the local or country markets, are not fully carried out, but so far as they are applied, they serve to guarantee that commodity prices shall vary in accordance with the quality or condition of the articles sold.

The efficiency of the inspection and grading system in a market, largely determines the size and prosperity of that market. The inspection must be carried on by reliable and competent men, and the grading must be honestly done. The difficulty of grading tobacco so that a definite contract grade could be established upon which trades for the future might be made, has limited the organization of a tobacco market. It is nearly impossible to keep track of individual lots of this commodity and prevent its being mixed with inferior lots in the warehouse. Therefore no buyer will accept a certificate of inspection which purports to be a guarantee that the tobacco he buys is of a specified grade. The same is true also in regard to eggs, apples and potatoes.

10. *State bureaus of inspection.*—To win the confidence of the public as regards the inspection of great staple commodities, many states have established bureaus where the inspection is done by public officials. Grain inspection is a case in point. In Illinois, the State Board of Railroad and Warehouse Commissions supervises this work. In Minnesota, there is a similar commission. A certificate of inspection from a body like this is a state guarantee of excellence. In the export trade of Duluth it is particularly important that such a board be in charge, because, owing to the fact that the Duluth standard for grain is higher than that of the Atlantic seaboard, the temptation of sellers to pass off poor grain is correspondingly greater. Therefore those who buy grain at Duluth to sell it in Europe, watch carefully to see that a poorer grade than they bought is not substituted between the time the grain leaves Buffalo and the time that it is loaded on the transatlantic steamer.

Each market has its own standard, and as a consequence there are many different grades. Many attempts have been made to establish for wheat a uniform grade that would apply to all markets, but without much success.

11. *Chicago and Liverpool grades of wheat.*—The following grading for wheat in a few of the large markets will illustrate to some extent at least, the variety of grades.

Chicago's "contract grades" of wheat, which form the basis for transactions in the pit, are No. 2 red winter wheat, No. 1 northern, and No. 2 hard winter. In Minneapolis the contract grade is No. 1 northern. In the Duluth market, No. 1 northern is the contract grade, but No. 2 northern may be delivered on contracts at 5 cents a bushel under the price of the former. The contract grade in the Kansas City market is No. 2 hard winter wheat—not less than fifty-nine pounds —but the seller is allowed to deliver No. 2 red if he wishes to do so.

There are at least nine varieties of wheat deliverable on contracts in the Liverpool market. The fact that the wheat comes from all parts of the world makes the work of establishing uniform grades very difficult. This important business of inspecting and grading devolves upon a special committee of fifteen members, which is elected by the directors of the Liverpool Corn Trade Association. There is perhaps no position in the business world where a man's judgment counts for more than it does in that of inspector and grader. It is the grader who decides by what standard the various products shall be measured. And when one considers the millions of bushels and millions of pounds of products that are entering the market, and the fact that their selling power is in a large part predetermined by the inspector's judgment, one can readily see how an incompetent or an unscrupulous inspector could establish a wrong purchasing power for products, by assigning them to a grade in which they do not belong.

12. *The Federal grain inspection law of 1916.*—Congress passed a law which became effective on August 11, 1916, giving the Federal Department of Agriculture, authority to establish grades for grain shipped in interstate commerce, and a system of licenses and inspection. Grades have now been established for corn and wheat but not for oats and other grains.

It is, however, clear that the Act has at least the possibilities of surprising changes. It may eventually do away entirely with the system of grading which has grown up in response to the needs of trade, under the supervision of state authorities. That it will have such results seems unlikely. There is great probability that the State systems which have been well developed will be changed but little. There is a possibility that the State inspectors will receive Federal licenses, and if this takes place, the change will be in name only. It is generally believed that the new Federal system will seek to utilize what is best not only in the principles and methods of the state system but the personnel as well.

THE PRODUCE EXCHANGES 193

13. *General methods of inspection and grading.*—
The method of inspection is much the same in all markets. All cargoes of grain that come into Chicago from country points are promptly reported by the railroad companies to the grain inspectors. These men visit the cars and secure samples of grain that fairly represent the grain in each car. Every car so inspected is then sealed by the inspector, and the samples are turned over to the grain merchants to whom the cars were consigned from the local shipping center. The grain merchant displays his samples in the market-place of the exchange building, and the grain is sent to the elevator. A warehouse receipt is issued upon the acceptance of the grain by the elevator company, and this receipt, together with the sample of grain, becomes the basis for the sale and purchase of that particular amount and grade of grain. When the grain is sold, the warehouse receipt is delivered instead of the actual grain, each new owner indorsing the receipt when he receives it. If the holder of the warehouse receipt wishes the grain itself he can obtain it by presenting the receipt to the elevator company. Only those firms, however, can issue warehouse receipts that have been declared "regular"— that is, only such firms as conform to the Board of Trade rules covering the inspection, handling and storing of the grain. The warehouse receipt thus becomes a very important instrument of trade, and a heavy responsibility rests upon the superintendent of the warehouse, for he has charge of the grain and is

expected to keep it from deterioration. The various grades must be kept distinct, altho the identity of any particular lot may be lost.

The object of grading is to separate a commodity into grades according to difference in soundness, color and freedom from impurities. First, there are seasonal and color variances, which are often one and the same thing. The classification of winter wheat differs from that of spring wheat according to substance, color (white or red) and location (northern or western). Secondly, the appearance, the inherent quality of the grain, and its condition—its brightness, plumpness and sweetness, and the soundness of the berry—must be considered.

Thirdly, the question as to whether the grain is free from foreign substances, such as chaff, and from any admixture of other kinds of grain, is also carefully considered by the inspector before the product is assigned to a definite class.

REVIEW

In what way are produce exchanges more important than stock exchanges?

Where are the principal produce exchanges and what staples are traded in on each?

Why is "future" trading an important feature of produce exchanges and how does it differ from "spot" trading?

Have "futures" any legal status? Discuss.

What do you consider the value of a warehouse receipt?

What is the object of inspecting and grading wheat and cotton?

Describe the work of state bureaus of inspection.

CHAPTER XIV

THE PRODUCE EXCHANGES (*Continued*)

1. *Hedging.*—The economic usefulness of future trading cannot be fully understood unless one first obtains a thoro grasp of the very important subject of hedging. This process consists in matching a purchase with a sale, or vice versa; in other words, it consists in making a purchase or sale for future delivery to offset and protect an actual merchandising transaction. There are many varieties of hedging processes; some of them are based on sound principles, and some of them are entirely unsound. In the grain and cotton trades, however, there is an enormous amount of absolutely legitimate hedging, which could not be carried on without the aid of the future system. Curiously enough, while the future market is usually called the speculative market, futures are extensively used to avoid speculation.

Hedging is used as a safeguard against risks by those who take part in the various commercial activities of the cotton and grain trades. Suppose a concern that handled wheat in one of its stages buys 10,000 bushels of spots at $2.00 a bushel. It may be several days, weeks or even months (in the case of a manufacturer) before the wheat is passed on to the next stage. But the price may have fallen to $1 a bushel by that time, wiping out the trade profit of a few cents a bushel which the concern (elevator, mill or whatever it may be) expected to make. To prevent this loss, the concern sells 10,000 bushels of future wheat short when it buys an equal amount of spot wheat.

2. *Relation of hedging to future trading.*—The chief economic argument in support of the future trading in the wheat markets relates to the hedging operations of the elevator companies, the mills and other grain interests. The local elevator companies, for example, place their hedges as soon as they begin to accumulate supplies of grain. In the Northwest this happens about the first of September. Having paid cash for their wheat and put it in the elevator, they order their broker to sell for December delivery. If some of this wheat is delivered by the elevator company when December arrives, the hedge of course is not bought in; but the wheat that must be carried still further into the year must again be provided for. The December lot is bought in the pit and an equal amount is sold again for May delivery. The number of these hedging transactions that depend upon elevator companies are very numerous because of the organization of the elevator business. Beginning with the country, or out-of-town elevator companies, which are buying or selling against their cash transactions in grain, there is a steady volume of hedging sales running thru the months from September 1st to January 1st. But these hedges are again bought in when the

wheat is sold to the elevators in the big markets. Now when these terminal elevator companies buy the cash grain, they go thru the same process of hedging as did the out-of-town elevator companies. They sell in the pit against purchases of cash grain from the country elevator, and buy in the pit as they sell the cash grain to millers or exporters.

Several of the terminal elevators have storage facilities for a million bushels of wheat. A fluctuation in price of only two or three cents during the months the wheat is stored there, would result in a big loss to the company. It makes little difference to an elevator if wheat rises or falls fifty cents a bushel, provided its holdings have been hedged. It seeks a warehousing, not a speculative, profit. Grains that are not hedged—such as barley and rye—are handled on a much wider margin of profit by the elevators, than when hedging is used, the wider margin being the only means by which they can protect themselves against loss.

It must not be assumed that the protection afforded by a hedge is complete. It would be perfect if spot and futures were always at the same price. But a small difference or "spread" usually exists, altho the prices tend to become uniform as the delivery day approaches. But the possibility of a spread is never so strong as the possibility of a rise or fall in the price of the commodity itself.

3. *How millers hedge.*—It is now the miller's turn to use the conveniences of the pit. His first step is

to buy his supply of wheat in Duluth for which he pays $1.90 a bushel. Between the purchase date, say the first of September, and the date when the wheat has been turned into flour is a long time. Before that time has elapsed the price of wheat may fall to $1.80 which of course lowers the price of flour. In this case the miller would have to sell flour made from $1.90 wheat in competition with the millers who could buy at $1.80. His second step is taken to protect himself against losses of this kind so he sells in September upon the Chicago market, for February delivery, the same quality of wheat for the same price at which he purchased it, $1.90. Then, when February arrives he goes in the Chicago market again and makes good his delivery contract by buying the wheat at its market price, $1.80.

From this latter transaction it will be seen that the profits gained by the miller equal his losses in the former. This operation is known as "hedging" or "covering." By means of it the miller has eliminated all element of risk from price fluctuations in wheat.

Flour mills are not in the business of storing grain. That is expert work that is done by elevators. But the miller sells flour in advance, and he therefore has to agree on a price with his customer in advance. But how is he to know what the price of wheat will be several months from the date of contract? Suppose that in December he agrees to deliver flour at a certain price late the next May. He bases his price on the May wheat future, and by hedging he is able

THE PRODUCE EXCHANGES

to hold to it. If he did not hedge he would have to charge more for the flour to protect himself against fluctuations in the price of grain. Of course, this sort of hedging does away with the possibility of any sort of speculative profit, but there are many middlemen and manufacturers in the great grain industries who are seeking only a trade profit. Estimates have been made that as much as 90 per cent of the wheat that reaches the primary markets is hedged.

4. *Shifting the risk.*—Thus, it will be seen that the first great function of futures, and that of the great volume of pure speculation that goes with them, is to shift the risk inherent in the ownership of all soil products from the producer and actual merchandiser to a body of professional risk-takers. It is only the existence of a tremendous amount of speculation that provides at all times a continuous market, and consequently plenty of persons who are willing to take the other side of a mill or elevator-hedge transaction. The speculator does not consciously assume risks, but he assumes them nevertheless.

5. *Future trading steadies prices.*—Still another service which futures perform in the grain and cotton markets is to steady prices and regulate the speed at which the year's crop is consumed. Future speculation creates a steady and constantly active market for produce and commodities of all sorts, irrespective of the temporary demand of the present.

If all the farmers were to sell their products at one time, it is obvious that, because of the law of supply and demand, the dumping of so much produce on the market would depress the price to a ruinous extent. This state of affairs is prevented by the process of selling futures, which operates to spread or distribute the produce over periods prior to maturity so as to equalize the supply and stabilize and level prices. If it were not for future selling, prices would sometimes decline decidedly and monopolists, taking advantage of the temporary situation, would pile up commodities in their warehouses to resell them later at an exorbitant price when the demand for them arose.

6. *Service of future trading illustrated by the grain business.*—The proof of these statements is to be found in a study of grain prices. The future system enables the farmer to get as much for his crop by selling in the fall as by holding till spring. Speculation not only makes prices more or less uniform thruout the year, but also makes them less abrupt over short periods of time. One of the most admirable explanations of this point is that of Dr. Weld in his "Marketing of Farm Products":

The reasons for the relatively gradual fluctuations in the wheat and cotton markets are to be found in the tremendous pressure brought to bear on both sides of the market by speculators. The shorts, or bears, are always trying to depress the market; longs, or bulls, are always trying to raise it. The unfortunate thing for either of these classes in realizing their desires is that sooner or later the short sellers have to become buyers, and the bulls, sellers. Speculative short sellers, for example, sell large quantities for future delivery, hoping to see the price go down; but the only way they can make any profits from a fall in price is to begin to cover, i.e., to buy again, and their purchases tend to obstruct a further decline, and possibly to cause the price to begin to rise again.

Professional speculators are content with extremely small profits in each transaction. Just as soon as the price begins to fall, there are shorts who begin to buy; and on the other hand, just as soon as the price begins to rise, there are bulls who begin to sell in order to take their profits. In other words, just as soon as the price begins to move in either direction, even by eighths of a cent (in the case of wheat), there are strong counteracting forces which hinder and often completely obstruct the price movement. As a consequence, extreme fluctuations in the prices of those commodities which are dealt in speculatively, are exceedingly rare under normal conditions, and this level influence is of great value to those engaged in merchandizing the commodities.

7. *Adjusting prices.*—But the future market, thru speculation, performs still another important service. It adjusts prices between different markets by means of "spreading," a process which, on the produce exchanges, corresponds to the arbitrage of the stock markets. If prices are lower in one market than in another, speculators take advantage of the difference, as has already been explained under the head of arbitrage. Thus there is a constant tendency to adjust prices and keep them uniform in any one country and even to establish prices that shall hold for a number of countries.

8. *What the farmers think of the exchanges.*—The farmers in the eight grain states—Illinois, Indiana, Iowa, Kansas, Nebraska, South Dakota, North Dakota and Minnesota—have a Farmers' Cooperative Grain Dealers' Association which represents the far-

mers' elevator movement. Its headquarters are at Chicago. The Association publishes an official organ called the *American Cooperative Journal,* which is owned and operated by farmers and for farmers. This excellent journal has devoted some large special issues to "Grain Exchange Facts." These articles are the fullest statement in print of the views of informed farmers. The following extract is both interesting and enlightening:

We have circularized the entire cooperative trade, in our search for opinions, and are able to announce with more than ordinary authority that cooperative grain dealers are well satisfied with the modern methods of handling grain.

In the pages of the *Journal* the public may find full information concerning prices, and a detailed record of grain transactions.

There is no doubt that organized markets are necessary for the protection of the public. Thru organization men have been able to secure competitive bids for grain, to establish grades, to maintain standards, to enforce prompt settlements, to bring together the world's buyers, to find better markets; in short, by means of organized markets with their speculation men have been able to reduce the handling of grain to a science, and to render many services to the trade which they could have supplied in no other way.

9. *Activities of the exchanges.*—In the article already referred to, "Grain Exchange Facts," there is also the following vital discussion of the activities of the exchanges: "The commission merchant," says

the report, "renders a service of great value to the country shipper. He finds the lowest freight rate and the highest market price for the shipper's grain." The selling end of the business is of extreme importance. Competition is keen. Commission men "struggle on the floor of the exchange to find the best market and the highest price for each car." Their commission, being fixed by the exchange, is very low. They loan money to country shippers, and this transaction plays an important part in financing the grain movement and in the process of getting money from the money market to the country bank. "It is clearly to be doubted whether there is any other business handled on so close a margin, when you consider the money risk involved and the many services rendered by the commission merchant." Or, to put it more picturesquely, the report continues:

Here is where salesmanship comes in. Here is where steel meets steel, and it is a tussle between buyer and seller. The commission merchant storms, stalls, bluffs. He says he has a better bid, or that he knows where he can send the car and get a better price for it. He may call up long distance, or wire, or he may take it to fill an order which he has previously received. All forenoon they circulate back and forth on the floor. Expert buyers representing the world's markets are in the exchanges looking for wheat. The maltsters are there looking for barley, the feeders looking for feed, bidding, barking, bickering, jollying, jesting, joking, but all the time trying for the high market.

Is speculation an economic benefit? This question is asked by a farmer, and answered in the *Journal,* to the effect that speculation shifts the risk from the farmers and millers to the speculators, thereby raising prices for farmers and lowering prices for the consumers.

10. *Farmers' participation in the business of exchanges.*—The members of the Farmers' Cooperative Grain Dealers' Association in northwest Canada are also members of the Winnipeg Grain Exchange. The Farmers' Equity Union of the United States is represented on the Omaha Grain Exchange by Mr. C. Vincent, of the Beal-Vincent Grain Company. At the fifth annual national convention of the Equity Union, at Omaha, December 15, 16, 17, 1915, a resolution was adopted that a seat be purchased on the Kansas City Board of Trade. In short, farmers are coming to realize that they can learn more and accomplish more by securing places in the grain exchanges than by waging a campaign of destruction from the outside.

Economic evolution has produced the grain exchange, and benefits resulting directly from the establishment of this institution are uniform grades in grain, honest weights, ample storage, large drying and cleaning capacity, adequate banking facilities, and uniform and equitable trade rules. Farmers who have visited the exchange and studied its methods know that it offers an opportunity during war or peace, for the sale of any volume of grain of any kind, no matter what its grade or condition.

In general, there is a far wider margin—or differential or profit—in industries where organized speculation on a large scale does not exist than in those where there is such speculation. We often hear the complaint that there are too many middlemen in the agricultural industries. And yet in the manufacturing industries, where distribution to the consumer is more direct, and there is no organized body of speculators, the margin of profit is vastly greater. Many persons who buy manufactured articles would probably be very much surprised if they knew how little is the cost of manufacture.

If speculation in grain and cotton were done away with, the man who actually does the merchandising would want a larger margin of profit, just as the manufacturer does who is unable to shift the risk to a body of speculators. The grading and inspection system, the central warehouse systems, central organized markets and the future system—all these serve to establish steady national and world markets for grain and cotton. Every now and then a suggestion is made that future trading be abolished by law. It is well to bear in mind that this has been attempted without success in both Canada and Germany. Manitoba abolished future trading, and also the grain exchange itself, in the spring of 1908. The buyers then hedged by paying the farmers less for the grain, with the result that the exchange and future trading were restored before the close of the same year. Germany likewise abolished future trading both in grain and in cotton under her Börsengesetz (Bourse Law) of June 22, 1896, thinking thus to do away with speculation. But speculation, thus disorganized, increased in volume, and prices fluctuated more violently than before. "This law," says the Hughes Report, "not only failed, but, as we have seen, it added a darker hue to evils previously existing." It is interesting to note that in coming back to the American practice of future trading Germany has, in the "Constitution, By-Laws and Clearing House Rules of the Bremen Association for Future Business in Cotton," followed closely the plan so long in successful operation in the New York Cotton Exchange. The German experiment is more fully explained in a later chapter.

The system of futures was devised primarily to aid the individual farmer, and to spare him the risks involved in the fluctuation of prices. The farmer is assured a certain price and needs to pay attention only to the physical problem of growing his crop and not to the financial question of securing a reasonable price for his produce.

11. *Influences that govern the price of grain.*—Speculation in commodities, like that in stocks, is concerned with the future rather than with the present. To ascertain what will take place in the future as regards wheat, corn, cotton and the like, requires a study of every element and condition involved in the growth of these great staples. For this reason the Board of Trade and every other produce exchange undertakes to collect and distribute broadcast a de-

tailed and intricate mass of economic information.

Altho we have not yet studied the influences that affect the price of stocks, it is apparent that the stock and the produce market differ radically in one respect. Which is the more difficult to understand, interpret and forecast, it is impossible to say. General financial and money market conditions, wars, disasters and prosperity, or its reverse, naturally affect both markets. But besides these general conditions, it is necessary in the stock market to study the status of individual corporations, of which there are thousands. The case of the produce markets is different. They handle only four or five different commodities, and the chief characteristics of these are easy to comprehend. There is a mass of technical detail, however, connected with the innumerable and intricate agricultural conditions affecting the various crops.

The market price of wheat is an equation between supply and demand. Nowhere else, perhaps, does the law of supply and demand work out so clearly and openly. If there is a huge crop of wheat and people do not want much wheat, obviously the price will fall. If the crop is damaged so that harvests are small, and consumers want a great quantity of wheat and have the money to pay for it, clearly the price will rise.

The problem of supply is much more intricate than that of demand. The recent war appeared to have increased the demand for grain products but in reality, the supply having been cut off from certain countries by naval operations, other consuming countries demanded more from the few producing countries that were still free to carry on export trade.

12. *Foreign influences: the Liverpool market.*—The price of wheat is determined by international rather than by local or even domestic influences. Many countries in all parts of the world produce wheat, and harvest the crops during no less than ten months of the year. Since wheat can easily be shipped from one part of the world to another, the price is largely the result of the variations in the supply that comes from many different countries. Certain countries consume more wheat than they produce, and consequently must import from countries that produce more than they consume. The principal importing countries occupy a relatively small area of the earth's surface, and are all crowded together in western Europe. Great Britain does the most importing, and Liverpool is the principal wheat market in that country. Thus surplus wheat tends to flow toward Liverpool, and the Liverpool price dominates the world markets.

Indeed, prices in even the smaller markets always tend to approximate the Liverpool price, minus freight, handling, insurance and other charges. If, then, every producing country has a large crop, Liverpool does not have to pay much to attract wheat. If, on the other hand, all producers have small crops, Liverpool must pay exorbitantly. If most of the growing countries have small crops and a few have large crops, the few will, of course, receive a big price

THE PRODUCE EXCHANGES

for their large crops. The question is often asked whether farmers are better off with small crops and large prices, than with large crops and small prices. The answer depends not on one country alone, but upon the conditions in the world markets.

The supply of wheat is dependent upon many conditions: droughts, floods, early frost, black rust, and insect pests are all fatal to the wheat crop. Thus an estimate called attention to the following facts:

> Every inch of rainfall above four inches in the Dakotas, California, Washington, Kansas and Nebraska in May and June means an increase of $15,000,000 in the wheat crop, and every inch of rain above three inches in July, in Indiana, Illinois, Kansas, Iowa, Ohio and Nebraska increases the value of the corn crop by $160,000,000.

13. *Sources of market information.*—The Federal government, thru the Department of Agriculture, publishes frequent crop reports. These constitute the most important single source of information. But there are countless other sources. Grain houses employ crop experts, who scour the country in search of data. Their activity has become a sort of joke in financial circles because they often discover more damage than actually exists. The railroad companies whose lines run thru crop countries also issue reports. And there are countless facts gathered from the correspondents of banks, brokers and newspapers located in different sections of the crop area.

There is always uncertainty as to the final harvest of any product until it is actually garnered. While the crops in the United States are growing, the market may have half a dozen crop scares. Meanwhile, the operators watch the growing crops in other producing countries such as Canada, Russia and the Argentine. The situation is complicated by the fact that when any estimate is made as to what prices should be, the "visible supply"—meaning the amount in storage, or in transit which has been left over from last year—must always be taken into consideration. Of course this "visible" varies from year to year. And in addition, the broker and the speculator must watch the prices of wheat on all the exchanges—no easy task, for there are nearly a dozen of them in this country. Moreover, the prices of various commodities affect each other. Corn affects pork. Pork affects lard. Lard and cotton affect cotton-seed oil.

14. *Newspaper accounts of market fluctuations.*—An excellent description of a typically active wheat market appeared in the Chicago and Minneapolis newspapers of August 10, 1916.

Chicago, Aug. 9—Heavy crop losses in the United States and Canada sent the wheat market today nearly straight skyward. At one time the ascent of prices amounted to 11¾ cents a bushel. Trading closed in a whirl of excitement, showing net gains of 10⅝ to 11⅜, with the September option at $1.44¼ to $1.44½ and with December at $1.42⅜ to $1.48.

Something of the strain involved and of the far reaching consequences may be realized from the fact that, according to the United States Government crop report, which was the principal cause of today's excitement, the domestic yield of wheat for 1916 will be 358,000,000 bushels smaller than

THE PRODUCE EXCHANGES

the production last year. No such shortage had been foreseen by even the gloomiest prophets. Black rust spreading in Canada, and indicating that the crop there would be cut down 136,000,000 bushels from the 1915 total, made the situation still more acute. Canada and the United States have been furnishing six-sevenths of the world's breadstuff supplies to the countries that in the face of war difficulties have been able to import.

Foreign buying on a high scale apparently had much to do with the extreme prices in the last hour of today's session. It was estimated that export business today totaled 1,500,000 bushels for immediate shipment, not including big purchases made of options on future deliveries. The late buying also seemed to make clear that many bearish speculators who had attempted to capitalize the chance of a downward immediate swing in prices were badly punished for the tactical error, and had promptly decided to accept heavy losses rather than to risk waiting for possibly better or worse fortune tomorrow.

Gossip of big individual profits gained by the sudden rise in the market was extremely indefinite. The best ground for guesses was the circumstance that since July 31 the principal options of wheat have risen more than 23 cents a bushel.

Minneapolis, Minn., Aug. 9.—Minneapolis September wheat showed an advance of over 6½ cents today from the previous close on the Government crop report. The Winnipeg market for December wheat was up 10 cents a bushel.

Chicago, August 28.—Rumania's declaration of war smashed the wheat market. Opening prices today showed a fall in some cases amounting to 5¾ cents a bushel. The September delivery, which closed Saturday at 1.51¾, started today at 1.46 to 1.48½. Other options also broke wildly.

Before the drop in prices could be checked, losses that reached to 8½ cents a bushel were shown for the principal trading month, December, which sold as low as 1.45½, as compared with 1.54 at Saturday's finish.

General rushes to sell took place, which were increased by the increased chances of a general railway strike in the United States.

Bear traders generally took the view that the action of Rumania was likely to prove a big factor in forcing a more speedy end of hostilities, or would at least tend to hurry the opening of the Dardanelles and so release huge Russian shipments of wheat.

REVIEW

What is hedging and what do you consider its value?

How does a miller hedge and why does he resort to the practice?

What service do "futures" perform?

Describe a farmers' cooperative grain exchange, showing how it benefits the farmer.

Do you believe it wise to prevent speculation in grain and cotton? Give reasons.

Should trading in futures be prevented? Discuss.

What influences play a part in determining the price of grain?

CHAPTER XV

THE CHICAGO BOARD OF TRADE

1. *Why Chicago has the largest market.*—Chicago is the world's foremost clearing house for grain, and the largest shipping point for wheat. Not only does the grain business form a large portion of its commercial activities, but Chicago's enormous trade in many products which depends upon the cereals, such as live stock, cured and dressed meats, pork, lard, hides, cheese and butter, is due to its dominance in the grain trade.

Chicago is close to the great wheat and corn states. It is centrally located for rail and water transportation. Naturally the most important produce transactions in wheat far exceed the country's actual crop; in addition to the trading in wheat, are transactions involving hundreds of millions of bushels of corn and oats. Trading in excess of the crop is made possible thru speculation in futures which assures dealers the world over an opportunity at all times to buy or dispose of any quantity of grain, wheat especially.

Thus the Chicago Board of Trade has become the foremost speculative market in the world for grain, and next to the market of Liverpool, tends to dominate the prices for this produce. Some idea of the importance of the Board of Trade may be had when we reflect that the volume and the value of the grain crops have an immense influence upon railroad traffic and earnings, upon money rates and prosperity generally.

The country miller of Illinois, the grain buyer of Iowa, the elevator manager of any center, the big Minneapolis miller, the terminal elevator company of Chicago, the exporter of New York and Argentina, and the importer of London, Liverpool, Amsterdam and Antwerp—all come here to buy or sell wheat as a "hedge" against transactions in their regular business activities.

We have seen that futures play a leading part in the grain markets. These markets also have clearing houses that still further reduce the actual delivery of grain, just as the stock exchange clearing houses reduce the delivery of stocks. "Ring" processes which are described later in the chapter still further reduce actual delivery. At the same time there must always be present within easy reach a large supply of wheat. It is estimated that the storage capacity of elevators contributory to the Chicago Board of Trade reaches fifty million bushels.

Grain houses are of three kinds: (1) the country and (2) terminal elevator companies already described, and (3) the commission houses. Some of these do only cash or "spot" business, others handle only futures, still others both spots and futures. Some houses handle mostly speculative business, others buy for the big mills and for export. As on the stock

FLOOR OF THE CHICAGO BOARD OF TRADE

The picture shows two of the four pits on the floor, in the foreground the corn pit, in the background the wheat pit

THE CHICAGO BOARD OF TRADE 215

exchange there are commission brokers, members who execute orders for other members, and traders, who are the professional speculators. These latter are sometimes called "scalpers."

2. *Methods of trading, spot and cash.*—The transactions on the exchange are of the two general kinds: the "cash grain" business and the "future" business. Under the former come all the dealings which pertain to the actual grain—wheat, corn, oats, etc.—selling it by sample. One side of the exchange room is given up to this "cash" business. Here the samples are laid out for the inspection of the various buyers.

The rest of the exchange floor is given over to the future markets. The four points about which the buyers and sellers habitually congregate are called "pits." The pit corresponds to the "post" or "crowd" on the stock exchanges and consists of a circle of steps leading up from the outside and down into the centre. It is arranged so that a maximum number of people on different levels can see and hear each other in a minimum of space. Telegraph operators sit on raised platforms near the pit and transmit quotations. The word "pit" permeates the phraseology of the Board of Trade. Instead of "room" or "floor" traders we have "pit" traders; pit is almost a synonym for market. Business is carried on by mere gestures, single words, nods and even finger signs.

Sales involving thousands of dollars are consummated by a single spoken word, by a nod of the head, or by a distinctive gesture; and each party merely jots down on a little card a memorandum of the transaction. In no other business, except perhaps in stock trading on the exchanges, are such important deals made with so little bickering over details, or with such implicit confidence that the contract will be faithfully carried out.

On the floor of the exchange, there are the wheat pit, the corn pit, the oat pit and the provision pit. During the busy time the combined markets present a scene of activity, intenseness, seriousness and often excitement that gives the impression of impending tragedy, and which is seen nowhere else except on the floor of the New York Stock Exchange. During a very active market the wheat pit is crowded with some 350 struggling, shrieking men endeavoring to execute their orders; and at such a time every one in the exchange room seems to have a realizing sense of the importance of the momentous volume of business that is being done. It is a time when moments are valuable, and a few seconds suffice to complete transactions. This necessitates the greatest possible rapidity and alertness physical and mental that human beings are capable of, and the aid of all the mechanical appliances that may be had. Orders are continually coming to the floor by telephone and by telegraph, and messengers are speedily delivering them. From the time the gong sounds in the morning until it announces the close in the afternoon there is no time or thought during an active market for anything but the business of the moment. What happened a minute ago is past,

THE CHICAGO BOARD OF TRADE

and that which is to be done a minute hence will be attended to when it is reached.

The orders received by the brokers in the future markets come from every conceivable source. Broadly speaking, however, these orders may be divided into two classes. (1) Those which are sent by men who intend to receive or deliver the actual grain at some time in the future. These men take advantage of the market which offers them an opportunity to insure themselves against loss of profits which may arise due to a change in the price of some commodity upon which their business depends. This method of insurance is termed "hedging" and has already been described. (2) There is another class of orders received, however, which the senders never intend shall be filled by receiving or delivering the actual grain. They expect to get rid of either obligation by selling on a basis of "differences." That is, instead of delivering the actual commodity which the contract calls for, the seller, for example, gives the buyer the difference between the price of the commodity on the delivring date and the price agreed upon when the contract was made. Such orders are called speculative, as they are sent in by men who buy and sell without expecting to use the grain or even to see it. They hope to "sell out their trade" at an early date and to reap a profit by a change in price.

3. *Methods of payment.*—The methods of payment in the board of trade are made to conform to the system of future trading. It would be a bungling sys-

tem indeed if every purchaser had to make payment in full whenever the price changed during the time the contract was running. It is possible, however, by a system of differences to make only partial payments until the final delivery is made. The amount paid over each day would therefore depend upon the price fluctuation. This is shown in the following case quoted from Professor Sparling's chapter on the Exchanges in his book on "Business Organization."

Suppose on March 10th A [1] sells B 5,000 bushels of wheat for May delivery at 95 cents. On each day thereafter this price fluctuates, and as the price rises above 95 cents, B, having the wheat, would thus be the gainer as the market advances, and A the loser; so A would pass checks to B for differences in value figured on the basis of the closing market prices each day. As market prices go lower, B would pass checks to A for differences shown. Let us suppose that by April 20th the price had gone up to $97\frac{1}{2}$ cents per bushel. Then A would have paid to B a total of $2\frac{1}{2}$ cents per bushel, and B decides to sell to C, who finds on May 1st that the price is still $97\frac{1}{2}$ cents. A would then deliver the wheat to B in the form of warehouse receipts which call for the actual wheat, and for these C would give A payment for the total on a basis of $97\frac{1}{2}$ cents per bushel; but he has already paid B $2\frac{1}{2}$ cents a bushel, so, while the wheat costs C $97\frac{1}{2}$ cents, A realizes but 95 cents for it, B having taken the difference. B is in this case purely a speculator, having judged that conditions of supply and demand would bring about higher prices, and acted on his judgment. B may have, however, sold to D, and D to C, and C to K, and K to X, of the same wheat between March 10th and April 20th, each of these traders having gained or lost as the market price fluctuated from day to day. These various parties whether trading

[1] In this illustration, A might be designated a "bear," and B a "bull."

directly for themselves or thru brokers, were thus speculators, though not one of them in selling knew whether or not in selling to C he was dealing with the actual receiver of the wheat, or just another speculator.

We have seen in a previous chapter that warehouse receipts form a basis of future trading in wheat and cotton. The receipts are not actually passed from hand to hand each time a contract is sold. The seller is permitted to issue a so-called "delivery" or "transferable" notice in which he notifies the buyer that he stands ready to deliver certain receipts in fulfillment of the contract. The receipts are actually tendered only when a contract is closed out by a delivery of the actual grain or cotton which it represents.

The board of trade rules provide that delivery may be offset by some corresponding trade or contract, if such offset is consented to by all parties, and that balances shall be payable immediately. Thus two contracts which agree in all particulars except price may be offset and may be settled by a payment of price differences. Contracts may in this way be closed out by direct settlement between the parties concerned, by so-called "rings," and thru a clearing house.[1]

[1] The Supreme Court of the United States holds that "set-off has all the effects of delivery." In the decision of May 8, 1905, the following opinion was rendered.

When the Chicago Board of Trade was incorporated we cannot doubt that it was expected to afford a market for future as well as present sales, with the necessary incidents of such a market, and while the State of Illinois allows that charter to stand, we cannot believe that the pits, merely as places where future sales are made, are forbidden by the law. But again, the contracts made in the pits are contracts between the members. We must suppose that from the beginning as now, if a member had a contract with another member to buy a certain amount of wheat at

4. *Ringing out.*—A ring is formed where a whole group of traders gets together. A has sold 5000 bushels to B; B has sold a like amount to C; C has sold to D; and D has sold to A. It will be noticed that a ring has been formed, in that the last one in the chain has sold to the first. If all the sales had been made at exactly the same price, these four traders would merely agree to cancel the transactions with each other without the payment of money. However, since the prices usually differ, some will have net balances due them and others will owe on balance. These balances may then be settled by a few payments involving small amounts.

Let us suppose that A sells to B a given quantity of a commodity of contract grade at a price of 90 cents per unit. The ownership of this is evidenced by a warehouse receipt. The future market closes that night at 91 cents, so A passes to B a check for one cent per unit. The next day B may sell to C, and he, through others, to K, and the market closes that night at 90½ cents. Checks are passed between all

a certain time and another to sell the same amount at the same time, it would be deemed necessary to exchange warehouse receipts. We must suppose that then, as now, a settlement would be made by the payment of differences, after the analogy of a clearing house. This naturally would take place no less that contracts were made in good faith for actual delivery, since the result of actual delivery would be to leave the parties just where they were before. Set-off has all the effects of delivery. The ring settlement is simply a more complex case of the same kind. These settlements would be frequent, as the number of persons buying and selling was comparatively small.

The fact that contracts are satisfied in this way by set-off and the payment of differences detracts in no degree from the good faith of the parties, and if the parties know when they make such contracts that they are very likely to have a chance to satisfy them in that way and intend to make use of it, that fact is perfectly consistent with a serious business purpose and an intent that the contract shall mean what it says.

parties for differences between prices at which purchases and sales are made, with K having paid ½ cent to J. The process continues up to X, who buys when the market is at 95 cents. Differences have been passed, until X has had to pay to W, from whom he made purchase, 5 cents per unit, and to A, 90 cents per unit. In this way the ring is made complete, each trader intervening between A and X being able to secure his profit or pay his losses promptly hence obviating the necessity for the clearing house.[1]

5. *Clearing-house.*—This is the most improved method for facilitating the settlement of contracts. It resembles bank clearing-houses in large financial centers. The economic importance of the clearing-house system rests in the saving of time and friction which frequently arise in the settlement of a large number of accounts, by affording a central office with an organization of trained officials where the numerous transactions can be cleared. The clearing-house is an independent organization with its own set of officers, rules and regulations. Its function is to keep a record of the sales and to open up accounts with the exchange members.

In order to facilitate the settlement of contracts by offset, each member is required to keep a "settlement book," in which shall be entered the names of parties with whom settlements have been made, the dates and terms of the trades included in such settlements, the terms of such settlements, the prices at which the commodities were originally sold or purchased, the amounts due to or from him or them on each separate

[1] S. E. Sparling's Introduction to Business Organization, page 189.

settlement, and also the net amount due to or from him or them on all settlements.

When the business day ends the members go to the clearing house and pass in their accounts or "reports." If the clearing house sheet as made up shows a credit to the owner of the "report" a draft for the correct amount is drawn on the clearing house. If the day's dealings have netted the member a loss he passes a check for that amount to the clearing house. The clearing house performs the settlement and obviates the necessity of each member hunting out those with whom he has made contracts during the day. In the above supposed case:

when C traded with B, then C's name appeared at the close of that day's business on the clearing-house records, and when C made an opposite trade with D, then D's name appeared on the clearing-house records, but C's obligations were closed and his name dropped. This process continued, showing always the original trader A and the last trader up to X, who, on delivery day, was shown to be the actual purchaser of the commodity. The clearing-house clerk would pass these promptly to Mr. X, and instruct him to make full payment to Mr. A, and thus become the new owner of the commodity.

Thru the buyer's offsetting or canceling his purchase by a sale and by means of the clearing house and ringing out, few future trades remain to be carried out but there are always some longs and some shorts who are left at the end of the delivery month. In these cases actual delivery is made.

6. *Commissions.*—A margin may be required up to

10% of the contract price and the usual commission is ⅛ of a cent a bushel. If transactions are made for members or for firms with one member on the board, the rate of the commission is reduced by half. Corporations have the privilege of getting half commissions when they have one director or stockholder who is a member of the Board of Trade.

7. *Government and management.*—The Chicago Board of Trade was formally organized on March 13, 1848, at a time when Chicago was reached by small tugs and boats on Lake Michigan and by wagon. The purpose of the Board was expressed as follows:

to maintain a commercial exchange; to promote uniformity in the customs and usages of the merchants; to inculcate principles of justice and an equity in trade; to facilitate the speedy adjustment of business disputes; to acquire and to disseminate valuable commercial and economic information; and generally to secure to its members the benefits of co-operation in the furtherance of their legitimate pursuits.

Unlike the New York Stock Exchange, the Chicago Board of Trade is an incorporated institution, having received a special charter from the State of Illinois, in 1859, nine years after the original date of incorporation. Under the regulations enumerated in the charter the members are authorized to transact business and are permitted to "establish such rules, regulations and by-laws for the management of their business and the mode in which it shall be transacted, as they may think proper." The business of the Exchange is done between the hours of 9.30 a. m. and 1.15

p.m. All transactions must be completed before or at the latter hour.

The government of the Board of Trade differs little from that of the stock exchanges. Of course the main difference is that instead of having a stock list committee the Board of Trade has committees to supervise the inspection, weighing, grading and sampling of grain. The Board of Trade publishes elaborate annual statistics concerning grain prices.

The membership numbers between 1700 and 1800 and includes a representative of nearly every important grain commission and elevator company in the country, many of the big millers, some of the New York Stock Exchange members, even a few European importers, several hundred local grain commission men, elevator managers, flour merchants, insurance men, grocers, shipping merchants, lawyers, lumbermen, several capitalists and bankers and owners and representatives of the packing houses. Memberships have recently sold at $4,700, the price depending upon the demand for membership seats.

8. *Other American grain exchanges.*—Altho Minneapolis has the second largest grain market, those in Kansas City, Duluth, New York and St. Louis are important. The New York Produce Exchange occupies a large building and has nearly 1900 members. Besides grain, it deals in many other products, including hay and straw, cotton seed oil, flour, provisions, lard, seed, petroleum, pig iron, hops, butter and cheese. The Exchange also takes an active part in

furthering New York's commercial interests and has committees on canals, bills of lading, exports and railroad affairs.

New York is an important export point for wheat and is the third largest milling centre in the country. Trade in flour is comparatively large, and such trading in wheat as takes place is done chiefly by brokers acting for nearby mills. New York has long ceased to be a primary market for grain, the development of other export points making it less important than formerly. The completion of the barge canal across the state may, however, restore some of New York's prestige in the grain trade.

The hours of trading are 10.30 a. m. to 2.15 p. m., which, allowing for difference in time, correspond exactly with those of Chicago, Minneapolis, Duluth, St. Louis and Kansas City. Wheat is normally about 6 cents a bushel higher in New York than in Chicago, representing the difference in transportation rates and other costs.

An interesting feature of the Produce Exchange is the fact that members may send substitutes on the floor for limited periods of time. While the produce exchanges generally maintain a high standard of membership, there are generally less severe restrictions regarding the occupations of members than obtain on the leading stock exchanges.

The produce exchanges of the Middle West have their specialties. Besides its important wheat market, Minneapolis has a large barley market,

Kansas City specializes in futures for hard winter wheat, St. Louis in winter wheat and Toledo in red winter wheat. An interesting feature of the Minneapolis Chamber of Commerce is its large illuminated dial that immediately records all the trades made in the pit. There are 550 members in this important exchange, the seats of which cost about $3,500.

REVIEW

Why is Chicago the foremost speculative market in the world?

What can you say in regard to the pit and its transactions?

Describe the two main classes of orders received by brokers in the future markets.

Describe an imaginary transaction that will show the method of payment in the Board of Trade.

What are the nature and function of the Clearing House?

Give a brief description of the Management of the Chicago Board of Trade.

CHAPTER XVI

THE NEW YORK COTTON EXCHANGE [1]

1. *Importance of cotton.*—Cotton is today one of the most valuable of the world's crops as well as the most diversely used. In normal times the world consumes each year nearly eight pounds of cotton per capita. In the United States the consumption is thirty pounds per capita. Either the raw material or the manufactured product goes thru the routes of commerce to every part of the world.

While Egypt, India, China and Russia are fairly large producers of cotton, their crops do not approach the production of the United States, where nearly two-thirds of the world's supply is grown. Next comes India, which produces 17 per cent of the total crop. Nearly two million persons in the United States are engaged in cotton-growing. In production, Texas surpasses all the other states of the cotton-growing belt, a district 1500 miles long and 500 wide. The American crop ranges from 12 to 17 million bales of nearly 500 pounds each.

There are tens of thousands of ginneries and two thousand mills in the United States. Moreover cotton furnishes a huge volume of business to railroads,

[1] A note is appended to this Chapter describing the operations of the New York Coffee Exchange.

steamship lines, banks, merchants, factors, brokers and exporters, and normally constitutes the most valuable item of American foreign trade. The price of the staple is therefore of importance to millions of people. Some idea of the position which the New York Cotton Exchange holds may be had from the fact that seats cost more than on any other exchange in America, except on the New York Stock Exchange and, at times, on the Boston Stock Exchange.

2. *Primary markets.*—Both the New York and the New Orleans cotton exchanges were incorporated and granted charters in the same year, 1871. Their machinery for the conduct of affairs and their methods of trading are almost identical, consequently a description of the New York Cotton Exchange will apply also to the New Orleans and other similar exchanges.

The New York, New Orleans and Liverpool cotton exchanges are the world's primary cotton markets, Liverpool being the chief distributing point for American exports. The world's great consuming centers are Manchester, England, and Fall River and New Bedford in Massachusetts.

In the United States, the cotton-picking season lasts from September first to January first. The active cotton months (futures, deliveries, options) are January, March, May, July, August, September, October and December. Even before our entrance into the war, cotton, in recent years, varied between five and a half and twenty cents a pound. The long season during which the cotton market is active and the wide fluctuations in the price afford, of course, great opportunity for speculation.

3. *Government and membership.*—The New York Cotton Exchange is managed much as the other American exchanges which we have already studied are managed. Instead of the grading committees of the produce exchanges the cotton exchange has a classification committee. The governing body is known as the Board of Managers. Membership is limited to 450. Seats have cost as high as $25,000, a more usual figure being from ten to fifteen thousand.

4. *Unit of trading.*—All trading in cotton is either in "spots" or "futures." Cotton is shipped in "bales," each bale weighing on the average 500 pounds. Cotton is quoted at so many cents a pound, varying somewhat in price according to the month of delivery; spots always vary more or less from futures. For example, on August 24, 1916, the highest price for October cotton was 15.89 cents a pound. To get the price of one bale, multiply 15.89 cents by 500; to get the price or a trading contract multiply by 50,000.

Fluctuations are recorded in "points," one point being one one-hundredth of a cent. The highest for "October" on the day mentioned was 15.89 cents and the lowest was 15.41 cents. Thus "October" rose on that day 57 points, or about half a cent a pound or $2.50 a bale. Obviously a point in cotton is much less than a point in stocks. A ten-point rise in a stock is sensational, but ten points for a pound of cotton is only half a dollar a bale, which is of little importance.

The commissions charged vary according to the price. The commission for members is one-half of that charged non-members. An additional charge is made for members and non-members residing outside the United States and Canada. See Editor's note on page 241 for further detail. Margins vary greatly but are usually about one-half cent per pound, or $250 a contract.

5. *Methods of settlement.*—There are two methods of settlement, "direct" and "ring." If a broker sells cotton on contract for future delivery for one customer and later in the month buys an equal amount for another client the settlement would take place directly, which means that one transaction would offset the other. Here the principle of a clearing house is applied.

"Ring" settlements are a more complicated procedure and may involve as many as twelve parties. A, who is a member of the cotton exchange, sells to B 1000 bales of cotton for future delivery. But B has already sold, or will soon sell, to C who may in turn sell to A. If we assume that these transactions took place during the same month, a settlement will be effected among the three or more parties. Each one has bought and sold futures for delivery during the same period with a view to realizing the difference between cost and selling price. Nothing else interests them at this point. The "ring settlement" makes it possible for them to liquidate their contracts and secure their profits long before the month of delivery.

Every transaction in cotton together with the time and price must be reported to the sales reporter of the exchange within ten minutes after the sale. Otherwise no record will be kept by the exchange. No statement of the total volume of cotton sales is published from day to day in the newspapers, as is the case with the stock exchanges.

6. *Cotton futures.*—Cotton is of many different grades. The proportion of the crop in each grade varies so from year to year that it would be impossible to permit deliveries of any single grade or even of two or three grades in fulfillment of future contracts. If such deliveries were permitted, the buyer would find it comparatively easy to corner the small amount of cotton that falls within each grade. Consequently the price of one grade (Middling Uplands) is selected as a basis for the prices of cotton futures, but in delivering on contract the seller may deliver not only middling but any one of a number of other grades, some of which are worth more and some less than middling. If a dealer delivers a better grade than middling, he must receive a premium therefor; if he delivers a poorer grade he must grant a discount. The difficulty comes in adjusting equitably these premiums and discounts, or "differences" as they are called. Since the seller has the option of tendering any one of a number of grades, the buyer must have some guarantee that he will at least receive cotton which is

worth all he has to pay for it. Because of the technical difficulties of determining premiums and discounts the cotton markets have for years been the center of all manner of disputes.

7. *The grades.*—To the layman the names given to the different grades and classes of cotton are most puzzling. Cotton is generally classified as follows:
1. White Cotton. Full Grades: Middling Fair, Good Middling, Low Middling and Good Ordinary.

    Half Grades: Strict Middling Fair, Strict Good Middling, Strict Middling, Strict Low Middling and Strict Good Ordinary.

    Intermediate Grades: (the value of which must be the mean of the adjacent full and half grades). Fully Good Middling, Barely Good Middling, Fully Middling, Barely Middling and Full Low Middling.

2. Tinged Cotton: Strict Good Middling Tinged, Good Middling Tinged, Strict Middling Tinged, Middling Tinged, Strict Low Middling Tinged and Low Middling Tinged.

3. Stained Cotton: Middling Stained.

Some of these terms require explanations. In general it may be said that grading depends upon three factors: (1) color, whether the cotton is white, tinged, or stained (2) comparative absence of extraneous substances and (3) general character of the fiber. The American cotton "staple" fluctuates in fiber length from ⅝ inch to 1½ inches. The longer the fiber, the greater is the value attached to the class. White is the normal color of cotton, when picked before the frost sets in and affects the plant. This grade of cotton possesses greater value than the tinged or the stained. The "tinged" color is produced by the light frosting of the cotton bolls prior to opening or by exposure to rain. The result is a change from white to a yellowish or golden orange color. When storms are heavy and the frosts severe, a deep orange or tawny color takes the place of white. The New Orleans Exchange recognizes more detailed differences in this respect as "spotted," "light tinged," "medium tinged," "light stained," etc.

As previously stated the average grade is called "middling." Consequently if there is less foreign matter in the cotton than the average grade possesses, the name assigned is " good middling." On the other hand if a larger amount of dust or husk adheres, the cotton is classified as "low middling." The full grades, half grades and quarter grades are designed to carry out the refinement of classifications still further.

8. *Cotton futures act.*—For some time prior to the date upon which the cotton futures act became effective, February 18, 1915, the two great exchanges used different methods of determining the "differences." The New Orleans Exchange used the "commercial" method and the New York Exchange the

"fixed" method. The commercial method of determining differences has been clearly summarized by a leading authority: [1]

> The premiums and discounts allowed for better and poorer grades delivered on contract are fixed by the actual selling prices of the different grades that exist in the spot market at time of delivery.

This system of commercial differences was substantially the method employed by the New York Exchange in early days, but it was abandoned in 1888 for two reasons: first, the amount of actual cotton arriving at New York had begun to decrease, owing to direct shipment to northern mills from the South, and to the development of cotton manufactories in the South itself, so that there was not enough spot cotton bought and sold in New York to afford sufficient basis for close determination of differences (a real difficulty, by the way); and second with the amounts of actual cotton, it became increasingly easy to manipulate the prices of the various grades, and hence the differences between grades. For these reasons the method of commercial differences was supplanted by that of fixed differences, whereby the premiums and discounts are fixed arbitrarily by a committee at stated intervals. At first the differences were adjusted once a month (for the nine most active cotton months), but in 1897, the meetings of the revision committee were limited to two a year. Except for a change to quarterly revisions, this method persisted until 1915 when it was prohibited by the United States Cotton Futures Act.

The method of fixed differences caused much dissatisfaction. The United States Bureau of Corporations made a careful study of the problem, and issued a comprehensive and conclusive report, in which it concluded that the present New York system of fixed differences is uneconomic, in defiance of natural law, unfair, and like all other attempts to defy natural law, results in such complex and devious effects that

[1] L. D. H. Weld, The Marketing of Farm Products, pp. 331–333.

the benefits of its transactions accrue only to a skilled few. It was found that the differences as established by the committee became out of line with the differences in the spot market, and that therefore some grades would be overvalued and some undervalued by the arbitrary values established by the committee. Whenever cotton was delivered on contract, the seller, having an option with regard to the grades to be delivered, naturally delivered such grades as were most overvalued by the arbitrary differences. In other words, he delivered cotton which the revision committee said was worth ten and one-half cents in settlement of a contract, whereas the cotton was really worth only ten cents in the spot market. Buyers naturally tried to protect themselves by paying less for the future contract in the first place, with the general results that future prices were artificially depressed, this depression caused confusion in all markets, and it largely destroyed the value of the future market for hedging which is the principal value of a speculative market.

The United States Cotton Futures Act abolished the method of fixed differences by placing a prohibitive tax of two cents a pound on all future trades which did not comply with certain specifications, including the use of commercial differences instead of fixed differences. Realizing that the spot transactions in any one market might not be of sufficient volume to make possible an accurate determination of commercial differences, the law provides that in this event these differences shall be determined by the actual commercial differences on the sixth day prior to the date of delivery in the spot markets of not less than five places designated for the purpose from time to time by the Secretary of Agriculture.

In actual practice the Department of Agriculture has designated some eleven cities where bona fide spot markets exist. A recent bulletin of the Department shows that futures now fairly reflect the great spot markets of this country instead of being much lower, and also conform to the Liverpool market. Indeed since handling of freight charges are included, futures now tend to be higher than spots. As future trading dominates the price situation it is maintained that the farmers are greatly benefited and hedging is rendered a fairer and more satisfactory process.

9. *Use of futures.*—The usual method of marketing the cotton crop is for the planter to sell out, in advance of harvesting, with the condition that delivery of his crop will not be made for several months. There are several different channels thru which the farmer may dispose of his cotton, but the system as a whole must involve the use of futures on a large scale. It is especially necessary for the southern mills to employ futures in their hedging operations. The alternative is to buy cotton and own it for a great length of time, because of the insecurity of the trend of future prices. This entails a heavy outlay of capital, besides storage and insurance expenses and loss in the weight of cotton.

Since cotton buyers in nearly all cases must hedge and employ the future market for the purpose, they have never felt that they could pay much higher prices than those made in the future market, and while many spot markets have always existed in the South, the growers receive in the main, lower prices than were made in those markets. It is this anomalous situation which the Futures Act has already begun to remedy. While the judgment of the thousands of buyers and their representatives as to the numerous grades in different parts of the South naturally differs from time to time, there is a constant tendency for the price paid to farmers to approach the future price minus freight, insurance and handling charges.

10. *Factors that determine cotton prices.*—Altho artificial causes appear to have affected the price of cotton, for reasons already mentioned, it is unquestionable that the great underlying movements of cotton prices respond to the law of supply and demand. As stated by Hunter A. Gibbes, in a prize essay published in *Commerce and Finance:* [1]

It is, doubtless, true that during periods of active speculation the price is pushed up or down by the artificial influence of trading in futures. In such a case the successful speculator simply takes advantage of a condition by exaggerating the condition in the minds of the investing public. For example, before the maturity of the crop of 1910, the indications were that the crop would be short. The increased demand for cotton for manufacturing purposes made it highly probable that the price would be above normal. The farseeing speculator impressed this condition upon the minds of others, and thereby succeeded in pushing the price for a time to about seventeen cents per pound. Fortunately for those on the bull side of the market, the early diagnosis of the situation was correct. The crop was in fact short, and as a result of the active period of speculation in futures the average price for the crop of 1910 in the United States was 13.95 cents. In 1911, the situation was reversed. On account of the high price of 1910, a larger acreage was planted during the succeeding year. The early crop reports indicated a large yield. The wide-awake speculator again took advantage of the conditions, and on the bear side of the mar-

[1] Vol. V, No. 31, August 2, 1916, page 870.

ket hammered the price downward. The average price for the crop of 1911 was only 9.56 cents per pound.

In 1914, the crop of the United States was the largest on record, being 16,134,960 bales, including linters. The early forecast of the crop and war conditions in Europe gave the wise dealer another opportunity. The result of his activities was an average price of 7.33 cents per pound for the 1914 crop.

In 1910, the high speculative prices caused the average price for the year's crop to be in excess of the average actually justified by the law of supply and demand. In the years 1911 and 1914, the average price was doubtless lower than that actually warranted by the law of supply and demand. The abnormality of average price for each year was due to psychological processes. We feel the same influence in every other phase of business activity. Men are like sheep. They follow one another. In case of a real estate boom the influence of speculators on one another causes prices to go upward, but temporarily only. In the excitement of an auction sale of jewelry or furniture, the subtle influence of the auctioneer often makes a price much higher than that justified by the actual worth of the article sold. In each case, however, it should be borne in mind that the marked influence on price is for a relatively short period.

It is, therefore, clear that if we figure out the average price of cotton for a period of say five or ten years, the result will be a price actually justified by the law of supply and demand. For example, the average price of cotton in the United States for the five years ending with the season embracing the 1914 crop was 10.96 cents per pound. This price certainly represented a fair margin of average profit for the period. It is safe to say that such price was the result of the average economic and financial conditions in their relation to actual supply and demand and that what may be styled the psychological influence was eliminated by its counter neutralizing effects.

**11. *Reading the cotton market.*—A particularly exciting market is indicated in the following account adapted from the *New York Times* of August 26, 1916.

More than 16 cents a pound, or $80 a bale, was paid for cotton on the New York Cotton Exchange yesterday for delivery next year. Earlier options closely approached the 16 cent price. That rate is the highest at which cotton has sold since the Civil War in times of normal market, and only twice has it been exceeded. In the Sully campaign of 1903-04 prices were carried to a 17 cent basis, only to drop precipitately. In the Patten-Hayne-Scales-Brown corner of 1910, shorts in the August option were squeezed up to 20 cents as the month ran out.

Yesterday's speculation was the most animated of any day of the year, and brokers said the public interest in the market was as great as ever before. There had been days of larger advances in price, but none in which the market advanced so impulsively on general rather than clique speculation.

At one time prices of most of the options were up more than 60 points, or $3 a bale, over Thursday's close. The close showed advances of more than $2.50 a bale to be the rule. There was heavy buying for foreign account, for spinners and for shorts as well as for bullish speculators. Scores of reports from the South had it that planters were inclined to hold out for higher prices.

The 16 cent range compares with a price of 10 cents at which it was aimed to steady the cotton market two years ago when in the first month of the war the Cotton Exchange closed, and cotton sold below 7 cents or $35 a bale. It was then expected the Teutonic markets would be closed. With that expectation realized, cotton is now more than 100 per cent higher. Two years ago, also, there was formed a $135,000,000 pool to steady the cotton market. Now the market is natural.

Reports from southern centres said that the picking of the bolls showed the cumulative effect of the use of inferior or scanty fertilizer for two years in succession. Damage from drought was also reported, and the bulls said there would be no late pickings because the soil, having had insufficient moisture last winter, had not since been replenished. Predictions were made that the Government crop report on August 31, would indicate a crop even less than the scanty 12,000,000 bales, which lately has been an accepted estimate.

Liverpool again furnished a surprise by sending cables which were about 18 to 20 American points higher than due. Spot cotton was 16 points higher at 9.42d for American Middling. The local market made more than a full response to cables and opened at an advance of 23 to 31 points, with trading active and excited.

The New York Coffee Exchange

Almost a billion pounds of coffee are consumed annually in the United States. This fact explains the existence of an important coffee market in New York. The principal source of supply for the United States as well as for other countries is Brazil, especially the states of Rio and Sao Paulo. The United States is the largest per capita consumer, the number of pounds being 14, whereas Germany consumes 6½, France 4.3 and England .69.

Coffee is generally classified and graded according to quality and the source of production. The names of the leading grades are as follows: La Guaira, Rio, Santos, Mocha, etc. In addition there is a further subdivision of first, good first, regular first, extraordinary first, second, etc. The size of the bean and its cleanliness and color offer means for classfication.

The New York Coffee Exchange was incorporated in 1887, the same year that the Havre Exchange began operations. Its present official title is "The Coffee Exchange of the City of New York." One of its duties is to classify and grade coffee through a special staff created for the purpose. Unless otherwise specified, the quantity of coffee taken as a unit is 250 bags, each weighing approximately 132 pounds or 32,500 pounds in all. The commission charges are as fol-

THE NEW YORK COTTON EXCHANGE

lows: 2 cents per bag to members, or $5 for the execution of purchase or sale of a unit, and 4 cents to non-members. As regards margins required by the broker, no definite amount is stipulated. The amounts range from $200 to $500 on a contract. The minimum fluctuation in the coffee market is five points, representing $16.25 on the standard unit.

REVIEW

What are some of the facts that prove the importance of the cotton industry in this country?

Describe the two methods of settlement used in cotton transactions.

Discuss the methods employed in the grading of cotton.

What was the object of the Cotton Futures Act, passed February 18, 1915?

Comment upon the factors that determine cotton prices.

What do you understand by the term, "reading the markets? Illustrate.

What are the functions and the importance of the New York Coffee Exchange?

Editor's note to page 230: Commissions charged to non-members are: $10 for buying or selling 100 bales when price is below 13.01 cents per pound; $12.50 when price is within a range of 13.01 cents per pound to 25 cents inclusive; an additional $2.50 when price is within each range of 5 cents per pound above 25 cents per pound. Commissions for members are one-half of the above rates. In addition to the above rates, $2.50 is charged for non-members residing outside of the United States and Canada, and $1.25 for members residing outside of the United States and Canada.

One dollar is charged when name of principal is disclosed at or before the close of the Exchange on the day of the transaction provided the price is below 13.01 cents per pound; $1.25 when the price is within a range of 13.01 cents per pound to 25 cents per pound; an additional 25 cents when price is within each range of 5 cents per pound above 25 cents per pound.

CHAPTER XVII

ABUSES OF SPECULATION.—THE BUCKET SHOP

1. *Speculative refinements lead to abuses.*—The perfection and refinement of the machinery of exchange must have been impressed upon all who have read the previous chapters of this book. It has indeed reached a high pitch of achievement. By means of it vast operations are carried thru without a hitch. Everything conceivable has been devised by it to facilitate huge transactions in stocks and produce. No sensible person will doubt that great economic services are performed by this elaborate mechanism. But like other human institutions, it lends itself to abuses which arise both within and without the exchange. It is the purpose of this chapter to consider certain abuses.

The whole modern tendency in business is toward saving expense. For this purpose all intermediate and unnecessary steps are cut out. A merchant orders an article for a customer from a manufacturer and it is delivered direct to the customer without the merchant ever seeing it. As the system of accounting grows more refined, many forms of transactions are settled on paper and business is transacted to an increasing extent by means of ledger balances and differences.

THE BUCKET SHOP

Even in the real estate market parcels of property often change hands many times thru the use of options before the title is transferred. No wonder this whole tendency has gone far on the stock and produce exchanges, where one share or one bushel is just like every other and therefore lends itself readily to the substitution. The stock exchanges have their clearing houses and their "street" certificates but the produce exchanges go even further with their settlements and ring outs.

Is it not natural, then, that with speculation made so easy on the legitimate exchanges irresponsible parties should make it still easier off the exchanges? Thus we have the bucket shop, where one may gamble in stock or grain quotations without any buying or selling whatever taking place. It is a fungus growth upon the institution of exchange speculation, an abuse and a pest, but one which would hardly have been devised had the speculative machinery not been what it is. On the other hand if bucket shops had not catered to the gambling instinct it is likely that some other institution would have done so.

2. *What is a bucket shop?*—Like many another word the term bucket shop which we use to designate any place where men gamble on stock prices, by fictitious sales and purchases, has been used in varying senses at different times. As nearly as can be ascertained it was soon after 1870 that the expression was brought to us from England. It seems to trace its origin there back to the custom in London where

gangs of vagabonds used to drain kegs which had been thrown out of the public houses. When they had gathered enough of this delectable liquor and a few cigar stubs, they used to withdraw to a hovel where they made merry. Their hovel was called a bucket shop and in time this name was used as a term of reproach for those places where stock and produce dealings were feigned.

Nor does the bucket shop as we now know it always operate in the same field. At one period it deals mostly in stocks, at another in grain. If killed in one place it breaks out in another, altho the warfare against it gains strength from year to year, and ultimately may conquer it.

The distinctive features of this form of gambling consist in the fact that stocks are not usually purchased or sold for the customer, and selling and buying does not take place with a view to delivery. The intention of the customer is merely to pocket the difference between the price which he pays and the price which the stock rises. Otherwise expressed, the customer wages against the bucketer on the price of a stock. The owner of a shop always takes one side of a deal, whether the patron realizes and consents to it or not, and in the long run comes out the winner as is the case in most gambling establishments. The dealings are simply in profits and losses, not in the securities themselves. As prices fluctuate the differences flow into the pockets of the winners. The interest of

THE BUCKET SHOP

the bucket shop is always opposed to that of its patrons, as the profits of the shop are measured by the losses of the patrons.[1]

It is evident that bucket shops exist only when they are able to secure the quotations made on legitimate exchanges. Occasionally the bucket shop is obliged, for reasons to be explained later, actually to buy or sell stocks. But in that case a contrary order is put in for a like amount, so that in no event does the shop carry stocks. Legitimate stock exchange brokers have been known to "bucket" their orders—accepting the customers loss or paying him the profit without any

---

[1] Section I of the Wisconsin law prohibiting bucket shops defines the institution: "A bucket shop, within the meaning of this act, is defined to be an office, store, or other place wherein the proprietor or keeper thereof, either in his own or its own behalf, or as the agent or correspondent of any other person, corporation, association or co-partnership within or without the state, conducts the business of making or offering to make contracts, agreements, trades, or transactions respecting the purchase or sale, or purchase and sale of any stocks, grain, provisions or other commodity, or personal property, wherein both parties thereto or said proprietor or keeper, contemplate or intend that such contracts, agreements, trades or transactions shall be, or may be, closed, adjusted or settled according to, or upon, the basis of the public market quotations of prices made on any Board of Trade or Exchange, upon which the commodities or securities referred to in such contracts, etc., are dealt in, and without a bona fide transaction on such Board of Trade or Exchange; or wherein both parties . . . shall contemplate or intend that such contracts, etc., shall be or may be deemed closed or terminated when the public market quotations or prices made on such Board of Trade or Exchange for the articles or securities, etc., shall reach a certain figure; and also any office, store or other place where the keeper thereof, either in his, or its own behalf, therein makes or offers to make with others contracts, etc., for the purchase or sale of any such commodity wherein the parties do not contemplate the actual or bona fide receipt or delivery of such property, but do contemplate a settlement thereof based upon differences in the prices at which said property is, or is claimed to be, bought and sold."

real buying or selling—but the punishment on all exchanges is sure and swift if the authorities discover any bucketing.

The majority of bucket shops advertise that stock can be actually delivered, but as their patrons call for delivery only in rare cases, they can afford to buy the stock thru genuine brokers to fill these occasional demands. On the real exchanges not only are all stocks delivered, except where the clearing houses make an offset, but vast quantities of stock are actually transferred every day from one owner to another on the books of the companies. Even where the broker on a legitimate exchange has the gambling instinct he is forced by the rules into an actual merchandising transaction.

3. *Extent of bucketing.*—It is difficult to say whether bucket shops have catered more to gambling in grain or in stocks. In the Middle West, grain is the favorite, on the Atlantic seaboard, stocks. There is no way of estimating the number of shops existing at any one time. In 1910, the Federal Department of Justice closed 250, and about the same number were driven out of business in 1915-1916. At one time there were 54 bucket shops in Boston alone. It is said that in a single city in New York State 8300 shares of a certain stock were "bought and sold" in the bucket shops in one day, altho only 1350 shares changed hands on the New York Stock Exchange. A further illustration of the size if this illegitimate business is shown by the fact that in one state the bucket shops

THE BUCKET SHOP

once traded in 50,000,000 bushels of wheat a year.

4. *Margins or stakes.*—Bucket shops usually require a margin of only 2 per cent. This is really the customer's stake in the game. The proprietor holds the stake and appropriates it when the price of the stock, which is the object of the bet, falls to the limit of the deposit, unless of course, the customer puts up another sum. As will be remembered, a legitimate broker rarely charges less than 10 per cent. Superficially then, one might suppose the advantage to lie with the bucket shops, and hastily come to the conclusion that for the public at large they offer greater benefits.

It cannot be denied that the man who pays 2 per cent of the value of a stock loses less than the one who pays 10 per cent, but the latter has five more chances to recover a loss. Time and again it has been demonstrated that stocks are apt to drop at the beginning of the day because of overnight rumors, but after the effects of the rumors have worn off prices recover their losses. The 2 per cent man would be wiped out while waiting for prices to recover. Just as important is the fact that the 10 per cent man is transacting legitimate business with responsible and honorable individuals who are not likely to break their pledges and flee the town overnight, as so often happens in the case of the bucket shop owners.

5. *When bucketers flourish.*—Bucket shops thrive best in a falling market, because the majority of customers wager that stocks will rise. It is in the in-

terest of the bucket shop owners to have prices fall that they may pocket the differences; otherwise they lose. During the war, speculation on the exchanges surpassed all expectations and stocks shot upward as seldom before. This fact explains why so many bucket shops closed up during the past four years.

To prevent loss and ruin many bucketers often unite and make a drive against the market to force down prices and thus ruin their customers. A bucket shop keeper, it must be remembered, is in the business only to make money.

Suppose several of these concerns have orders to "buy" a large number of shares of a given stock. Technically they are short of the market. It is perfectly feasible for them to go to regular brokers, if the brokers will take their business, and if not directly, then thru dummies, and sell a great block of stock short, thus breaking the market and wiping out the margins the customers have on hand.

Most of the bucket shops are controlled by unscrupulous men of large financial resources. In outward appearance, however, the bucket shops differ little from the establishment of a member broker of the Exchange. High sounding names are used such as Standard Stock Company. On the signs often appear such statements as: "Member of the Exchange," "Member of the Board," "Bankers and Brokers" and so on. Names of famous houses are imitated. The real backers often keep out of sight. Able lawyers with political influence are engaged to defend them.

THE BUCKET SHOP

One group of proprietors is said to have made $20,000,000. One firm alone had seventy branches. Many of the groups have gone by the names of "Exchanges" and "Syndicates." Their secret power and outward appearance cover up the degenerate nature of the business.

6. *Bucket shops and quotations.*—Prices quoted in these concerns are usually so fixed as to favor the proprietor. Moreover all advantage of fractions is against the patron as the house does business in a "rough-shod" manner. The organized exchanges wage relentless war upon the bucket shops and try to put them out of business by preventing quotations made upon the exchanges from reaching the bucketers. This requires the exercise of vigilance and the more powerful of the bucketers resort to endless legal controversies to defeat this aim.

The Federal Government also relentlessly fights the bucket shops and more have been closed by the Government than thru any other legal agency. The basis for Federal action is the misuse of the mails for purposes of fraud. In addition to governmental action nearly all the states have laws prohibiting these concerns. The test as to whether a business is operated as a bucket shop or not rests on the ability of the complainant to prove that it was not the intentions of the one party or both parties to the transaction actually to deliver the property, but merely to settle by a payment of the differences. Some states make it possible for a business to be so considered if it can be shown that only the proprietor had this idea of non-delivery of property while other states require proof that both parties had such intention.

7. *Evils of bucket shops.*—In actual practice it is not always easy for a customer to know whether his orders are really being executed or bucketed, altho of course there are very many brokers, who are above suspicion in such matters. To make sure the customer need only ask for the names of the brokers on the opposite side of the transaction, that is, the one from whom his security was bought or to whom it was sold.

On May 19, 1909, the New York Stock Exchange adopted the following by-law with regard to bucket shop operations on the part of members of the exchanges:

That any member of this Exchange who is interested in or associates in business with, or whose office is connected, directly or indirectly, by public or private wire or other method or contrivance with, or who transacts any business directly or indirectly with or for, any organization, firm or individual engaged in the business of dealing in differences or quotations (commonly called a bucket shop) shall on conviction thereof, be deemed to have committed an act or acts detrimental to the interest and welfare of this exchange.

Another of the great evils of the bucket shops is that all the money spent in them by the customer has little or no effect upon the market. The bucketer steals from his customer a most valuable asset, his effect upon the market. If a man buys 100 shares of a stock he is entitled to the strengthening effect which his buying has upon the price of that stock. But as the bucket shops buy practically nothing there is no effect. In a previous paragraph it was noted that customers of bucket shops bet on 8300 shares of stock in a single day when only 1350 were bought and sold on the exchange. If the entire 9650 shares had gone through the exchange the price would probably have risen far more than it did. Indeed, efforts have been made to show that the advance in stock prices during the years 1915–1916 was partly due to increased odd lot buying secured by legitimate brokers after the closing of hundreds of bucket shops. The pretended buying of hundreds of thousands of bushels of grain in bucket shops will not add a fraction of a cent to the price of the product, nor will the pretended selling of this amount either increase the supplies of the consumer or lessen their cost.

The real curse of the bucket shop is that so many people are willing to deceive themselves and are willing to act under false pretenses.

The stock of the Anaconda Copper Mining Company may serve to illustrate this point. The company is one of the largest producers of copper in the world. If one really believes such a business is to become more valuable in the course of months, and is prepared to stake a considerable sum on that belief, he is engaging in legitimate speculation. In that case a certificate of ownership in this vast copper-mining concern will be made out to him. But in the bucket shop a man simply guesses that in a few hours or days the person just described will buy enough of that stock to put it up, and he who has done nothing will benefit by the other man's action and bet upon its result. This is making a mockery of the great processes of industry and trying to live upon them without taking part in them.

REVIEW

Why and how have refinements in speculation led to abuses?

Explain the nature of bucket shop transactions.

What is meant by margins, or stakes, in connection with the bucket shop business?

Under what conditions do bucket shops flourish? Explain.

What can you say in regard to the bucket shops and quotations? Upon what grounds do the organized exchanges and the government take legal action against the bucket shops?

In regard to the effect on the market, what is the chief evil of bucket shop transactions?

Why are bucket shop deals unethical from a business standpoint?

CHAPTER XVIII

MANIPULATION

1. *Difficulty of the subject.*—The word "manipulation" is commonly used in a broad inclusive manner with a meaning that is vague and elusive. The operation itself is more easily seen than defined since it is always easier to see something in retrospect than when it is actually taking place. Yet no subject relating to brokerage is more hotly debated and none possesses, perhaps, so much intrinsic interest.

Probably the most comprehensive explanation of manipulation is this: "Putting up prices by virtue of ability to do so." Manipulation almost invariably conveys the idea of artificiality. It always connotes skilful and ingenious management. It is in a sense an art. Usually a group of men, a pool perhaps, or at any rate interested parties, buy or sell securities or produce in such a way as to give the public the idea that the activity involved in such buying or selling is the result of natural forces. This is the usual meaning of the word but there are many others. As John G. Milburn, counsel to the New York Stock Exchange has said:

The term manipulation is one of comparatively recent origin. Like all such terms it is necessary to define it to avoid confusion in its discussion. We get nowhere if it has different meanings to different minds. It has been so much used of late that it should have a definite meaning and application; but that is far from the truth. It has, for instance, been applied argumentatively before this committee to transactions to which it does not at all apply. It is also improperly confused with speculation. It is not easy to say what the meaning commonly attributed to it is, because it is generally used as a term of vituperation rather than as description of a definite class of transactions. Perhaps as accurate a definition as can be given of it is, the giving by the same man or group of men of contemporaneous, or practically contemporaneous, orders to various brokers to buy, and to other brokers to sell the same security at the market price whatever it may be, from time to time, for the purpose of realizing a speculative profit, in some cases from an expected or intended rise in the price, and in other cases from an expected or intended fall in the price, the vice of such a system of orders being that their execution may not involve a change of ownership.

In popular imagination and in the interested attacks of certain self-styled reformers almost every extraordinary movement of prices on the exchange is explained by the magic word manipulation. It is a common and ancient custom to ascribe to manipulation the increase in the price of any of the great staples. Any one identified with such operations, it is said, is an enemy of society. Did not they try to mob James A. Patten in the Cotton Exchange in Liverpool for the part he played as a leading "bull" in one of the cotton campaigns about eight or ten years ago?

If there is a wild opening in a certain stock and it rises abruptly there is said to be manipulation, altho the real cause is the foolishness of certain buyers and their brokers in placing all their orders at one moment instead of biding their time. A much advertised example was the Rock Island episode of December 27, 1909, when twenty brokers each buying 2,000 shares drove the stock up from the 50's to 90's in a few minutes. This was in no sense manipulation but the result of a freak order given by a capitalist at the end of a long Christmas Eve party.

Thomas F. Woodlock, a widely recognized authority on stock exchange subjects, says that manipulation as an independent factor in price-making may almost be neglected. "It is an auxiliary factor to a small extent."

2. *What is manipulation?*—The present writer treated the subject of manipulation in an address given before the American Economic Association at Princeton, New Jersey, in December, 1914, in which he said: [1]

Now there may be manipulation on the Stock Exchange, but it is only fair to observe that the great fundamental changes in prices of the exchange appear to bear little if any relation to manipulation, or to any artificial influence. These changes, in recent years at least, and going back for a number of years, have been due to the *changes in the value of the properties* the stocks represented. It is maintained by numerous economists that speculation arises from changes in the value of property, and certainly there is ample evidence that the great price movements, which after all are perhaps the best test of what is going on, have been due to the rise or fall in the value of certain corporations.

The long decline in New Haven stock was clearly not due to stock market manipulation. It may have been due to

[1] *The American Economic Review,* Vol. V, No. 1, Supplement, March, 1915, pp. 86–87.

manipulation of the property by so-called "insiders," or it may not; that is not the question for us to settle. But certainly it is admitted that confidence in the property was for a time at a low ebb, and that is the reason the price of the stock declined. Exactly the same is true, in a greater degree even, of Rock Island, Missouri Pacific, and St. Louis and San Francisco, and to a less degree of Baltimore and Ohio, where the gradually realized fact that a bad investment had been made in the Cincinnati, Hamilton and Dayton property, together with the enormous distribution of Baltimore and Ohio stock by the Union Pacific, has forced the price down. On the other hand the tremendous speculation in such stocks as Lehigh Valley, Union Pacific, and Reading were largely due to knowledge, later transmuted into extra dividends, of the riches of these companies. Much has been made of Reading, but why should not the stock have been active when everyone with any familiarity with such matters knew perfectly well that some day the company would probably distribute a great extra dividend in the form of its coal lands (it owns 40 per cent of the country's anthracite coal) either voluntarily or because forced by the government? Indeed I imagine that the very year in which Reading's stock was dealt in forty times over was just before the regular cash dividend was largely increased. Why should there not be active speculation in a stock of this character? Certainly if speculation was ever warranted, it was in this case; and the same remark applies to Lehigh Valley and Union Pacific, in both of which the big burst of speculation took place shortly before big extra dividends were paid.

It is largely in these stocks that the great, fundamental price changes have occurred, and I submit that heavy speculation was warranted by facts. During the last year or two I have answered for various periodicals, perhaps a thousand letters from investors. And I can assert that speculation on the Stock Exchange seems small to me as compared with that in other fields.

3. *Kinds of manipulation.*—But it must not be sup-

posed that manipulation is an unimportant subject. It includes under its broad meaning all intentional corners, a description of which will be given in the next chapter, and many other forms of speculative excess and abuse which we shall now discuss.

4. *Extreme or excessive speculation.*—When speculation runs to excess it is often incorrectly termed manipulation. The fact that certain stocks are dealt in more than they are transferred on the companies' books is taken as proof that manipulation exists. Such is far from being the case. Professional traders buy and sell "in and out" several times a day, and handle stock much as they would a ten dollar bill. Their intent may be that of a gambler, but that is quite a different matter.

5. *Rumors.*—The spreading of false rumors is often described as manipulation, and it is that, most certainly. The whole subject of the effect of rumors upon stock prices is intensely interesting and important. There have been countless instances where false rumors or those with only a grain of truth in them have affected prices. Over the circulation of such rumors exchanges naturally have no authority, except in the most obvious and flagrant cases. Speculators go to extremes, discard all sense, judgment and reflection and impetuously rush to ruin upon the circulation of any plausible whisper.

Often the spreader of rumors intends to deceive. State laws forbid the circulation of untruths, with the avowed intention of injuring property. But tho it is a penal offense, conviction is most rare and difficult, except possibly where the standing of banks is affected.

6. *Pools.*—A pool is formed by a number of persons uniting or joining their interests for the purpose of buying or selling and thus increasing or depressing the price of one or more securities, or commodities. The members of the pool divide the loss or profit. Often the word is used in much the same sense as syndicate. The word "clique" has also much the same significance. A pool in and of itself is simply a joint venture of various individuals managed by some individual or firm selected for that purpose. This individual or firm is given the sole authority to direct the buying and selling for the persons in the pools. The practice is of course perfectly proper and is open to criticism only when the methods employed are questionable.

A member of a pool is naturally prohibited from selling or buying for his own account any shares of the stock in question as long as the pool is in existence, and any attempts to evade this rule often result in the collapse of pools and frequently in litigation.

7. *Directors' and officers' manipulations.*—The stock exchange is most active in requiring publicity as regards the declaration of dividends, new stock issues, bond issues, etc. But it cannot prevent directors and officers of corporations from declaring larger or smaller dividends than conditions warrant or in other wise abusing their trust. In other words there is

nothing, and there can be nothing provided in the machinery of the exchanges to prevent corporate abuses and misuse of trust. The destiny of the corporation lies in the hands of its directors who may or may not declare dividends and who may speculate to destroy the value of the company. They may, if unmindful of their trust, secure control of the company by forcing the stock down in an indirect way and buying the securities at a low price. An unscrupulous director, too, will take advantage of his "inside" knowledge and his resulting stock market operations may be included in the term "manipulation."

Should directors take stock market advantages of their knowledge of perfectly proper corporate transactions prior to the rest of the stockholders? Some hold that a director acts in trust for stockholders and should take no advantage, even when the results are harmless from the stockholders' viewpoint. Others say that a director is but poorly rewarded at best and could not afford the time and trouble if he had no pecuniary advantages.

8. *Wash sales.*—The manipulation of stock by means of "wash sales" is extremely rare upon the Stock Exchange. These fictitious transactions are the result of collusion and conspiracy and are both deceitful and malicious. Broker A arranges with broker B to bid high for a stock when A offers it. Other brokers unaware that A and B are confederates are misled in believing that a real market exists for the stock. Formerly "washing" was said to be common

on the curb. The committee appointed by Mr. Hughes when he was governor of New York, to report on speculation, had this to say on wash sales:

> So far as manipulation is based upon fictitious or so-called "wash sales," it is open to the severest condemnation, and should be prevented by all possible means. These fictitious sales are forbidden by the rules of all the regular exchanges, and are not enforceable by law. They are less frequent than many persons suppose. A transaction must take place upon the floor of the Exchange to be reported, and if not reported does not serve the purpose of those who engage in it. If it takes place on the floor of the Exchange, but is purely a pretence, the brokers involved run the risk of detection and expulsion, which is to them a sentence of financial death.

9. *Matched orders.*—A much more common and important form of manipulation of the market consists in matching orders. This is a practice which deserves careful consideration. It is manipulation in the strictest sense of the word. It corresponds to Mr. Milburn's definition referred to earlier in this chapter. An operator who desires to advance or depress the price of a stock does so by matched orders. In these transactions he uses different brokers some of whom he instructs to buy and others to sell, naming the price limit in each case. By simultaneous or substantially simultaneous orders to buy and sell, the market is given an appearance of activity. In the words of Mr. S. A. Nelson, the well known writer on stock exchange subjects, the manipulator "will cover his tracks with the skill of an Indian." In most cases the brokers to whom these tasks are assigned are ig-

norant of the object in view and execute their transactions in good faith. Nevertheless a large operator with ample resources can by this measure secure the same ends as he formerly attained with wash sales. The only disadvantage is that he may be obliged to absorb a large amount of stock which is offered by outsiders and which is naturally purchased in good faith by the innocent broker in preference to that offered by his unknown ally. This stock must of course be paid for in the regular way. The purchase of the stock at high prices, however, materially reduces the profits of the operator in his stock market campaign.

From the foregoing description it is readily observed that a sharp line of demarcation exists between wash sales and matched orders.

10. *Defense of matched orders.*—Many brokers have defended vigorously the practice of matching orders. They say that where a stock is both bought and sold on a varying scale, or at the prevailing market price, the market is rendered more steady and is always active enough to permit investors to buy or sell without serious loss. "It makes a constant liquid market," says one broker. Another says:

It is a species of advertising. People begin to study the earning capacity and possibilities of the property, the shares of which are being made active.

The dry goods merchant manipulates when he prepares a bargain sale and advertises the same. The real estate operator does the same, either by word or mouth or by advertising, or by the purchase of property in the vicinity. It seems to me that without manipulation none of us would want anything but the sheer necessities of life.

11. *Evils of manipulation.*—Brokers freely admit, however, that manipulation may be overdone and abused. This abuse ranges all the way from moderate efforts to stabilize a market to outright fraud. Obviously, excessive manipulation defeats the very purpose of a stock exchange, because the market established in a stock is no longer the result of normal supply and demand. A further adverse point to be made is that all manipulation in new securities is not for the laudable purposes set forth but often to enable the "insiders" to sell out. In the case of established properties the manipulation may be to discount some favorable news known only to a chosen few, or to keep up a favorable market to let the "insiders" out if bad news is coming.

But this abuse tends to correct itself. Excessive manipulative efforts usually fail and ruin the perpetrators. Matched orders moreover, are very expensive. Especially on the produce exchanges advancing prices often incite so much selling from farmers as to ruin the operator.

12. *Prohibition of manipulation.*—At the 1913 session of the legislature of the State of New York, a law was passed (Laws 1913, the 476, sec. 951. In effect May 9, 1913) prohibiting operations of this character. If it develops from any inquiry that an outsider has abused the facilities of the Exchange in this respect, the Exchange must report him at once to the district attorney. Whether there have been any matched orders since this law was passed or

whether there can be in the future, it is difficult to say. It is generally conceded that manipulation of all descriptions has diminished in recent years.

The New York Stock Exchange has always waged war against "fictitious" transactions. Section 8, of Article XXIII of the Constitution, By-Laws and Rules of the New York Stock Exchange holds that: "Fictitious transactions are forbidden. Any member violating this rule shall be liable to suspension for a period not exceeding twelve months." On February 5, 1913, the following rule on sales with no change of ownership was adopted: "that no Stock Exchange member or member of a Stock Exchange firm, shall give, or with knowledge execute, orders for the purchase or sale of securities which would involve no change in ownership." Violation of this provision makes the offender "liable to suspension for a period not exceeding twelve months." Eight days later further restrictions were enacted to this effect: "that reckless or unbusinesslike dealing is contrary to just and equitable principles of trade and the offender shall be subject to the penalties, etc." In addition it has been a standing rule of the Stock List Committee to decline the listing of securities, a reasonable volume of which was not in the hands of the public. By this means it was intended that new issues might not become the subject of manipulation *en bloc*. There is no doubt that the Exchange authorities can and have prevented extreme and continuous cases of manipulation.

13. *Some celebrated plungers; James R. Keene.*—It is no simple matter to present typical cases of manipulation, because the critics and defenders of the exchanges rarely agree as to whether a given case is manipulation or not. It may be said in a general way that the machinations of the pools and plungers who attempt to "rig" markets usually ruin the promoters in the long run.

James R. Keene, the greatest manipulator of all time, died a relatively poor man and the last venture of this kind in which he engaged, the Columbus and Hocking Pool, was a complete failure. Keene made and lost many millions in his deals. In 1880, he tried to corner wheat. But the farmers sold more than he had expected and he lost $5,000,000. It took him years to sell all his wheat and he was obliged to ship some of it to foreign countries. In his next venture in 1895 and 1896, he netted nearly $5,000,000 by manipulating American Sugar stock. The next year Keene joined with another operator to put up American Tobacco. Each man became suspicious of the other and tried to sell out first. Keene bought his stock below par, and became distrustful of his confederate when it reached 150. He sold out at an average of 136. In 1903, Keene drove up the price of Southern Pacific. The deal would have netted him a huge fortune had the directors voted to pay dividends, as he believed they would do, but President E. H. Harriman would take no such step and the manipulators were confounded.

MANIPULATION

14. *A. O. Brown & Co.*—One of the most remarkable instances of an attempted speculative feat was the effort of a tottering firm, A. O. Brown and Company to regain its lost fortunes. This house was at one time heavily engaged in stock operations, but had lost a considerable sum through its investment in an outside water power project. To recover this loss the senior partner sold stock heavily short and to his dismay the market advanced. He helplessly awaited imminent ruin but another partner, not so easily daunted, devised a scheme of buying and selling an enormous quantity of stocks in a single session of the market and by thus preventing a further movement, either up or down, he thought that the firm would be able to cover its shorts. Therefore this single firm dealt in nearly one and a half million shares in the Saturday two-hour session. But the firm failed at once for two reasons: (1) the commissions were so enormous that they offset any possible gain in covering shorts and (2) the banks became suspicious and called in all the firm's loans.

15. *Matched orders, American Ice.*—This chapter will be concluded with three well known instances of matched orders. In the case of the American Ice Company, a prominent plunger and manipulator, thru his connection with various banks, was able to send matched orders to the Stock Exchange during the first months of 1906, from January to May, which are shown on the page following.

Month	Bought shares	Sold shares
Jan.	89,950	76,650
Feb.	35,000	33,900
March	88,800	89,281
April	145,300	145,100
May	108,000	80,000

16. *The Hocking pool.*—One of the most disastrous efforts to control the price of a stock by means of matched orders was the notorious Columbus and Hocking Coal and Iron pool conducted in 1909 by James R. Keene, together with the firm of Lathrop, Haskins and Company. In reality two pools were formed, each to buy 20,000 shares of stock. At least a dozen firms were involved. By means of matched orders an active market was made in the stock and from a very low price it was pushed up 92½. It remained around that price for a short time and then unexpectedly one day a large amount of stock was thrown on the market and the price fell in a few hours from 88 to 25, resulting in the failure of three firms and the disciplining of several others. Subsequently the stock fell to 2 and then disappeared from the trading list.

The remarkable feature of this case was the fact that few people outside the pool ever thought the stock had any value. Most brokers refused to buy it at all. Finally the astute Keene, altho the manager of the pool, unloaded his stock at the high price and then smashed the pool of which he was manager by selling

MANIPULATION

short. This was a case where the usual selling from outside was lacking. Collapse was due to the bad faith, bad judgment, lack of unanimity and lack of resources of the members of the pool. The testimony of Mr. Criss, specialist in the stock, is most enlightening:

Q. You bought 14,000 shares the last morning?
A. Yes.
Q. You were trying to keep up the market?
A. I was trying to support the market; yes.
Q. Where did all the stock come from?
A. It came in gradually at first, and after a while it seemed to come from all over the face of the earth. I could not say.
Q. Then you had to stand from under, did you?
A. I stayed there until they canceled my order, when I stopped trading in the stock.
Q. Then you were swamped?
A. Yes, sir.
Q. And your firm went under as a result of that?
A. As a result of that; yes.
Q. Did you gather from this flood of selling orders that somebody on the inside was selling out the pool?
A. I thought something like that, sir.
Q. You know stock exchange indications, do you not?
A. Well, sir.
Q. You know the danger signals?
A. I knew something was wrong but I could not help but obey my order.
Q. What did you finally ascertain was the cause of the breaking of the pool?
A. That Lathrop and Haskins failed and that somebody leaked on the pool. We said somebody had leaked on the pool.
Q. Somebody leaked?
A. Leaked pretty heavily.

Q. Did you find out who it was who had sold out the pool?
A. There has always been rather a mystery about it. Eventually Mr. Keene settled.
Q. What is that?
A. Eventually we made a settlement with Mr. Keene, so I had my own opinion of the matter.

17. *California petroleum case.*—The Pujo Committee [1] revealed an interesting episode in the history of manipulation, as illustrated by the case of the California Petroleum Co. In this case the efforts of certain brokerage houses were seen to have been devoted to stimulating speculation in the new security when it was introduced on the New York Stock Exchange. The account of the operation after the listing privilege was secured is described in the report as follows:

Thereafter an operation in the stock was conducted (principally in the common) on the New York Stock Exchange by Lewisohn Bros. for the joint account of the bankers, for the purpose, as described, of "making a market." Under the general direction of Salomon & Co., Lewisohn Bros. would put in separate orders to different brokers on the morning of every day to sell on a scale up and to buy on a scale down, so adjusted that at the end of the day they would have bought and sold, so far as market conditions permitted, substantially the same number of shares. There is in the record a table showing the purchases and sales by Lewisohn Bros. and the prices day by day from October 5, when the stock was listed, through the end of that month,

[1] This Congressional committee, known by the name of its chairman, Mr. A. P. Pujo, then member of the House from Louisiana, was organized "to investigate the concentration of control of money and credit." The report of this committee was published in February, 1913.

MANIPULATION

from which it appears that during that period of about 21 business days 163,000 shares were purchased and 172,000 sold by Lewisohn Bros. for account of themselves and associates.

Under the influence of this operation the price of the common stock, starting at about $62\frac{1}{2}$, quickly rose to 72. The total purchases and sales on the Exchange during these 21 days were 362,270 shares, which was equal to over three and one-half times the total outstanding common stock.

In order to make the explanation clearer the following statement of matched orders in California Petroleum during October, 1912, is given:

	Purchases	Sales
October 5	6,000	11,200
7	8,900	4,000
8	6,500	7,100
9	3,100	3,800
10	13,000	17,100
11	6,300	5,800
14	2,300	1,900
15	4,400	7,300
16	10,400	13,000
17	11,000	14,200
18	10,400	9,300
19	5,100	2,700
21	7,900	8,200
22	6,400	10,900
23	11,000	9,400
24	7,900	7,900
25	5,200	5,800
26	3,100	2,500
28	4,300	9,800
29	6,300	7,200
30	9,000	8,600
31	4,500	5,200

REVIEW

Do you consider that manipulation is ever justifiable?

What do you understand by the term "pool"?

How do you distinguish between wash sales and matched orders?

What are some of the well-known instances of manipulation? Do you think the failures of the manipulators might have been prevented? If so, how?

CHAPTER XIX

SPECULATIVE FEATS AND EXCESSES—CORNERS

1. *Corners defined.*—A corner has already been defined as the situation that exists when shorts cannot borrow stocks. Technically and strictly speaking, the definition is correct, but it is not comprehensive. A corner is a control or monopoly of a commodity or security, which has been effected for the purpose of raising prices. Those who engineer a corner aim to dominate a given market, such as that for a certain stock or metal, or for one of the staples, such as wheat, coffee or cotton.

The promoters of a corner usually aim not only to dominate prices, but also to create a situation in which they can actually dictate terms to the unfortunate persons who have become ensnared in their trap. The corner takes its name, of course, from the fact that the victims are at bay and must meet the terms of their captors. In other words, they are in a corner.

Corners may take place outside the field of organized speculation. Indeed, the first classic example of a corner, as well as of produce speculation, was the situation described in the Bible, when Pharaoh, upon hearing Joseph's dream, concerning the fat and the lean years, decided to accumulate grain in the period of plenty and good harvests, and to sell it at a higher price later on during a period of scarcity and famine. Speculation, in this case, was of simple character; it consisted merely of buying produce outright and holding it for an inevitable advance. The plan was carried to a successful conclusion, and the Pharaohs waxed rich.

Corners have been engineered in all manner of articles, and in reality are commoner in transactions carried on outside the exchanges than in those of the exchanges themselves. Nevertheless it is true that the conspicuous corners have taken place on the stock or produce exchanges. They are especially spectacular because of the plight of the short seller. The shorts, unaware of the secret efforts of those who are engineering the monopoly, suddenly find they cannot meet their contracts unless they pay the prices of those in control. A witness in court once described a corner as "a . . . combination to prevent people short of stocks from buying them."

2. *How corners are worked.*—Corners have often proved as dangerous for those responsible for them as for the intended victims, and very frequently the manipulators reap only financial disaster for their pains. Because of the creation of big corporations that issue an enormous amount of stock, and because of a wide distribution of the ownership of these stocks, the opportunity for cornering stocks is no longer frequent. Indeed there has been no important corner on the Stock Exchange in a number of years.

To take a hypothetical case, suppose that the issue

of B. T. & D. stock is 500,000 shares, of which A and B own 200,000. These two conspire to work a corner. Quietly, and without arousing suspicion, they begin to buy up shares of the B. T. & D. This unadvertised but active buying gradually boosts up the price of the stock to such a high point that short selling takes place. That is to say, speculators anticipate a slump from the abnormally high price, and consequently sell. When the shorts are requested to deliver the stock to A and B they find themselves in a peculiar position. They cannot deliver the stock because they sold what they did not own, and the only persons from whom they can borrow are A and B, the very persons to whom they sold. And of course A and B, since they have bought up all the available supply, will not loan stock on the usual terms.

There are only two alternatives open to sellers. One is to fail to deliver the securities, a method that entails expulsion from the exchange for breaking a contract. The other is to settle at a fixed price determined by the parties to the corner. This amount is known as the "settlement" price. In any case, if the corner succeeds the victims are caught, or squeezed. Usually the manipulators have lulled the suspicions of the shorts by previously lending stocks freely; then, when all is ready they suddenly call in their loans.

3. *Corners in stock.*—Corners may be divided into two classes, those that merely occur thru force of circumstances, without personal contrivance, and those that are the result of personally directed manipula-

tion. A group of individuals may find to their surprise that they control the whole supply of a certain stock at a given time, and realizing the power which this situation gives them, attempt to utilize it. Sometimes this power falls into the hands of an individual. In either case the event occurs without the consequences having been foreseen. Most corners, however, are the result of definitely planned speculation, the promoter or promoters intending to profit by the unique position of the debtors, whom they have forced into an embarrassing situation.

4. *Northern Pacific panic.*—The most famous case of an accidental corner was that in Northern Pacific stock, in May, 1901. Two opposing parties of very powerful capitalists sought control of this road, and began secretly to buy up the stock. The price rose by leaps and bounds; professional speculators, not aware of the cause and believing the price to be far above the intrinsic value of the stock, sold short. The thousands of shares thus called out were of course eagerly snapped up by the contending syndicates. When the shorts endeavored to cover, they found that there was practically no stock available on the market. The supply had been exhausted by the greedy demand of the rival syndicates. The shorts, in their efforts to cover, bid the stock up until it finally reached $1,000 per share.

Altho contending parties agreed to lend out enough stock to prevent a panic, they forced the shorts to pay heavily—about $300 a share. This price however, considering the fact that the shorts were cornered, was not exorbitant.

5. *Harlem corner.*—One of the most famous corners which was ever deliberately planned was that worked by Cornelius Vanderbilt in the case of the Harlem Railway stock. When Vanderbilt originally bought this stock he paid only $8 or $9, for each $50 share. By hard work and good management he so improved the road that the value of the stock jumped to $58 a share. After having thus effectively established the credit of his property, Vanderbilt decided to extend his system. As soon as he applied to the Common Council of New York City for the franchises necessary to carry thru these improvements, the public learned what was going on. Nevertheless, the franchises were eventually secured.

In the meantime because of the general knowledge of the advantages that would accrue to the road the price of stock advanced until it reached 117. The political interests which had been instrumental in securing the franchises for the railroad profited by this rise, having bought stock in anticipation of the event. They were not satisfied with their profit, however, but decided that there was another splendid opportunity awaiting them. Their asset was the complete control of a council that would do their bidding. They planned to sell the stock of the Harlem Railway short, at the high price then prevailing, and after this had been done, to have the council revoke the franchise which had been granted, an act that would cause consternation among the holders of the stock of the company, and a consequent heavy fall in its price. As soon as this occurred the politicians would go into the market and buy up the securities necessary to cover their short sales.

But somehow, Mr. Vanderbilt secured a knowledge of this scheme. He at once decided not only to block the move but to profit by the incident. All of the stock which the politicians sold short he purchased, so that ultimately he held options from the political syndicate for more than the total issue of the Harlem stock. He thus forced his enemies into a position where they promised to deliver more Harlem stock than was in existence. Mr. Vanderbilt had succeeded well in his venture. He simply waited until the options matured. When the time for delivery came the politicians endeavored to secure the shares, there were none obtainable in the market. The price of Harlem stock in the meantime had dropped to about 72. As soon as the political schemers discovered their predicament they began to buy stock at any price. Quotations advanced by leaps and bounds, until they finally reached 179. Here the price remained. Mr. Vanderbilt then disclosed to his rivals the full extent of their position. He dictated the terms on which he would settle the regranting of the franchise and a settlement at the figure then prevailing. The syndicate had no choice but to accept his terms.

The politicians, smarting under the costly defeat, cherished the hope that they might avenge themselves upon Vanderbilt. A short time later he secured control of the Hudson River Railroad and immediately set about preparations to consolidate this road with the Harlem. The politicians argued that Vanderbilt would take advantage of the opportunity to make money thru the rise in the price of the stock—a rise which seemed almost inevitable because of the advantages of a united property. It occurred to them that here would be a splendid opportunity to retaliate for that first corner in Harlem, which had been so disastrous to them. They consequently resolved to sell Hudson stock short and then, thru manipulation of the legislature, to balk Vanderbilt's scheme by refusing the necessary permission for the consolidation of the property.

But the railroad men soon became aware of this plan. As soon as they began their bear raid upon the prices of Harlem stock, buying orders came from every source by tens of thousands. Every option that was offered was purchased. The tremendous volume of transactions exhausted both sides and Vanderbilt was forced to extremes to raise the money necessary to purchase the stock that was for sale. In the meantime the politicians carried out their plan and persuaded the legislature to refuse permission for the consolidation. Harlem stock immediately fell from 150 to 90; Vanderbilt repeated his former tactics—simply sat still and waited. The shorts, as soon as they tried to cover their transactions, found that there was no stock available. The price jumped up by great leaps until it finally reached 285. Vanderbilt determined that this should be a costly lesson, and declared that he would not settle under $1,000 a share. The shorts could not purchase the stock, and therefore were at the mercy of the only person who had sufficient stock to enable them to carry out their contracts. Wall Street was in a violent panic, for every brokerage house realized that if settlement had to be made at Vanderbilt's figure it would mean universal ruin. Influence was brought to bear upon him to alter his decision, and he was finally induced to accept settlement at 285.

6. *Gold corner of 1869.*—Altho the famous gold corner was not a corner in stocks, it fits into this narrative because it took place in a period when operations of which it is typical were common. Speculation in gold was rife in 1868, owing to the government's adopting the policy of auctioning the gold to the highest bidder instead of selling it in private transactions, as formerly. The new method undoubtedly stimulated wide-spread speculation in gold; for that reason Wall Street protested, but to no avail.

Late in 1869, Jay Gould and James Fisk undertook to engineer a gold corner. Since the supply of gold outside the Treasury was limited, the success of the corner hinged on the promoter's ability to influence the Treasury Department not to sell gold in unusual amounts. This, Gould and Fisk proceeded to do. They persuaded the administration to keep the price of gold at a high level during the fall because the West was just beginning to move its crops and this high premium on gold would ultimately benefit the farmer by making his crops worth more in gold. In a few days, because the supply of gold was thus restricted, the premium on gold rose to 162. Thus the plans of Gould and Fisk were materially advanced.

But when the Secretary of the Treasury, Boutwell, observed this significant rise, he immediately ordered gold to be sold, and on "Black Friday," September 23, 1869, the price dropped to 135. On that day disaster overtook many, the corner was broken, and the clique was ruined by its own acts.

7. *United Copper corner.*—Another corner that resulted in disaster, not only for the projectors but for the country at large, was the United Copper Corner of 1907. A brokerage firm whose leading partner was a director in many banks, had a large interest in a mediocre copper company. This man had but recently sold another far more valuable copper property for the sum of $14,000,000, but he and his brothers, evidently not content with their newly acquired fortunes, dreamed of limitless riches.

The firm in question made arrangements to lend stock freely to shorts, and then suddenly called in all the loans simultaneously. It had made arrangements for other brokerage firms in collusion with it to do the same thing, and for a brief period the shorts were cornered. But the ownership which the head of the firm held in many banks caused widespread loss of confidence. Banks began to call loans made to the firm, several banks failed, the price of the stock slumped in spite of the elaborate arrangements to corner it, the firm itself failed, and the panic of 1907 was in full swing.

8. *Corners in products.*—The only difference between a corner in stocks and a corner in commodities is that in the latter case the clique buys up all the available warehouse receipts. Corners in wheat and cotton are of fairly common occurrence, and there has been at least one big corner in copper, which was known as the Secretan corner. Several capitalists now living, including James A. Patten, have been concerned in numerous cotton corners.

But while corners take place fairly often in cotton and wheat, the likelihood of financial success is small and the danger to the engineers is great. This is because the available supply can never be more than approximately determined. If a corner drives wheat up to $2 a bushel, farmers have a marvelous way of finding hundreds of thousands of bushels the existence of which had been unknown to all except themselves, and by placing this extra quantity on the market they seriously disconcert the promoters. Of course, unless practically all offers are accepted, the corner ceases to exist. The situation plainly differs from that in the stock market, where the amount of stock outstanding is always known, altho it may happen that the amount available for purchase cannot be definitely ascertained. Thus, while at a given time the total supply of a commodity may have been cornered, additional amounts may come into the markets which the shorts can purchase and with which they can fulfil their obligations. Since such are the circumstances, to corner produce a clique must assume great risks. The possible gain from the transaction must be discounted at an exceedingly high rate.

9. *Speculative corners.*—A sharp distinction should be made between real corners in actual grain or cotton, and the speculative corners that occur when the outstanding futures maturing in a particular month are bought up by a group of operators who suddenly threaten to require delivery. Only a temporary squeeze results, which lasts until the operators who sold short for delivery in that month settle up at an advanced price. An actual corner of spot grain or cotton would be a national calamity, but it is practically impossible to engineer one, because of the vastness of these crops and the stupendous amount of capital required. The price effects of speculative or one-month corners are short-lived because the victims quickly settle. Spot prices do not, as a rule, follow the inflated prices at which the futures of a particular month may sell during the period of a speculative corner. The evils of these prices lie chiefly in the losses of the speculative victims and an upsetting of legitimate hedging operations.

A leading example of a one-month corner on a large scale is that engineered by Messrs. Patten, Hayne, Scales and Brown in 1910, when the August option on cotton was squeezed up to twenty cents as the month ran out, and hundreds of thousands of bales of cotton were delivered to the pool. In this case the corner operators acquired vast quantities of cotton and resold at a profit, but their operations were confined to a single month.

Even if there were no system of futures, there would still be the same possibility as there is now of cornering actual wheat or cotton, because of the fact that at certain periods of the year only small amounts of these products are available. In other words, the existing evils of speculative corners are less than the appalling dangers of monopolistic operations in actual grain would be if there were no future system.

10. *Corners in wheat.*—According to the records, corners in wheat took place as early as 1879. In that year, as a result of the prosperity that existed, prices were artificially boosted far higher than the real value of the commodity warranted. But exports of wheat were blocked and eventually, the market fell thirty-four cents a bushel. In 1887, coffee and wheat were often cornered, but the experiment was always attended with disaster. In 1888, the price of wheat was raised to $1.85. The farmers, however, were able to sell a great quantity of the commodity at a comparatively high price and the corner broke down.

11. *Leiter corner.*—Joseph Leiter, a daring speculator, in 1902, became convinced that the wheat crop was much below its usual size, and that a world-wide scarcity would follow. He proceeded to buy up all

the wheat that dealers were willing to sell, and to arrange that it should be delivered upon a specified date. On the fatal day when, according to Leiter's estimate, the sellers would have to settle at his figures, the tide turned, and to his consternation his debtors acquired a supply of wheat sufficient to liquidate their contracts. At the last moment they had secured wheat from certain elevators which Leiter had apparently overlooked, and had rushed it post-haste to Chicago in order to fulfill their obligations. The result was that the famous operator lost millions.

REVIEW

What do you understand by the term corner?

By means of an imaginary case, illustrate how corners are worked.

What are the two kinds of corners in stocks? Explain the characteristics of each kind.

Describe the corner that precipitated the Northern Pacific panic of May, 1901.

What can you say in regard to the Harlem corner, engineered by Cornelius Vanderbilt?

What were the circumstances attending the panic of 1907?

How does the Leiter corner of 1902 illustrate the difference between a corner in produce and a corner in stocks?

What can you say in regard to the difference between speculative corners and other kinds of corners?

CHAPTER XX

BENEFITS AND EVILS OF SPECULATION

1. *Investment, speculation and gambling.*—It is the purpose of this chapter to clear up as far as a most difficult subject permits, the controversy as to whether speculation is a good or bad institution and whether, if possible, it should be abolished. But before we go more deeply into the subject it is necessary to clear the ground by making plain the essential features of three well-known ways of employing money —investment, speculation and gambling. These words have been used repeatedly in this book, and no doubt the reader already had his own idea of their meaning before taking up the Text. He, perhaps, gathered still further ideas about these terms from the many references made to them in these pages. But the time has now come to define and distinguish them in detail.

The three words are frequently confounded and even considered as synonymous. Indeed the three acts themselves are constantly being confused. Speculation is a certain aspect, it is true, of the broad term investment. It is often said that no stock is a good investment unless it is also a good speculation, meaning thereby that an investment should have a future as well as a past. In a hearing before the United

States Committee on Banking and Currency the late Charles A. Conant, a distinguished economist, was asked, "How much of a twilight zone is there between investment and speculation?" He replied:

> A very wide one necessarily. Some securities that were considered at one time absolutely non-speculative, like a distinguished New England railroad, sometimes become very speculative. There is nothing sure. As the gentlemen . . . said, you cannot give a policy of insurance with investments. You have to take your chances in the evolution of the financial and economic affairs of the world.

Another witness at the same hearing testified:

> Many who buy for investment buy partly on credit; and purchase for investment may have in it a speculative element determining the permanence of the investment. It is a common experience to buy for investment and yet sell on an unexpected rise in the market or when an expected rise takes place. It is not a criterion of the investment or speculative character of a transaction whether or not the security is bought partly on credit any more than it is in the case of purchases of real estate. Securities bought with a speculative purpose may be retained as investments. Any statement of the proportion of the transactions that are of an investment as distinguished from a speculative character is merely a worthless guess.

And yet investment and speculation differ widely not only in the words themselves but in the underlying principles involved. Let us first define speculation and then we can see how it differs from investment.

2. *Speculation defined.*—The word speculation is derived from the Latin "speculare" meaning to spy

out, to look out, to observe. This Latin derivation affords the best idea concerning the meaning and real significance of speculation. It involves nothing more or less than the desire of the individual to overcome the domination of chance and to penetrate into the future with a view of profiting thereby.

The speculator in his daily operations is obsessed with the idea which remains, permanent and all-dominant in his mind—how can he anticipate or spy out the future conditions of supply and demand, especially the former? He strives in this way to overcome the inevitable fluctuations of values and is successful in so far as he accomplishes this end.

Speculation is never artificially created. It exists only when property has fluctuating value. Fluctuations cause speculation. It must not be supposed that speculation alone deals in uncertainties. All business is fundamentally affected by demand and supply and these two forces constantly fluctuate. Especially in agriculture, upon which all other industries rest, the supply fluctuates. Among the other disturbing factors are fire, incompetency, miscalculation, corruption, depreciation, change of popular taste, new inventions and wars. Insurance may provide against some uncertainties, but only a few. Thus the professional speculator who has an equipment for his work equal to that of the highly trained business or professional man in reality assumes no greater risks than the farmer, manufacturer or storekeeper. In fact he quite properly assumes smaller risks in any given operation, i. e., he is satisfied with relatively smaller gains and losses, because the very nature of his business is to assume risks, and as in the analogous business of insurance, risks can safely be assumed only by making each one small.

To overcome future uncertainties is the task which the speculator sets before himself. In theory a speculator is one who is engaged in foretelling the powerful changes in prices, but in practice he puts his information into effect by purchasing or selling commodities or securities. His supposed ability to foretell prices is the foundation upon which he works. Speculation must involve reflection and careful thinking on the one hand and, on the other, the assumption of risk, conscious or unconscious, on the basis of this decision. The profits, if there are any, are the reward given for this reflection, foresight, forethought and knowledge of facts. We may distinguish the two relationships, investment and speculation, from no less than seven different points of view. These will now be discussed.

3. *Safety and risk.*—A man is said to have made an *investment* when the element of safety predominates in the enterprise to which he entrusts his funds. The undertaking is speculative if risk is involved to more than ordinary degree. The danger and greater liability to fluctuation does not make a very strong appeal to every one. But because it carries with it the expectation of a rise and a consequent source of

profit, there are found these who are willing to undertake the risk.

Practically speaking, it is often extremely difficult to differentiate these terms very clearly and to state at just what point one relationship merges into another. When is an enterprise sufficiently devoid of danger to call the placing of money in it an investment, and at what point may one unquestionably maintain that the peril to which the capital is exposed sufficiently warrants its being described as a speculative endeavor? To this question, no hard and fast rule can be applied except thru the standard set by *expert opinion*. The general convictions of veterans in industry and commerce, men who have learned some lessons in business life thru personal contact and experience, serve as good criteria of the propriety of including the undertaking in one of the two classes.

4. *Income and profit*.—The distinction between investment and speculation, leads to the use of the two words, income and profit, as applied to the revenue derived from the respective businesses. The former designates a steady and regular inflow, while the latter implies a return which fluctuates with external conditions. Two individuals, for example, have $10,000, one of whom buys United States Government 2½ per cent bonds, and the other, common stock in a corporation. One receives a yearly income of $250, the other obtains a profit, which, however, cannot be determined until the fiscal year is complete. Profits on the common stock may in one year rise to 40 per cent

BENEFITS AND EVILS OF SPECULATION

on the capital invested while, in a year of depression or crisis, they may be reduced to a low level or be omitted altogether. In the case of an investment, the individual expects to derive a definite sum during the year, which is not subject to any substantial changes. But when one is willing to be carried along on the waves of business prosperity, securing a larger sum when business is in a boisterous state and a much smaller amount when the storm breaks, he counts his varying yearly income as profit. That, at least, is the case when he retains the security. However, the ordinary security speculator does not usually purchase with the intention of retaining control indefinitely. He tries to sell at the earliest possible moment when profits may be realized. Securities are dealt in by him merely for their anticipated increase in value. The increase in them is called profit.

5. *Method of purchase.*—The investor, as a rule, buys securities or commodities outright. The speculator, on the other hand, buys on a margin. Investors may, it is true, occasionally buy "on margin," but speculators rarely buy in any other way. The amount of their capital is limited, but their operations are extensive. Placing small amounts here and there enables them to spread their capital over a wider area of the security market than would otherwise be possible, and aids in equalizing their risks and gains. The speculator realizes quite well his liability to ruin and tries to ward against it by "covering" and "hedging."

6. *Ownership of capital.*—Another point of difference between speculation and investment is the nature of the ownership of the sum put into the enterprise. This follows as a direct result of the methods of purchase. The individual who possesses a surplus at his disposal which he desires to invest does so for the purpose of making it productive. It must not be idle but should be converted into an income-bearing source. He invests the whole sum in a way that he believes to be feasible. On the other hand, the speculator buys on a margin because he does not want to tie up his limited resources indefinitely by buying outright. He must always be alert and active, prepared to buy at a moment's notice any active commodity or security which indicates a possible source of gain to him.

7. *Duration of investment.*—While the investor is content with a steady income and tries to avoid reinvestment, the speculator is incessantly changing the form of investment to meet the exigencies that constantly arise. Whenever, in his own opinion, the speculator believes that prices will rise, he buys and buys quickly. The retention of his purchases hinges on the course of succeeding events. As a rule, buying is a temporary matter with him and his decision varies according as the possibility of gain is close at hand. When indications all point to the advisability of retaining what he bought, no other alternative presents itself; the decision is made automatically.

When loss must be incurred, he immediately sets out to relieve himself of the burden, as quickly and shrewdly as is possible under the circumstances.

8. *Bonds or stocks.*—Investments are usually made in bonds, mortgages and preferred stocks whereas common stocks are the field of speculation. A bond is in reality a promissory note secured by the property of the concern itself. The stockholder tho he technically owns the property of the enterprise, has little voice in its management, which lies in the hands of the directors. Profits are only secured in the form of dividends when the board of directors votes to this effect. It may decide to accumulate profits, without declaring dividends, and there is no force on earth to make them act otherwise.

So far the picture is a gloomy one for the stockholder but there is a reverse side to it. The interest on bonds ranges from four to six per cent, but in the case of stocks no limit is set. In time of prosperity, the income rises very high but in dull times reaches a low ebb. The possibility of enormous gain is considered a recompense for the risk. Since dividends on common stock are thus subject to fluctuation, the prices of the stock are liable to equal vacillation thus opening up a great field for speculative efforts. An announcement of large orders in connection with the expectation of handsome profits causes a flurry of excitement among would-be purchasers; the article of security is eagerly sought, and, for a time, prices rise until the climax takes place. At this stage, particularly, cool-headedness and sound judgment are needed by the speculator.

9. *Gambling defined.*—All these distinctions serve to distinguish clearly between the two forms of business relationship. But we have to contend with another difficulty which finds its origin in popular confusion of mind. Speculation is often attacked on the ground that it is merely another form of gambling. How is it distinguished from gambling?

The gambler acts blindly and assumes risks whether the exigencies of the situation require that course of action or not. The speculator, however, assumes those hazards which must fall to someone's lot, if not to his own. Every business teems with risk and chance, and the speculator is best fitted by his training to cope with them adequately. It is not a question of an artificial institution; speculation is an inherent aspect of commercial intercourse and must be taken into account willingly or not. Moreover, speculation presupposes intellectual effort; gambling, only blind chance.

Both gambling and speculation, it must be admitted from the very outset, hinge on uncertainties in the fundamental laws underlying human action. Both, it is true, have a common lucrative purpose. In both cases, also, the object nominally purchased is often not actually in the physical possession of the owner at any given time. Furthermore, in each instance, the method of buying is identical, i. e. marginal payment. But there is all the difference in the world between gambling and speculation.

Gambling with cards entails a definite, concise loss on the one side and a corresponding gain on the other. Gambling on the stock and produce exchange is much the same. The gambler is reckless, assumes danger when there is no necessity for doing so, and employs little or no judgment and intelligence in the determination of where his money should be placed.

10. *Method of the speculator.*—In contradistinction the speculator employs a method. The profit of the speculator does not always imply a counterbalancing injury to the other party. What the normal speculator gains represents merely the difference between cost and selling price. He deals in "futures," for example, and buys up wheat crops from the small or large producers at a certain definite rate per bushel. The contract is a voluntary one and agreeable to both parties. The farmer in this case receives the prevailing market rate for his goods. Prices later rise, and, if the speculator unloads, he makes a profit. He performs a distributive function. The speculator assures the farmer the receipt of a definite sum and thus removes the element of risk from his shoulders. As recompense, the speculator gets the profit, if any exists, and a loss if the market goes against his expectations.

But it must be admitted that in actual practice much of what we may strictly define as speculation is carried on with a gambling intent. Even where the forms are legally those of speculation and all the objective phenomena are such, the intent and the social effects may be those of gambling. The rules of all exchanges forbid gambling as we have defined it:

But they make so easy a technical delivery of the property contracted for, that the practical effect of much speculation, in point of form legitimate, is not greatly different from that of gambling. Contracts to buy may be privately offset by contracts to sell. The offsetting may be done, in a systematic way, by clearing houses, or by "ring settlements." Where deliveries are actually made, property may be temporarily borrowed for the purpose. In these ways, speculation which has the legal traits of legitimate dealing may go on almost as freely as wagering, and may have most of the pecuniary and immoral effects of gambling on a large scale.[1]

11. *Evils of speculation.*—The great evil of speculation lies in the fact that persons who engage in it assume unnecessary risks and simply bet on fluctuations. There are too many amateurs in the business, too many unskilled adventurers without either the necessary capital or the mental equipment. The unskilled lose in this field as readily as in any other. They seek in a childish manner to make money without work, either mental or physical.

Possibly this evil of speculation on the part of ignorant outsiders can never be entirely abolished, but it can be greatly alleviated. In fact it is not as bad today as it was fifteen years ago; improvement is especially noticeable in the smaller markets like Duluth, Minneapolis and Kansas City. Moreover, many

[1] Report of Hughes Committee.

grain dealers have had gradual awakenings of conscience and have come to refuse absolutely speculative orders from outsiders who are not qualified to shoulder the risks involved. Others still cling to the old method of soliciting orders from any one and every one. However, the whole trend of opinion among the leaders of the organized exchanges is that many more safeguards should be established to prevent the "pikers" from taking "fliers."

12. *Excessive speculation.*—The charge is often made that speculation is harmful because of its great extent. A Congressional Committee, known popularly as the Pujo Committee, prepared tables showing that within any given period, certain stocks are "sold" on the Exchange at many times the amount of those stocks that are actually outstanding. One stock, for example, was dealt in six times over its amount in a single month. These figures are further fortified by the fact that dealings in certain stocks vastly exceeded transfers.

Such figures clearly indicate excessive speculation but there are counter considerations. Commonly these enormous transactions are confined to a few popular securities. It is the same on the London Stock Exchange and also to a certain extent true in Berlin and Paris. The great majority of stocks are never subject to such operations. As far as the fact that more stocks are sold than transferred on the company's books is concerned, it may be noted that many investors fear their ownership may be revealed if their stocks are transferred. In other words many operations, which appear on their face as being wholly speculative, are really of an investment nature.

13. *Effect of speculation on stocks.*—If dealings upon the various stock exchanges of the country were confined solely to the business of investors, it might be possible that a cut in the dividend of an investment issue would result in a hundred selling orders without a single buying order. Conditions upon the exchanges, however, do not follow any such one-sided plan. On any exchange there are always found both buyers and sellers for any stock which is listed. In this way one of the most useful functions of speculation is secured, that of counterbalance. The purchases made by the traders have a tendency to check or overcome the declines, and at the same time, give to the sellers an outlet for their stocks.

A pertinent illustration of this practice is shown in the case of a broker's customer who wished to dispose of some three hundred shares of Canadian Pacific. The market at the time was inactive with no sales of this issue. It was quoted at 185 bid and 190 asked, the bid coming from Berlin and the selling offer from Montreal. In an endeavor to secure the best possible price for his client, and having the necessary time in which to do so, the broker started in to work up interest in Canadian Pacific on the floor of the exchange. A man dealing in arbitrage raised the offer to 187 and made the asked price 189. At this juncture a well-known speculator made the market still narrow by quoting 188–189, whereupon another broker bid 188⅛ and offered to sell at 188⅞. The 300 shares were finally disposed of at 188¼, to a man who had no idea of buying Canadian Pacific one month previous, but who saw an opportunity for making a profit and was willing to buy a block of the stock. As a result of the interest aroused in this security by the broker, the customer received $975 more for the stock than he would have secured had there been but one buying order at the time when he wished to sell.

14. *Effects of speculation in general.*—The great services which speculation performs have been mentioned several times before. In briefest outline they are: (1) removing risk from other classes of producers; (2) steadying and leveling prices; (3) adjusting prices and regulating the flow of commodities between markets; (4) directing industries into profitable channels and liquidating those that are ill judged. Speculation is clearly the most elastic feature of the modern financial system. It takes the edge off panics and famines, for by putting up prices, it enforces economy ahead of future want, because the speculators discover a future shortage of grain before the consumer does. It tends also to prevent monopoly.

Speculation, moreover, softens the intensity with which great economic forces work by lengthening the time over which their influences extend. The speculator is accused of being a non-producer, a parasite. It is true that he does not produce goods. His main function is to bring about necessary adjustments in the business world. He hurries up and smooths out necessary processes. Thus he is really a producer of "time utility." As civilization expands and the means of communication increase, speculation has a tendency to destroy itself, because the field of certainty where business can be performed on an intelligent basis is always being widened. Thus, speculation is not permanent in any one branch of human activity.

15. *Survey of restrictions on speculation.*—In the Middle Ages, it was the common belief of philosophers that every commodity had a just and equitable price, and for one to charge a price above this mysterious point he incurred the displeasure of God and merited the punishment of man. English history is filled with examples of penalties inflicted upon merchants and tradesmen for attempting to carry out or in actually carrying out their plans to "bull" certain commodities. Men were imprisoned for storing away commodities in the hope that the market price might rise, and proclamations were issued by the sheriff as to the cause of the punishment administered, with an admonition concerning the future punishment that would be incurred upon a repetition of the act.

Among the earliest attempts to curb speculation, was the enactment of a law in 1707 licensing brokers and making illegal the transactions of unlicensed brokers. A year later, city ordinances were put into effect requiring brokers to give bonds to insure the proper and honest performance of their obligations.

After the South Sea scheme had ended in national disaster, considerable agitation arose to make impossible another calamity of this kind. The result was Sir John Barnard's "Act to Prevent the Infamous Practice of Stock Jobbing," with a preamble reading in this very interesting fashion:

Whereas great inconveniences have arisen and do daily arise, by the wicked, pernicious and destructive practice of stock-jobbing, whereby many of his Majesty's good subjects have been and are diverted from pursuing and exercising their lawful trades and vocations to the utter ruin of themselves and their families, to the great discouragement of industry and to the manifest detriment of trade and commerce, etc.

The essence of this piece of legislation was the prohibition of the practices now known as puts and calls, and what was most important of all, of short selling. However what seemed to be a panacea for existing evils was shattered by judicial decisions. The courts interpreted the law as applying to English public stocks only and this freed from the operation of the statute all foreign securities and all domestic securities not included in the category of "public."

John Barnard's law remained on the statute books, ineffective as it was, until 1860, when it was formally repealed. Seven years later the Leeman Act was passed with reference to the sale of bank stocks. It specified that the number of such certificates sold must be recorded and made known. Otherwise their sale was prohibited. Later, even this provision was repealed, and at the present time, no restrictions whatever exist with regard to speculation in the United Kingdom.

16. *Experience of Germany.*—In an attempt to place a curb upon short selling, the German government, in 1892, appointed a commission composed of government officials, merchants, bankers, manufacturers, professors of political economy and journalists to investigate the methods of the Berlin Exchange. This commission published in the following year a very conservative report in which it stated that the prohibition of short selling, called for by the popular clamor, would in its opinion, be harmful to German trade and interests. It was willing, however, to recommend the prohibition of speculation in industrials.

The bill recommended by the Commission was rejected by the Reichstag. This body, in 1896, passed a drastic law. The strong Agrarian party, believing that short selling lowered prices of agricultural products, insisted upon the prohibition of contracts for the future delivery of wheat and flour. Popular opinion also demanded an abatement of stock speculation. The law as passed prohibited all trading in futures in wheat and flour and in all industrial and mining shares. The law provided further that all persons who wished to speculate must register, and that speculative trades made by unregistered persons would be considered gambling contracts and therefore void. Public registry was required in an endeavor to prevent small speculators from assuming speculative risks, when they were unable to stand the losses such operations often entail.

The law failed of its purpose. Few persons registered. The small fry evaded it. Foreign brokers flocked to Berlin and established agencies for the purchase and sale of stocks in London, Paris, Amsterdam and New York. This resulted in the transfer of German capital to foreign markets, the passing into insignificance of the Berlin Exchange, and a general impairment of the financial standing of Germany.

Another defect in the law was found in the provision which required bankers and brokers to register, but which did not compel their customers to do so. As a result, the latter, thru different brokers, could speculate on both sides of the market, pocketing profits and "welshing" on losses. Men who had previously borne good reputations in numerous instances fell a prey to this temptation.

Still another defect in the law resulted in turning over to large banks much of the business previously done by independent houses. Persons wishing to make speculative investments in home securities applied directly to the banks, depositing satisfactory securities for their purchases. The banks, being largely promoters of new enterprises, could sell the securities to their depositors and thus finance enterprises with the deposits. In good times this business was profitable and safe, but since the claims of depositors were payable on demand, the practice in times of stringency was dangerous. As in the previous instance the law tended to encourage fraudulent practices since customers whose names were not on public register, could, if their speculation turned out badly, reclaim the collateral or cash which they deposited as security.

In 1908, the law was partially repealed by another law which gave the government discretionary power to authorize speculative transactions in industrial and mining securities of companies capitalized at not under $5,000,000. The law also abolished the Stock Exchange Register and declared that all persons whose names were in the "Handelsregister" (commercial directory), as well as all persons who dealt in securities, were legally bound by contracts made by them upon the Exchange. Furthermore, the law provided that while other persons were not bound by such contracts, yet on making deposits of cash or collateral security for speculative contracts, they could not reclaim them on the plea that the contract was illegal.

Germany still prohibits short selling in grain and flour. The effect, however, was different from what the supporters of this prohibition had anticipated. Without open markets and without continuous quotations, both buyers and sellers are placed at a disadvantage while prices fluctuate more than before the passage of the law.

17. *Why the German law failed.*—Dr. Henry C. Emery commented on the repeal of the law before the Senate Committee on Banking and Currency, February 11, 1914, and explained why it was ineffectual in carrying out its intended purpose. In his

testimony he introduced the following quotation from an earlier statement on his part:

(1) Fluctuations in prices have been increased rather than diminished. The corrective influence of the bear side of the market having been restricted, the tendency to an inflated bull movement was increased in times of prosperity. This in turn made the danger of radical collapse all the greater in proportion as the bull movement was abnormal. The greater funds needed to carry stocks on a cash basis further increased the danger when collapse was threatened. The result was an increased incentive to reckless speculation and manipulation. Says the report of 1907: "The dangers of speculation have been increased, the power of the market to resist one-sided movements has been weakened, and the possibilities of missing inside information have been enlarged."

(2) The money market has been increasingly demoralized thru the greater fluctuations in demand for funds to carry speculative cash accounts. The New York method is held in abhorrence by German financiers, who attribute to it in large part the wild fluctuations in New York call rates, the frequent "money panics," and the tendency to reckless "jobbery." In proportion as the new Berlin methods approached the cash delivery system of New York, these evils have appeared there.

(3) The business of the great banks has been increased at the expense of their smaller rivals. The prohibition of trading for the account made it difficult for the latter to carry out customers' orders, because the new methods required large supplies of both cash and securities. Furthermore, an increasing share of the business of the large banks came to be settled by offsets among their customers, and the actual exchange transactions became a proportionately small part of the total transfers.

(4) This has a twofold effect. Business within the banks is done on the basis of exchange prices, but these became

more fluctuating and subject to manipulation as the quantity of exchange dealings were diminished and were concentrated in a few hands. The advantages of a broad open market were lost. The object of the act had been to lessen the speculative influence over industrial undertakings. Its effect was to increase it.

(5) Finally, the effect of interference, increased cost, and legal uncertainty was to drive business to foreign exchanges and diminish the power of the Berlin Exchange in the field of international finance. The number of agencies, of foreign houses increased four or five fold, and much German capital flowed to other centers, especially London, for investment or speculation. This in turn weakened the power of the Berlin money market, so that even the Reichsbank has at times felt its serious effects.[1]

18. *Conclusion.*—It is apparent that thus far laws to suppress speculation have been failures. The Cotton Futures Act of 1915, the most recent law to regulate speculation, as explained in Chapter XVI is in no sense prohibitive, but it is designed to abolish certain purely technical abuses. Further legislation is more likely to take a similar form than to attempt any general suppression of speculation as a whole.

REVIEW

How do you distinguish between investment and speculation?

How do you account for the stigma which in past years has attached to the term "speculator"?

What in your opinion constitutes legitimate speculation?

What elements vital in all business are particularly important in speculation?

Assume that you have $1,000 on which you wish to secure profit. What type of stocks would you consider and why?

[1] *Yale Review*, May, 1908.

BENEFITS AND EVILS OF SPECULATION

Take the financial page of any reliable daily, as the *New York Times,* and work out "paper profits" on a few stocks; that is, determine some stocks which you would buy and test your judgment by the quotations for those stocks concerning a period of days or weeks.

CHAPTER XXI

INFLUENCES THAT GOVERN STOCK PRICES

1. *How far is speculation scientific?*—The future is always uncertain, but in so far as future movement of stock market prices can be foreseen, speculation is scientific. No system has ever been devised to foretell all fluctuations in prices, and the fate of the stock speculator who believes his method to be infallible is likely to prove like that of the gambler at Monte Carlo who endeavors by means of elaborate calculations to work out a system of beating the bank.

A moment's reflection will show that speculation cannot, on account of its very nature, be reduced to an exact science. At the end of the preceding chapter it was pointed out that as knowledge in any particular field becomes more precise, exact and complete, speculation tends to destroy itself. The same idea may be expressed in a more colloquial manner as follows: If speculation could be reduced to an exact science everybody would be right and there would be nobody left to trade with. In other words, if speculation could be reduced to an exact science—and many fakirs and charlatans pretend that it can—there would be no risks or uncertainties, and therefore no speculation.

In the first chapter strong emphasis was laid on the fact that stock exchanges serve the purpose of commercial barometers. They anticipate, or "discount" the swings of trade, the ebb and flow of prosperity. Now if the stock market is a barometer, how can any one pretend to foretell its movements? To draw up a rule to cover all the possible movements of stocks is like finding an instrument that will predict the movements of a barometer.

Countless forces play upon any large market. Each share of stock bought or sold affects the whole, and who can say why a particular share is bought or sold? Each loaf of bread eaten affects the price of wheat. These considerations are what a great economist has called "the imperceptibles of commerce." Who can weigh them all? The speculator must make a careful study of a large number of conditions that are only remotely connected with the earning power of any company, in order to be able to understand the fluctuations which occur in the prices of its securities. It has been aptly said that hardly an event occurs in the world which does not have some effect upon the prices of securities. Nevertheless the effort to foresee the future and make profit by so doing enters more or less into all business activities, and it can be proved that stock prices do not fluctuate so irregularly but that they can be foreseen, provided the speculator has the proper mental equipment and knowledge. Those who do possess this knowledge and equipment are, however, comparatively few.

2. *Influences affecting speculation.*—It will be noticed that stocks vary in price not only from year to

year, but from month to month, day to day and hour to hour. And it is a matter of common knowledge that stocks which are of the same apparent worth, and which pay the same dividends, differ enormously in price.

The price of a stock at a given time is the result of the interaction of the desires and necessities of buyer and seller, representing demand and supply respectively. Free bargaining takes place in the open market, and prices move according as these desires and necessities change from time to time. We have already seen that speculation arises largely from fluctuating property values, and it may be added that fluctuation in the value of property is the underlying, altho by no means the only cause of price movements of stocks. There are two great groups of influences determining the desires and necessities of buyers and sellers, which will here be considered.

3. *Extrinsic influences.*—Accidental, speculative, temporary and artificial factors may be called extrinsic influences. First, there are wars, fires, earthquakes, floods and wrecks on the sea and land. Then there are the artificial influences, including manipulation, one of the minor factors. There are also the speculative influences, which are more important. Speculation is itself due to fluctuations in the value of property and the course of the prices of stocks or produce depends to no little extent upon the volume and character of the speculation. This general relationship is often referred to in the market as the

"technical" conditions, which will now be discussed.

4. *Technical conditions.*—A man's physical condition depends principally upon certain influences such as amount and kind of food, and amount and kind of work and exercise. But if he once becomes very strong or very ill, this fact itself tends to affect later conditions of health. To change the simile; the movements of a machine are partly governed by the laws of the machine itself, its construction, materials, strength and defects, as well as by the steam or electricity which is the outside motive power. To draw an analogy, stock prices are, in the main, governed by fluctuating values. But once speculation sets in, prices are often largely determined, for the time being at least, by the laws of speculation itself—in other words, by "technical" conditions.

The speculator who has bought, may sell in order to close his transactions. When a large number of speculators have bought "long" the market is threatened with a large amount of sales which must sooner or later be made—and *vice versa* when speculators are generally short purchases must eventually be made to "cover."

The former condition is called an "overbought" market and the latter an "oversold" market. Both constitute a species of unstable equilibrium which is easily disturbed and always is distributed sooner or later. It is to this development that we must ascribe many of the sharp movements downward in a period of advancing prices and the sharp rallies in "bear" markets.

Experience shows that the price movement in either direction is constantly overrunning itself in this way and reacting, and it is an axiom in Wall Street that reaction is more or less proportioned to the action that it follows. Many people claim that on a fair average reaction will be somewhat about half the action previous.

The reactions that come from these various speculative endeavors constitute the technical condition. Thus, a stock may decline for a while wholly because of speculative or technical considerations, irrespective of any question of value. For example, a weak pool may boom the stock, and banks may later on call loans on the pool and force it to dump its holdings overboard.

In the discussion of speculative or technical conditions we may also include the question of whether the supply of stock in the Street is ample or limited. If there is a small supply in brokers' hands, speculators may easily shove up the price. Of course the fact that the floating supply is small is often attributable to the fact that the stock possesses intrinsic value and has therefore been bought up by discerning investors.

Last, among the extrinsic influences are those of a strictly temporary nature, such as false or unimportant rumors. Certain groundless fears or hopes play a part, at least temporarly, in the fixing of prices.

It will serve no purpose to examine further into extrinsic factors that govern stock prices. Because of them, speculation can never become an exact science, for even the most seasoned and experienced speculator can never foretell what effect these factors will have. Often their effect is just the opposite of what experience and reason would lead one to expect. Only professionals can make a living by the kind of speculation that rests upon profiting by such changes. They are able to do so only because they have no commissions to pay and do not try to predict these unexpected price movements, and merely use their exceptional facilities to take advantage of them as quickly as possible. The average man in conducting his stock transactions, is sure of only one fact—that prices, in the long run, are governed by the changing values of property.

5. *Importance of extrinsic influences.*—The importance of extrinsic influences is well illustrated by a letter of Ex-President H. G. S. Noble of the New York Stock Exchange. This letter, which appeared in the *New York Times* of August 3, 1915, was Mr. Noble's reply to an editorial in the *Times* suggesting that the Stock Exchange suppress excited speculation in war stocks.

In the interest of arriving at a clear understanding of this question the following facts must be borne in mind: Any event tending to disturb the equilibrium of security values brings about a period of speculation which lasts until the equilibrium has been readjusted. The greater and the more far-reaching this disturbing event happens to be, the longer and the more excited will be the resultant speculation. A historic example of this can be found in the experiences of our Civil War. That great national convulsion, accompanied by a suspension of specie payments and the issue of paper money, created a speculation of unprecedented magnitude. The Stock Exchange of those days was a small organization doing business in a primitive way, and when the great war speculation came, it refused to enlarge its facilities to meet the new conditions, and thus virtually did what was in its power to impede the rising speculative tide. The result was that speculation, finding itself choked off from the regular organized channels, proceeded to form new and unorganized channels for itself, and a great continuous, and unregulated market was established in the open street to carry on the business that the daily "calls" of the stock exchange were incompetent to handle. The mania for trading on the war news of the day was such that the market did not close in the afternoon hours; but was transferred uptown to the lobby of the old Fifth Avenue Hotel, where it continued during the evening. Out of this unorganized market there grew the "Open Board of Brokers," which the old stock exchange was finally obliged to unite with in 1869.

At the present time we are witnessing events similar in principle to these happenings of fifty years ago. The great world-war has shaken the accepted adjustment of values like an earthquake. As a consequence of this there is likely to be speculative excitement in many fields. One of the first signs of it has been the rise in the stocks of all companies obtaining war contracts. This rise has not been confined to securities listed on the Exchange, for its most violent manifestations have shown themselves in unlisted properties. The stock of the Du Pont Powder Company, which was selling at about 170, has risen to 700 and fallen back to about 600.

6. *Intrinsic influences.*—That group of factors that are termed intrinsic influences is more susceptible of analysis than the first. The following classification will help to make clear what influences govern the intrinsic value or worth of a stock. Each of the headings given will be treated separately.

(a) Business and money market conditions, including the income-producing capacity of capital as represented by other forms of investment.

(b) The profitableness or fluctuations in profits of the general class of business engaged in. Some industries never make spectacular profits, but there are times when others, notably copper, oil, zinc and other mining companies, make huge profits, almost irrespective of the inherent soundness of the companies themselves.

(c) Management and character of the company— its financial structure; proportion of assets to capital; past, present and prospective earnings. This may be considered solely in relation to the company's position in its own special trade, as well as in connection with business and money market conditions.

(d) Anticipated or potential profits. Prices of stocks depend as much on these as on present or actual profits. If the dividends are limited, as in the case of many preferred stocks, then the primary price factor is the security of the dividend.

7. *Business and money market conditions.*—The whole body economic may be likened to an organism, in which every organ must perform its function if health and efficiency are to be maintained. If thru some mishap one organ becomes clogged, the whole organism suffers, to a greater or less extent, according to the nature of the trouble. In a similar manner, if there is a total or partial failure of crops, the stocks of railroads, milling and other industrial corporations fall in price. A decrease in a crop involves a corresponding decrease in the revenue derived from its transportation, and also less work for the mills. This is probably the simplest illustration that can be given of the "general business conditions" that affect stock prices.

The reader will rightly conclude that if, in order to forecast stock prices, it is necessary to survey the whole field of business, including the income-producing capacity of other forms of investment,[1] he has no light undertaking. He will realize the fact all the more vividly when he knows that this set of factors is only one of many that must be taken into consideration.

8. *Business barometers.*—Among the more important indications of the general business situation are: size and conditions of crops, railroad earnings and traffic returns, bank clearings, pig iron production, exports and imports, trend of commodity prices, probabilities of legislation on tariffs, trusts and other government regulation of business.

How the prices of stocks vary is shown by the chart on page 316. In this chart is given the average for each month of the highest daily prices of twenty railroads and twelve industrial stocks since January, 1906.[2]

In charts of this character the monthly average of

[1] Capital moves more or less freely from one form of investment to another, and if it yields more in real estate or private enterprise than in stocks, it tends to go to the more profitable channels.

[2] The stocks included in this compilation are *railroads*. Atchison, B. & O., Canadian Pacific, Ches. & Ohio, Lehigh Valley, Delaware & Hudson, Erie, Illinois Central, K. C. South, Northern Pacific, Louisville & Nashville, N. Y. Central, New Haven, Norfolk & Western, St. Paul, Pennsylvania, Reading, Southern Pacific, Southern Railway, Union Pacific.

Industrials: American Smelting, American Car & Foundry, American Sugar Refining, Anaconda, Central Leather, General Electric, General Motors, National Lead, Peoples Gas, U. S. Rubber, U. S. Steel, U. S. Steel Preferred.

After October, 1915, the General Motors is omitted from the industrial list and the average given is that of eleven stocks.

the lowest price is frequently given. This information is, however, only valuable when the charts are drawn on a larger scale than can be employed here. Where the scale is large the eye can grasp the range of variation, but on a small scale chart this cannot be done. The lines show peaks and valleys, as well as minor movements. The lines are broken for the months when the Stock Exchange was closed.

Now it is a well-known fact—one which the chart will serve to emphasize—that stock prices fluctuate more or less with varying business conditions. As time goes on, men will probably be able more accurately to forecast these conditions. This is indicated by the progress that has already been made in the study of the causes of crises, depressions and panics. It appears from these studies that there is a certain amount of uniformity in the intervals between crises and in certain of the accompanying phenomena. This fact has led to the suggestion that a law of their periodicity might be formulated. It is said that crises tend to recur, and that prosperity, crises and depression succeed each other with such regularity as to warrant the use of the word cycle in this connection.

Some of those most familiar with the subject attribute the ebb and flow of business to psychological causes. Others emphasize the action of certain forces of nature, which, they say, determine the crop yield and thus affect values. Still others, and by far the greatest number, emphasize the structure of modern life, the interdependence of its various elements, and

316   SPECULATION

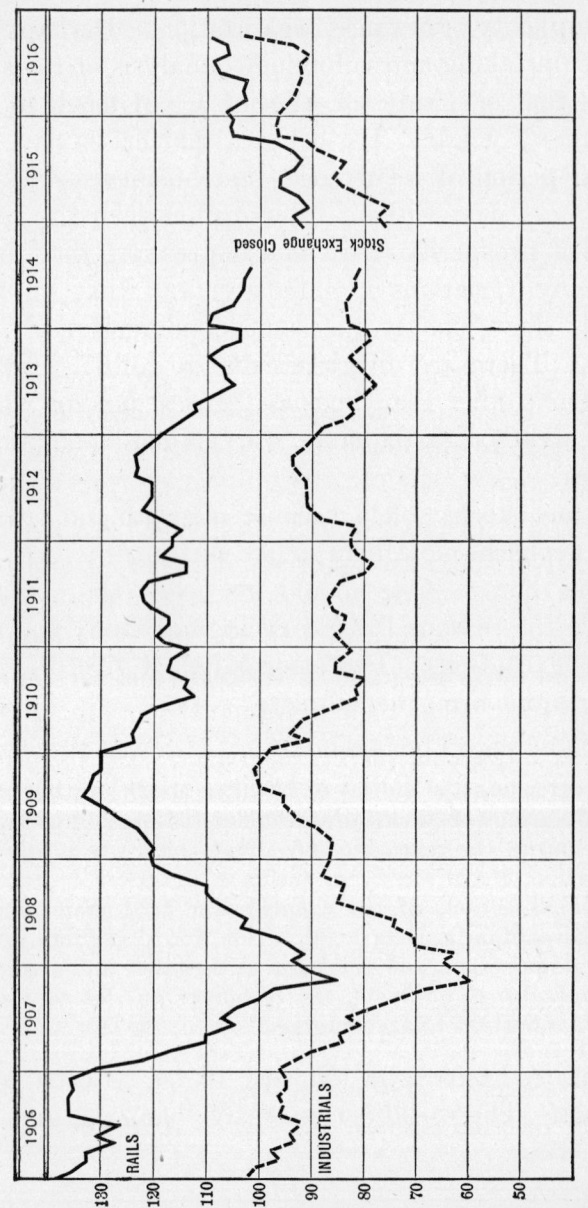

FIGURE 2. MONTHLY AVERAGE OF HIGHEST PRICES OF 20 RAILROADS AND 12 INDUSTRIAL STOCKS

WHAT GOVERNS STOCK PRICES

the complexity of business organization. Perhaps the most painstaking and voluminous analysis of the subject is that of Professor Wesley C. Mitchell in his "Business Cycles." He believes that crises have no regular period of recurrence, that business cycles do not always pass without interruption thru the same round of prosperity, crisis and depression, that there are many variations in intensity, and that no two periods show exactly the same combination of elements. There are diversities due to influences that arise from other than business causes, among which are the weather, earthquakes, war, epidemics and tariff changes.

To buy stocks solely because a graph indicates a certain cyclical movement is like putting the cart before the horse. One should go below the surface, analyze the reasons for the cycle, and study the numerous exceptions. Professor Mitchell gives the following opinion on the subject:

> This is scarcely one of the suggestions made for bettering or extending the indices of business conditions but calls to mind various obstacles which hinder the getting of trustworthy data—the reluctance of private interests to divulge information, the diversity of business practices in various trades and sections of the country, the continual changes going forward in business organization, the alterations in the relative importance, and still more in the kinds and qualities, of manufactured products, the technical puzzles of statistical classification and averaging.

That is, business is too vast to be reduced to a formula. The world is constantly changing, and the changes make it impossible to forecast the future accurately with only the past to judge by.

9. *Management and character of the company.*—If we consider the third great class of intrinsic factors, i.e., the company itself, it will be found that the price movements of many stocks, even whole groups of stocks, have little or no relation to any other influences. Thus, the shares of Standard Oil companies have gone up, during good times and bad, simply because of superlatively good management and an ever increasing demand for the products, whether times were prosperous or dull. On the other hand, express company stocks have declined for several years because in this industry the government regulation of rates and the installation of a parcel post service had reduced profits.

Usually even those stocks that are rising and falling because of the condition of the companies themselves, feel, to some extent at least, the great market movements which affect all securities. An extreme case of unusual, tho temporary, conditions, is that cited in a newspaper during the bull domination of the market in 1916.

If the speculator in stocks last week had taken no thought of intervention in Mexico, German submarines, Presidential politics, international diplomacy or the grand strategy of the war, but had bothered his mind with nothing more than the humdrum things of life he would have fared better than any of the wiseacres. Were his mind on sugar, he could have converted the demand for the necessity into a profit of 13 points in the stock of the South Porto Rico Sugar Company. Shirts would have given him a profit of 7 points thru the medium of the Manhattan Shirt Company.

In the same strain the article continues with illustrations of how given the upward trend of the market, the speculator, by means of the corporation stocks mentioned, could have drawn profits from collars, tea, tobacco, automobiles and other commodities.

10. *Limitations.*—It must not be assumed that any branch of knowledge concerning the movement of stock prices is complete as regards the temporary or minor movements. This statement applies just as much to the man who considers himself an authority on a particular corporation as it does to amateurs who try to "play the market" by means of "tape-reading" or the use of a chart.

11. *Potential factors.*—It may be well to amplify the statement that prices depend as much on potential or anticipated profits as on present or actual ones. It is often said that future earnings rather than present dividends make prices. In the previous chapter, reference was made to the Wall Street maxim that for a stock to be a good investment it must be a good speculation. Of course this is only another way of saying, what has already been emphasized, that the stock market acts as a barometer. Speculators attempt to anticipate, to foresee. The very meaning of the word speculation indicates that prices depend more upon future than upon present conditions. It is the future of which the speculator seeks to take advantage. Ex-president Noble of the New York Stock Ex-

change, in the letter from which we have already quoted, writes as follows:

> We are told by one conservative publication that the profits upon which these violent changes in price are based have not yet been secured. Speculation is always an act of anticipation, and if profits were secured and big dividends established investors would take these properties out of the market and speculation would disappear.

It follows, from these considerations, that stock prices often seem to act in a contrary manner. They decline as a result of good news and rush up when there is news of strikes and other supposed calamities. This is simply because the market discounts the future.

The various influences that have been described interact and produce a complex which is the price level of the moment. Now one set of influences seems to predominate, now another. One stock appears to react to this influence, another stock to that. Even where there is a close correspondence between intrinsic values, or earning power, and an upward movement of prices, it must not be inferred that values and prices change simultaneously or in unison.

Altho, as has been noted, the prices of stocks are influenced by a multitude of complicated influences, it is safe to lay down the general principle that values tend to fix prices for periods of time long enough to eliminate temporary disturbances. Price and value continually tend to approach each other. The exact real value, the absolute intrinsic value, nearly always remains intangible, indefinable and unascertainable.

But as the stock market represents the largest and best single body of collective opinion obtainable in regard to business, we find that the line of prices is never long or very far apart from that of values. Thus, during the period 1897 to 1902, the lowest prices of twenty railway stocks were less than 42, while the highest average price rose to nearly 118 on May 1, 1901. The difference between the lowest and the highest for the period was 76, which represented an increase of 180 per cent. Mr. Pratt uses this as an illustration in substantiation of his principle that this upward movement of stock corresponds very accurately to every possible test of value. He points out, for example, that during this same period the banks increased their clearings by 175 per cent. Furthermore, the value of the railroads, as represented by their surplus earnings available for dividends after all fixed charges and operating expenses had been paid, increased about as fast as the price. According to the reports of the Interstate Commerce Commission, the net earnings increased from $492 to $1,190 per mile, or approximately 140 per cent, while the dividends actually paid out increased from $484 to $725 per mile. This comparison shows that the increase in surplus earnings available for dividends was not so much less than the increase in price as reflected on the New York Stock Exchange.

12. *Classification of price movements.*—One of the best known classifications of price movements is that of Charles H. Dow, one of the founders of the *Wall*

Street Journal, who was himself credited with being a very successful speculator. This classification is based on the principle, generally accepted as sound, that in the long run prices are governed by the intrinsic value of the security, and the variations are the result of extraneous influences. Dow's classification is threefold:

1.—The "primary movement"—governed by intrinsic values,—which is the most powerful of the three.

2.—The "secondary movement," or the "swing"—governed by manipulation, by current reports and by the market machinery.

3.—The "tertiary movement"; in other words, the daily fluctuations in the market, which are caused by the most trifling circumstances—rumor, the operations of room traders or some other similar influence.

The "swing" may continue for weeks or even months. Prices of securities may be artificially inflated or depressed by the operations of a powerful syndicate, or clique, the members of which have created unnatural conditions in carrying out a policy for which they have banded together.

Mr. Dow claims that the primary movement, or that based on value, lasts the longest and is ultimately the controlling factor in speculation, as it is in investment. The only speculators who have had any long-continued success in the market are those who follow the primary movement. They disregard daily fluctuations and carry their securities with a very heavy

WHAT GOVERNS STOCK PRICES

margin, or pay for them outright, waiting for the real value of the property to be reflected in the price of the security. Those who gamble upon the daily fluctuations or who stake their hopes upon the success of manipulative efforts sooner or later come to grief.

The primary movement in either direction usually covers a considerable period of time, and often it is several years before its effect is consummated. A careful study of the variation in the prices of securities over a period of years shows that at more or less regular intervals, averaging perhaps four or five years, there is a reversal in the prices. Starting from a low point, securities will advance with some degree of steadiness to a high point, and will then decline with more or less suddenness. Altho during the years while the securities are running this range there will, of course, be many retrogressions, nevertheless the general tendency is unmistakably apparent. These more or less regular intervals of change are spoken of as "cycles" of advancing or declining prices.

The late Sereno S. Pratt, in his "Work of Wall Street" treats the subject of market movements in concise, picturesque language:

A bicycle rider starts over a new road. The actual distance is twenty miles, but his cyclometer, at the end, registers thirty, owing to the fact that he has not traveled in a straight line, but has gone from one side to the other in an endless succession of curves in order to avoid teams and ruts, and perhaps because he has been maliciously misdirected. In a like manner, prices travel thru an endless succession of daily curves and fluctuations and sometimes miss the road altogether, and, misled by manipulation, travel a long distance astray, but in the end they arrive at the true destination-value.

In this Text frequent reference has been made to the fact that the greatest evil of speculation is the presence of unfit amateurs who regard speculation as an easy way of getting money without working. It also has been pointed out that the risks taken by properly equipped professional speculators are probably no greater than those necessary in all lines of business. The speculator with capital as extensive as that of the large manufacturer and with the same expert knowledge, often makes reasonable profits. Probably in no other business are conservative methods and abundant capital so much needed.

Unquestionably the general public does not make money by active, in-and-out trading, and keep it. To attempt to "catch the turns"—that is, to follow every eddy, tide and swirl—is ruinous, except, as already stated, for professional floor traders. There are periods when even "the public" wins, especially those persons known as the long-pull, speculative investors. At other times even the professionals lose wholesale. Often they "fight a rise" and sell short and subsequent events prove that they should have bought instead of selling.

Another disputed question is whether the great capitalists, men like the late E. H. Harriman and J. P. Morgan, make large profits thru speculation. The probabilities are that many such men do speculate

WHAT GOVERNS STOCK PRICES

successfully, but in connection with constructive work along other lines. On the other hand, it often happens that costly speculative mistakes have been made by those who would seem to be best fitted to forecast the future. Frequently corporation managers and directors and bankers are actually too close to corporate affairs and too much occupied with details to get a clear view of speculative possibilities. They cannot see the forest for the trees.

13. *Mistakes of speculators.*—By reason of the difficulties which surround their operations, speculators are prone to fall into many errors of judgment. Perhaps the most conspicuous of these mistakes are:

1. Failure to reckon chances properly.
2. Overtrading as to amount.
3. Trading too often.
4. Overconfidence.

The chances for the speculator are not, as many think, even. The market goes up and down, it is true, but to enter it he must pay commissions and interest. By reason of these factors a slight change in the market against the speculator causes him more loss than he would gain from an equal change in his favor.

To assume risks not justified by the capital of the speculator is one of the most common mistakes, and one of the most frequent causes of loss. Trading on very narrow margins forces the speculator frequently to take a loss which would have been avoided had he not aspired to too large a profit, and made his transactions on a broader margin.

Akin to the failing above noted is the tendency to too frequent trading. Men become obsessed with the desire to take advantage of every turn of the market. The result is that they act too frequently for their actions to be well considered. Speculation, a perilous occupation at the best, leads inevitably to ruin unless it is based on careful, close analysis of all available information.

Experience shows, moreover, that speculators are reluctant to take losses, they are disposed to let them grow, tho they are quick and eager to take profits even when they are small. They are sanguine of temperament and lack the resolution to follow the familiar maxim of the street, "Cut your losses—let your profits run." But this is not the only case where traders exhibit the overconfidence which too often brings disaster in its trail. The only confidence on which it is safe to rely is that rooted in knowledge, and the present Text has been written in vain unless it has made clear, that no one can be ever quite sure that he has all the knowledge necessary to a true appreciation of just how prices will move in the future.

14. *Qualities necessary for success.*—The task of the speculator is difficult and many pitfalls beset his path. To accomplish it with a fair degree of success requires special qualifications and traits of mind. Mr. Woodlock has summarized the desirable qualities of the successful speculator as follows:

First: The speculator must have a clear idea of what he is trying to do, i.e., he must have some clear notion of what he expects the market to do and how he expects to operate so as to profit thereby. This implies original knowledge of stock values, money values, and speculative market conditions.

Second: The more moderate his operations in proportion to his capital, the greater his prospect of ultimate success.

Third: He must have the strength of mind to resist the temptation of cupidity, and the patience to wait until the chances favor him, sacrificing many apparent opportunities for the sake of safety.

Fourth: He must be more vigilant as to his losses than as to his profits, and inexorable in accepting a loss whenever he is in serious doubt as to his position, never allowing a large loss to accumulate.

With such disposition, with continual application of mind and careful study of financial winds and waves, and with abundant capital, speculation can be scientifically carried on as a profession. But it is a most difficult profession to learn —and not an easy way of making money.

It might be added that the speculator must be cool under excitement and often oblivious to all manner of verbal and printed advice. If he has other affairs to look after, he had better keep away from Wall Street. To be successful in this hazardous and thrilling occupation requires, what can be described in no other way, cool nerve. Otherwise a sanitarium will be the only outcome. It is perhaps a characteristic of many Wall Street men to be nervous and excited over trivial affairs, but to receive the news of great pecuniary losses and gains with the impassible calm of the proverbial Indian. That is the temperament needed by the market operator.

Special fitness in both character and knowledge is

essential to speculative success. The fact that countless persons, many of them well satisfied with their previous achievements along wholly different lines, have failed in speculation only proves the contention.

REVIEW

Why cannot speculation be made scientific?

In buying stocks what classes of influences would interest you?

What aspects of business are shown in a "business barometer"? Which are the more important?

What force have potential factors on price? What influence does value exert on price?

How may price movements of securities be classified?

INDEX

Agriculture, Produce Exchanges, 2, 177–212; Percentage of exchange deals, 4; "Future" trading, 180–86, 195–206; Grain elevators, and receipts, 186–87, 196–99; Inspection and grading, 187–94; Hedging on futures, 195–99; Weld on "Marketing of Farm Products," 200–01; Farmers, and "Grain Exchange Facts," 201–06; Prices of staples and influences that govern, 206–10; Chicago Board of Trade methods, 213–24; Grain exchanges and specialties, 224–26; Cotton markets, and N. Y. Exchange, 227–41

Arbitrage,
New York and London quotations, 108–11; Produce exchanges adjust prices, 201

Averaging, Mitigates losses, 107–08

Banks and the Security Market, 62–79;
Loans to brokers, 62–64; Time loans, 64–65; Call loans, 65–66, 67; Bank loan methods, 66–67; Collateral for loans, 67–69; Reserve and speculation, 69–70; Certification and the National Bank Act, 71–73; One-day unsecured loans, 73; Interest rates and call money, 75–76; Call loan system, 77–78; Money rates affect stocks, 78–79

Barnard, John,
Comments on short selling, 94; Law to prevent stock jobbing, 299

Benefits and Evils of Speculation, 284–304;
Investment, speculation and gambling confused terms, 284–87; Income and profit, 288–89; Purchase methods denote difference of intent, 289–91; Gambling versus speculation, 292–94; Pujo Committee on excessive speculation, 295; Effects of spec-

Benefits—continued
ulation, 296–98; Preventive measures, and John Barnard's law, 289–90; Germany curbs short selling on Berlin Exchange, 300–02; Henry C. Emery on German prohibition, 302–04
See also Speculation

Berlin Bourse, Speculation and government regulation, 167–68, 205–06, 300–04

Board, or Stock exchange, 29

Boston Stock Exchange, Commission rates, 144–46

Brokers,
Classes of, on N. Y. Stock Exchange, 21–26; Margin trading, 50–59; Legal relation to customer, 60; Sources of loans, 62–67; Short selling transactions, 85–100; Failures and consequences, 115–17; Commission rates on Curb Market, 138–39; and Jobbers, on London Exchange, 156–59; Trading rights on Paris Bourse, 170–74

Brown, A. O., and Company, Stock manipulations of, 265

Bucket Shops—Abuses of Speculation, 242–52
Gambling features, 244; Wisconsin prohibition law, 245; Extent of, 246; Margins, 247; Unscrupulous men and methods, 247–49; Federal action to prevent, 249; Evil effects upon market, 250–52
See also Benefits and Evils of Speculation

Call Loans, 62, 65–66, 67;
Interest and renewal rates, 75–76; Advantages of, 77–78

Calls,
Short selling methods of, 101, 102, 103–04; Factors that govern privileges, 105–06

Canadian Exchanges,
Stock sales on, 143; Future trading abolished in Manitoba, 205

INDEX

Chicago Board of Trade, 213–26;
Foremost grain market in world, 213–14; Grain houses, 214; Cash and future trading, 215–17; Sparling on payments, 218–19; U. S. decision on delivery, 219–21; Ringing out, 220–21; Clearing house for contracts, 221–22; Government and management, 223–24

Chicago Stock Exchange,
Important stocks of, 146–47

Clearing House,
Delivery price and speculative stocks, 112–14; Paris Bourse methods, 174; Settling contracts, 221–22; Chicago Board of Trade methods, 221–22

Conant, Charles A., on Investment and speculation, 285

Consolidated Stock Exchange of New York, Operations and history of, 140–42

Continental Bourses, 165–75;
And American exchanges, 165–66; Berlin Bourse regulates speculation, 166–68, 300–04; Paris Bourse under government control, 168–69; Membership, and methods of Paris Bourse, 269–75; Produce exchanges, 178, 180, 205–06; Germany's attempt to regulate speculation, 300–04

Corners—Speculative Feats and Excesses, 271–83;
How worked, 272–73; Classes of, 273–74; Northern Pacific case, 274; Harlem Railway corner, 275–78; Gold corner of 1869, 278–79; United Copper Corner of 1907, 279–80; In cotton and wheat, 280–282; Leiter speculation 282–83

Cotton Exchanges,
See New York Cotton Exchange *and* New Orleans Coton Exchange

Cotton Futures Act, 233–35, 304

Curb Market,
Location and methods, 130–32; Organization and membership, 132–33; Relation to Stock Exchange, 134–35; Functions of, 135–39; Valuable stocks listed, 137; Commission rates, 138–39

Dow, Charles H., Classifies price movements, 321–23

Emery, Henry C., Comments on repeal of German law, 302–04

European War Affects Exchanges,
Stock Exchanges closed, 10–11; Foreign securities listed, 31; Baltimore and Pittsburgh activity, 146; European markets, 149–51; Grain supplies and exports, 207–08; Effect on bucket shops, 248; Noble on war stocks, 311–12

Federal Reserve Act, Banks and brokerage loans, 64, 77

Foreign Securities,
Trade in since the war, 31–32; Arbitrage, New York and London prices, 108–11; War's effect on London Stock Exchange, 150–51

Futures,
U. S. Bureau of Corporations defines, 180–81, 185; "Contract" trading, 181–85; Legality of contracts, 185–86; Warehouse receipts and bank loans, 186–87; Hedging, on produce exchanges, 195–99; Speculation steadies prices, 199–209; Chicago Board of Trade methods, 213–24; Cotton Futures Act, 231–36

Gambling, Relation to speculation, 94, 292–94
See also Benefits and Evils of Speculation
See also Bucket Shops

Gibbes, H. A., on Speculative cotton prices, 237–38

Government,
Control of securities issued, 32–33; British rates on government securities, 162; Stock regulations on German Bourse, 167–68; Control of Paris Bourse, 168–69; Wisconsin law on bucket shops, 245; Federal control of bucket shops, 246, 249; Manipulation prohibited, 262–63, 268–69; Germany's experience, 300–04

Hedging,
"Future" trading in grain, 195–99; Insuring grain orders, 217; Cotton Futures Act, 233–36

Huebner, Grover S., Favors grain inspection systems, 189

Huebner, S. S.,
On Organized markets, 7; Justifies short selling, 95–96

INDEX

Influences that **Govern Stock Prices**, 306-28;
Science of speculation, 306-07; Extrinsic influences, 308-11; Intrinsic factors, 312-13, 318; Business conditions, and charts, 313-17; Potential factors, 319-21; Price classification, 321-23; Capitalists who speculate, 324-25; Woodlock on successful speculation, 326-27

Inspection and Grading,
Arguments in favor of system, 187-90; State bureaus for, 190; Variety of grades, 191; Federal law of 1916, 192; Methods and objects of, 193-94; Cotton grades and the Futures Act, 232-35

Interest Rates,
Brokers' charge on margins, 55-56; On call loans, 75-76; Short sale transactions, 89-91, 93; Consolidated charges, 142; Commissions on Boston Exchange, 145-46; British tariff to regulate, 162; Paris Bourse commissions, 173-74; Chicago Board of Trade, 222-23

Investment
See Benefits and Evils of Speculation

Jobbers, Importance of, on London Stock Echange, 156-59

Keene, James R., and Hocking Pool manipulation, 264, 266-68

Listing Securities on the Stock Exchange, 29-49;
What listing means, 29-30; Classes of securities admitted, 31; Committees on applications, 32; Government should determine merit, 32-33; Supervision ceases after listing, 33; Exchange does not guarantee securities, 34; Listing promotes marketability, 34-37; Bank loans on listed securities, 37; Typical listing, 37-49

Loans, Banks and the security market, 62-79

London Stock Exchange, and New York Exchange, 149; War's effect upon, 149-51; International trade, 151; Lombard Street, 152; First home of, 153; Organiza-

London Exchange—continued
tion and membership, 153-56; Distinction between broker and jobber, 156-58; Publicity and ticker service, 159; Fortnightly settlements, 160-61; Commission charges, 162; Listing securities, 163

"Long" and "Short" Sellers, 84
See also Short Selling

Manipulation,
J. G. Milburn's definition of, 253-54; Excerpt from address on, 255-56; Excessive speculation, 257; False rumors on stock prices, 257; Pools, 258; Directors control corporations, 258-59; Wash sales, 259-60; Matching orders, 260-61, 265-69; State laws to prohibit, 262-63; James R. Keene's operations, 264; A. O. Brown & Co.'s failure, 265; Pujo Committee report, 268-69

Margins,
Trading on borrowed funds, 50-52; Legislation dangerous, 52; Advantages of, 53; Risks and decline, 54; Amount required, 55; Broker's charges, 55-56; Partial payments, 56; When broker may close, 57-58; Legal decision on contracts, 59-60; Sources of brokerage loans, 62-64; Basis of, on Paris Bourse, 173; Bucket shop stakes, 247

Markets and Exchanges, 1-13;
Development of, 1; Stock and produce exchanges, 1-2; Why limited to securities and agricultural products, 2-3; Theodore H. Price on synonymous terms, 3-4; Three great exchanges, 4; New York Stock Exchange, 5-6, 12; Functions of, 6-10; Transactions in securities, described by S. S. Huebner, 6-7; Function of news agencies, 7-8; Real and quoted price, 8; Investment regulated by, 9; Speculation and price changes, 9-10; Domestic and foreign exchange, 10; Evils offset by benefits, 10-11; N. Y. Curb Market, 130-39; London Stock Exchange, 149-63; Continental Bourses, 165-75; Produce Exchanges, 177-212; New Orleans Cotton Exchange, 179, 228, 233-35; Chicago Board of Trade

INDEX

Markets and Exchanges—continued
213–26; N. Y. Cotton Exchange, 227–41
See also Other American Stock Exchanges

Matched Orders,
Price manipulation, 260–61; American Ice Co., deal, 265–66; Hocking pool, and testimony, 266–68; California Petroleum Co., 268–69

Milburn, John G., on Manipulation, 253–54, 260

New Orleans Cotton Exchange,
Trading in one staple, 179; Incorporated in 1871; Commercial method of grading cotton, 228, 233–35

New York Coffee Market, Functions of, 240–41

New York Cotton Exchange,
Cotton an important staple, 227; Primary markets, 228; Board of Managers, 229; Unit of trading, 229; "Direct" and "ring" settlement, 230; Cotton futures, and grades, 231–33; Commercial grading, by L. D. H. Weld, 234–35; Use of futures, 236; H. A. Gibbes on prices, 237–38; N. Y. *Times* market report, 239–40

New York, National Financial Center, 12

New York Produce Exchange,
Grain and cotton market, 179; Extent of activities, 224–25

New York Stock Exchange,
Beginnings of, and extensive organization, 5–6, 12; Membership requirements, 14–16; Building, 16–17; Main floor, 17–18; Purchase and sale methods, 18–20; Floor brokers, 21–22; Commission brokers, 22; "Two-dollar" brokers, 23; "Odd-lot" brokers, 23–25; Room traders, 25; Specialists, 26; Trading members, number of, 26; Government and committees, 27–28; Relation to Curb Market, 134–35; Absorbs railway stocks and mining industries, 144–45; Chicago stocks traded in, 147; Pittsburgh stocks absorbed by, 148; and London Stock Exchange, 149–52, 163; Provision against extreme manipulation, 263

Noble, H. G. S.,
On War stock speculation, 311–12; Price influences, 319–20

One-Day Unsecured Loans, and Overcertification, 73–74

Other American Stock Exchanges, 140–48;
Consolidated Stock Exchange of New York, 140–42; Stock sales on exchanges outside New York, 142–44; Canadian exchanges, 143; Boston Stock Exchange, 144–46; Chicago Stock Exchange, 146–47; Philadelphia Stock Exchange, 147; Pittsburgh Stock Exchange, 147–48

Over-Certification, Bank credit system, 70–74

Paris Bourse,
Relation to American exchanges, 165–66; Government control of, 168–69; Membership and government, 169–70; Rights of stock brokers, 170–72; Trading methods, 172–73; Margins and commissions, 173–74; Coulisse trading, 174–75

Philadelphia Stock Exchange, History of, 147

Pits, on Chicago Board of Trade, 215–16

Pittsburgh Stock Exchange, Stocks traded in, 148

Pools, and Manipulation, 258

Pratt, Sereno S., on Markets and speculation, 323–24

Prices, Influences that govern, 306–28

Produce Exchanges,
Scope of activities, 2, 4; Weld's summary of membership values, 16; Speculative activities of, 177–78; Principal exchanges and staples, 178–79; Spots and futures, 180–87; Inspection and grading, 187–94; Hedging, a safeguard, 195–97; Millers' profits in covering, 197–99; Future trading and grain speculation, 199–201; Organized markets protect trade, 202–04; Farmers and the grain exchanges, 204–06; Prices, and supply and demand, 206–09; Sources of market information, 209–11; Grain exchanges, 224–26; N. Y. Produce Exchange, 224–25

INDEX

Publicity,
International news agencies, 7–8; Listing securities provides a market, 34–37; Stock and news tickers, 119–26; London Stock Exchange Methods, 156, 159; Department reports and newspapers, 209–12; Chicago Board of Trade statistics, 224; N. Y. *Times* on cotton trading, 239–40
See also Use of Information on the Exchanges

Purchase and Sale,
N. Y. Stock Exchange methods, 18–21; Classes of brokers, 21–26; Unit of trading, 24; Advantages of listing, 34–37; Buying on margin, 50–61; Wall Street methods, 80–117; Speculative privileges, 101–07; Stock sales outside N. Y. City, 143; London jobbers, 157–59
See also Short Selling

Puts,
Speculative nature of, 101, 102–03; Privileges, and factors that govern prices, 105–06

Pyramiding, Dangerous "paper profits," 108

Room Traders, Operations of, on N. Y. Stock Exchange, 25

Short Selling,
Methods and illustration of, 85–89; Loaning rates, 89–90; Effect on market, 91; Dangers and advantages, 92; Laws to prevent, 93; John Barnard on, 94; Hughes committee on, 94; S. S. Huebner on, 95; Arguments against, 96–100; Corners and speculation, 274–83; Germany's experience, 300–02; Emery comments on failure of German law, 302–04
See also Benefits and Evils of Speculation

Sparling, S. E., on Chicago Board of Trade payment methods, 218–19, 220–21

Speculation,
Extensive stock trading on N. Y. Exchange, 5, 6, 8; Price indications, 9–10; Gambling practices, 11; Buying on margin, 51–55; Banks and the security market, 69–70, 78; Bulls and bears, 83–84, 85, 95, 98; Short selling, 85–100; Puts, calls and straddles, gambling privileges, 101–07;

Speculation—continued
Pyramiding unstable, 108; Clearing house, and bank loans, 112–14; Curb Market listing, 136–37; Settlements on London Exchange, 160; London jobbers' methods, 156–59; Regulations on Berlin Bourse, 167–68, 300–04; Coulisse of Paris, 174–75; and Produce exchanges, 177–78; "Future" trading, 180–86; Hedging safeguards, 195–99; Farmers' Cooperative Grain Dealers' Association, 201–06; Chicago Board of Trade and grain futures, 213–24; Cotton futures, 231–36; Celebrated plungers, 264–69; Corners in stock and products, 273–83; Definition of 285–87, 292; Gambling, 292–94; Speculators' methods, 293–98, 325; Influence on stock prices, 306–28
See also Bucket Shops
See also Benefits and Evils of Speculation

Stock Exchanges,
Three great markets in U. S., 4; Beginnings and extensive scope of N. Y. Stock Exchange, 5–6, 12; Functions of, 6–10; Transferring securities, 6–7; Effect of closing, 11; Safeguards that prevent abuse, 11; Relation of N. Y. Stock Exchange to Curb Market, 134–35; London Exchange of international scope, 149–63; Continental Bourses, 165–75; New Orleans Cotton Exchange, 179, 228, 233–35; Chicago Board of Trade, 213–26; New York Cotton Exchange, 227–40; N. Y. Coffee Exchange, 240–41
See also Markets and Exchanges
See also Other American Stock Exchanges

Stop-Loss Orders, When prices decline, 107

Straddles and Spreads, Speculative privileges, 101, 102, 104–06

Tickers, Stock and news bulletins, 119–26; London exchange publicity, 159

Time Loans, 64–65

Trading Methods,
"Regular" transactions, 80, 81; "Buyers' " and sellers' option," 80–82; Selling short, 85–100;

Trading Methods—continued
  London jobbers', 156–59; Paris Bourse, exclusive rights of, 170–73; Future trading on produce exchanges, 180–206; Hedging, 195–99; "Cash grain" and "future" business, 215–17

Transferred Securities,
  Corporation stocks and bonds, 6–7, 10; Credit in lieu of gold, 10; Protecting transfers by street certificates, 114–15

Use of Information on the Exchanges,
  Value of news, 118–19; Stock tickers, 119–22; Quotation companies, 122–23; Time tickers, 123; News tickers, 124; Bulletin service, 124–26; Newspapers and financial quotation, 126–29
  See also Publicity

Wall Street Ways, 80–117
  Four trading methods, 80–82; Commission rates enforced, 82–83; Bulls and bears, 83–84, 85, 95, 98; Short selling methods,

Wall Street Ways—continued
  85–90; Effects and advantages of short selling, 91–92, 93–100; Legal prohibitions, and arguments for and against short selling, 93–100; Puts, calls and straddles, 101–06; Stop orders and averaging to prevent loss, 107–08; Pyramiding dangerous, 108; Arbitrage, 108–09, 111; London quotations and N. Y. equivalents, 109–11; Delivery of stock, and price, 111–12, 113; Clearing house methods, 112–14; Transferring securities, 114–15; Insolvent brokers, 115–17; W. P. Hamilton on the London jobber, 158–59

Wash Sales, Condemned by Hughes Committee, 259–60

Weld, L. D. H.,
  on Uniform prices in future trading, 200–01; Commercial method of grading cotton, 234–35

Woodlock, T. F.,
  on Manipulation, 255; Successful speculation, 326–27

THE·PLIMPTON·PRESS
NORWOOD·MASS·U·S·A